JAPAN
AND THE
UNITED STATES

COUNCIL ON FOREIGN RELATIONS BOOKS

JAPAN
AND THE
UNITED STATES
Challenges and Opportunities

Edited by
WILLIAM J. BARNDS

A Council on Foreign Relations Book
Published by
New York University Press · New York · 1979

Copyright © 1979 by Council on Foreign Relations, Inc.

Library of Congress Cataloging in Publication Data
Main entry under title:

Japan and the United States.

   "A Council on Foreign Relations book."
   Includes bibliographical references and index.
   1. United States—Foreign relations—Japan—
Addresses, essays, lectures.   2. Japan—Foreign
relations—United States—Addresses, essays,
lectures.   3. United States—Foreign economic
relations—Japan—Addresses, essays, lectures.
4. Japan—Foreign economic relations—United States
—Addresses, essays, lectures.   I. Barnds,
William J.
E183.8.J3J317   327.73′052   79-1551

ISBN 0-8147-1020-4
ISBN 0-8147-1021-2 pbk.

Manufactured in the United States of America

Preface

This book grew out of a series of discussions held at the
Council on Foreign Relations during 1977-78 on new developments in Japan and in America's position in East Asia, and
on the implications of these developments for U.S.-Japanese
relations. The discussions were prompted by an awareness that
both countries were encountering serious economic problems
which, while differing in nature, were likely to create growing
strains in their relationship. In addition, America's changing
military posture and policies in the Western Pacific, as well as
the growing Soviet military presence in Asia, were causing a
growing number of influential Japanese to question the value
of the U.S. alliance and to examine the need for a Japanese
military buildup.

Japan and the United States had forged a remarkably successful relationship over the past three decades, demonstrating
an ability to overcome the specific strains and differences that
periodically occurred. But American economic and military
power had enabled the United States to maintain its dominant
role throughout this period even while making gradual adjustments to accommodate Japan's growing strength. Now, the
erosion both of America's economic competitiveness and of its

military supremacy in the Western Pacific are creating more basic and possibly more enduring strains than the difficulties of the past. Redefining the respective roles of the two countries in a way that protects their respective interests and preserves their ties poses a major challenge to the leaders and peoples of both countries over the next several years.

Specialists on Japanese affairs and on U.S.-Japanese relations were asked to prepare papers to aid the group in assessing the implications of recent events and to address key issues that are likely to affect the course of U.S.-Japanese relations. Several of the authors were also asked to set forth their own ideas regarding the appropriate policies for the United States to follow in dealing with Japan, its major Asian ally and largest overseas trading partner. No attempt was made to deal in a comprehensive way with all aspects of U.S.-Japanese relations in these essays. Thus such matters as cultural changes in each country and cultural differences between the two, as well as the history of Japanese-American relations, are considered in passing only as they affect political, economic and security affairs.

David MacEachron of the Japan Society discusses the combination of mutual interests and contrasting national backgrounds and characteristics that have influenced U.S.-Japanese relations, the evaluation of the relationship, and the issues that are challenging its future. Professor Gerald Curtis of Columbia University analyzes Japanese domestic political trends and the way in which these trends effect the positions of the country's political parties on Japan's foreign policy stance. Robert Feldman of Chase Manhattan Bank and William Rapp of Morgan Guaranty Trust describe how Japan's past economic successes have created structural problems that have weakened the economy at home without reducing its international competitiveness, and assess the implications of these developments for the United States. Professor Martin Weinstein of the University of Illinois appraises the changing Japanese perceptions of their strategic environment, their declining confidence in the American security guarantee, and describes the type of circumstances which could lead Japan to become a major military power. I. M. Destler of the Carnegie Endowment for International Peace examines issues in the bilateral relationship, especially the trade imbalance and the U.S. efforts to deal with it, in order to appraise the likely outcome of particular approaches in dealing with different types of problems. In the final chapter, I analyze the key issues facing both the United States and Japan in Asian affairs, and suggest how the two countries should deal with these matters in order to advance their respective interests without undermining their alliance.

The book looks at internal political and economic developments in Japan in a systematic way while devoting little attention to internal U.S. affairs. This asymmetry of approach was adopted because the book was written primarily for American readers, whose knowledge of Japan is limited. Japanese readers are unlikely to be seriously handicapped, however, because knowledge of the United States is quite extensive in Japan.

The group which met at the Council was chaired by James W. Morley, and included Morton I. Abramowitz, Michael H. Armacost, Gerald L. Curtis, I. M. Destler, J. R. Drumwright, Robert Feldman, Richard W. Fisher, George S. Franklin, Richard A. Freytag, Frank B. Gibney, Susan A. Goldberg, Selig S. Harrison, Lt. Col. Richard Head, USAF, Robert S. Ingersoll, Louis Kraar, Winston Lord, David MacEachron, Maynard Parker, Herbert Passin, Hugh T. Patrick, Nicholas Platt, William Rapp, Robert M. Ruenitz, Martin Weinstein, and Donald Zagoria.

We were also fortunate to have William Diebold, Jr., Peter Drysdale, Harriet Hentges, Fuji Kamiya, and Henry Scott-Stokes present at individual meetings. All the authors benefited from these discussions and wish to thank the members of the group for many useful suggestions. The views expressed in the book, of course, are the authors' own.

I wish to express my appreciation to James W. Morley for his excellent work as chairman of the group and to Timothy Curran for his work as rapporteur. John C. Campbell and Andrew Pierre, Directors of Studies while this volume was in preparation, provided continued counsel and encouragement, as did my colleagues on the Council's Studies Staff. Robert Valkenier's assistance went far beyond that of simply editing the individual papers, and all the authors express their appreciation to him. Thanks are also due to Janet Rigney and the other members of the library staff for their assistance in locating books and documents, and to Lorna Brennan and her staff for arranging the meetings. I am particularly indebted to my research associate, Helen Caruso, for providing valuable assistance on many of the topics analyzed in the book, and to my secretary, Carol Richmond, for her assistance with the manuscript.

I also wish to express my thanks to the editors of *Pacific Community* for permission to use material from an article of mine that appeared in their journal.

February 1979   W.J.B.

Contents

[ONE]

New Challenges to a Successful Relationship

David MacEachron

Japan and the United States, so dissimilar in many ways, have steadily become more deeply involved with each other over the past three decades. As a consequence, both nations have benefited substantially. Interdependence, however, has its hazards, especially when it involves two such large and dynamic nations. A U.S. congressional committee's casual release of allegations of illegal payments by the Lockheed Corporation to prominent Japanese political figures produced a storm in Japan which dominated public life for over a year. The Japanese quest for economic growth, pursued with intelligence and zeal, but without adequate regard for its effects on others, periodically produces economic dislocation in the United States and strained relations between the two countries.

Japan and the United States will exert a strong influence on each other as far into the future as one can foresee, and the skill with which they manage their relations will be of profound importance to Asia and the world. Yet during 1977 and 1978, the relationship was seriously strained by what may prove to be more basic and enduring problems than those that underlay the periodic troubles of the past. For example, productivity is rising much more rapidly in Japan than in the United States. This complicates bilateral economic adjustments, and leads to dwindling Japanese respect for the United States and to American suspicions that Japan is following devious and short-sighted economic policies and practices. There is reduced opposition within Japan to the U.S.-Japanese security treaty, and military cooperation between the defense forces of the two countries is increasing. Yet there are growing Japanese doubts about the reliability of the United States as a protector in view of the declining U.S. military presence in Asia, and there is a widespread Japanese belief that the U.S. lacks a coherent policy toward East Asia. In view of such troubling developments, what are the prospects that these two large industrialized democracies will continue their close ties? What are the issues that will strain the relationship, and how are these issues likely to be handled? Before attempting to assess the Japanese scene and the outlook for U.S.-Japanese relations, however, it is important to look at certain basic characteristics of the two countries.

The Unlikely Allies

Fundamental to any appraisal of the future of the Japanese-American relationship is an understanding of the shared and divergent values and interests which will color and control its evolution.

The divergences of history, geography, and culture are

[2]

much more striking than the similarities. The United States, vast in area and (until recently) rich in virtually all natural resources, has inclined to extravagance and the conviction that a new beginning on the frontier was always possible. Japan has always felt itself to be a small enclosed world, possessed of little fertile land and bereft of most natural resources.

Americans are immigrants or the descendants of immigrants from every continent, and racial and ethnic differences and the sentimental ties of many to the land of their origin both enriches and complicates American life and its international role. History has drawn a thick veil over the origin of the Japanese, and with the exception of the few remaining Ainu and several hundred thousand Koreans, the Japanese are one people, composing by far the largest homogeneous nation in the world. The differences between alien and countryman are blurred for many Americans, but for Japanese the line between Japanese and foreigner is bright and sharp.

America was created as an act of will by Europeans—the signing of the Declaration of Independence was a culmination as well as a beginning. The system of government and many of the ideals which provide the framework for American life were conscious intellectual efforts by individuals with a profound knowledge of European history who sought to frame a new society. The legitimacy of the United States rests on a continual reaffirmation of these ideas. In contrast, Japan evolved step by step over centuries. No other group of people that is a major actor in the world so completely shares a life which extends without break into pre-history.

Americans speak the predominant international language. The Japanese grow up speaking a language almost completely unrelated to any other tongue and using a written communication (partially derived from the Chinese and partially indigenous) which is the most complex of any used by a major nation. Americans expect others to speak English if they are educated; Japanese are still astonished to discover even a smattering of the Japanese language in a foreigner's repertoire.

Americans are talkative, litigious and make a virtue of being outspoken. Americanisms expressing approval of brutal candor abound: "talking turkey," "straight from the shoulder," "telling it like it is," "letting it all hang out," etc. Confrontation is common if not always relished, and subtlety of expression is not necessarily considered a virtue. The Japanese are skeptical about the efficacy of explicit verbal communication, often preferring implication, indirection, or even silence. Among people who have lived together so closely for so long, much is understood or taken for granted which Americans would have to articulate. Open confrontation is to be avoided if at all possible.

Americans have been the world's optimists—at least until recently—confident that a special Providence looks after their country. Americans feel at home in the world and, as a nation, inferior to no one. The confidence and optimism inclines Americans to assume that they can solve any problem, given enough effort and money. Americans are inclined to try to remake the world when it fails to suit them. In contrast, the brevity and uncertainty of life is a fundamental part of Japanese thought. The Japanese experience with the world, especially since Perry's ships sailed into Tokyo harbor in 1853, has created in the Japanese a sense of isolation and vulnerability, feelings more likely to give rise to aggression or circumspection than to international leadership. Japanese seek to adapt to the world as though it were completely exogenous, even though the Japanese economy through its size has become a major determinant of that external world.

The huge American domestic market meant that until recently the United States needed imports mainly for variety and luxury and—except for agricultural products—treated exporting as a marginal activity. Once Japan became committed to industrialization, the country was fated to become deeply dependent on world trade. Standing amid the ruins of their cities at the end of World War II, the Japanese said to themselves, "Export or die," and that urgent imperative has dominated Japanese economic life for a generation. Although Japan's foreign trade is a lesser percentage of its GNP than is the case for many European countries, the essential nature of Japanese imports (e.g., virtually all petroleum and half of food needs) makes dependence on world trade acute.

This catalogue of differences suggests the extent of the historic paradox in the close partner relationship. Even beyond these national differences, asymmetries in the relationship add to the problems of this unlikely alliance. The United States is a military superpower, whereas Japan is so lightly armed as to be virtually totally dependent on the United States for its defense. The United States sees itself as the defender of the non-Communist world with forces stationed around the world. Japan is not as yet willing even to commit its limited forces to a U.N. peace-keeping effort. The dollar, however beleaguered, is a major world currency, whereas the yen, in spite of its strength, is still cautiously guarded from the perils of becoming a full-fledged international currency. The multinational corporation for many years was virtually synonymous with American business, whereas the Japanese multinationals have only recently emerged. The United States played and continues to play a crucial role in the United Nations system and its many related organizations. (The U.S. withdrawal from the International Labour Organization caused deep worry throughout the international community precisely because it was feared that it represented a lessened commitment to the entire U.N. structure.) Japan, while deeply committed to the U.N. family

[5]

of organizations, is still cautious about assuming more than a quiet and low-profile role.

If the differences listed above were the whole story, there would obviously be little basis for the U.S.-Japanese alliance. However, Japan and the United States share certain fundamental values—and, equally important, certain basic interests. Both countries have an interest in a peaceful and pluralistic world order. Both place a high priority on international stability, and both recognize (to a degree) that no international system can be stable unless it can accommodate change. Japan and the United States also have broadly similar interests in maintaining a balance of power in East Asia, and each regards the Soviet Union as an adversary if not an enemy. Both countries accord central importance to preserving an open international economy in which trade can move across national boundaries without excessive governmental regulation. Access to the other's market is important to each country, although these interests make their economic relationship competitive as well as cooperative. Both have a declaratory policy of aiding the poorer nations. After a long and commendable record the United States's effort has flagged in recent years, and the Japanese have not yet fully matched their words with deeds. This combination of broad shared interests creates a mutual dependency which provides the foundation upon which the alliance rests.

An enduring alliance usually requires some shared values as well as mutual interests, however, and Japan and the United States are fortunate in this respect. Both are strongly committed to democracy and freedom for the individual from arbitrary dictates of government. There are, of course, differences in the way each nation exercises its democratic faith. The domination of the Diet by the Liberal Democratic Party for nearly a quarter of a century has seemed to some an

[6]

indication that democracy is weak in Japan, but Gerald Curtis in Chapter 2 makes clear that a vigorous political life goes on. The great power of the Japanese bureaucracy and the hesitation by the Japanese press to engage in vigorous investigatory reporting have led some Americans to conclude that Japan's commitment to democracy is weak. More fundamentally, Americans are inclined to see individualism as an inherent attribute of democracy, and are skeptical of the democratic credentials of the group-oriented Japanese with their penchant for consensus. Japanese point out that the U.S. Congress has been controlled by the Democratic Party in all but four years since 1933. They observe that most Americans depend largely upon television for their news, and thus their information about the world is controlled by a much smaller group of people than is true in Japan, where newspapers are more important. Further, they point out that income inequalities, which are greater in the United States than in Japan, are inherently undemocratic. In short, democracy has different strengths and weaknesses in each country, but the commitment of both peoples to this most difficult way of governance is of overriding importance.

Another similarity is that both nations are industrial societies with a high regard for technology. The ideal of efficiency is still strong, although many in both countries worry that this ideal is eroding. Among the many influences which create or prevent a sense of community among various peoples of the world, the extent of their involvement with and dependence on technology is among the most important. Citizens of Tokyo and New York, who literally could not live without the highly elaborate technological support available to them, share a more similar daily life than they do with their own countrymen, whether in a Japanese farm village or in a small midwestern town. (Three-quarters of all Japanese and

Americans are urban dwellers.) Both populations are highly educated. Literacy is virtually universal in Japan and is very high in the United States, and formal education in both nations in extensive.

Both nations are affluent, and affluence/poverty is another great fault line in human society. At a yen-dollar ratio of 200:1, per capita income in Japan is roughly comparable to that in the United States. The United States, of course, has had the advantage of a much higher level of income for well over a century, so accumulated wealth is substantially higher in the United States. Overall economic growth and real capital accumulation, however, continue to be substantially higher in Japan.

Continuity Amidst Change

These shared interests and values have sustained the alliance, but it is nonetheless impressive that two nations with such differences in style and outlook—and with the vast changes in their respective positions in the world since 1945—should have managed their relations for three decades with so little trouble. A brief review of the period will recall the difficulties successfully overcome, appraise the legacy of the past, and lay the groundwork for assessing whether the nature of the problems between the two nations is changing.

Few nations have faced greater disarray than did Japan after World War II. Having experienced little contact with foreigners, this society was suddenly placed under an alien authority full of naive self-assurance and bent on making fundamental changes in key aspects of Japanese life. The Japanese accepted the American presence in a wholehearted way, but later this created problems in the relationship since

[8]

the Americans neither fully understood nor accepted the reciprocal commitment which the Japanese expected. The U.S. occupation was basically successful, and laid the groundwork for the ensuing cooperation.[1]

The Peace Treaty signed in San Francisco in September 1951 ended the state of war and, more importantly, the occupation.[2] The widespread Japenese satisfaction with these developments did not, however, extend to the signing of the U.S.-Japan Security Treaty, which the U.S. government insisted upon as the price of ending the occupation. The alliance had been formed and a sustained American military presence in Japan legitimized, but prolonged and vociferous attacks on the treaty by the growing Japanese opposition parties created serious questions about its durability.

The first crisis in U.S.-Japanese relations occurred when a stronger and more self-assured Japan faced the issue of renewing the Security Treaty in 1960. The riots which protested the treaty's renewal and frustrated President Eisenhower's planned visit were evidence that the unquestioning acceptance of American domination was ending, and raised new questions about Japanese reliability. Yet the Kishi government's willingness to ratify the treaty even at the cost of its own political life was also a sign of growing maturity as well as continued recognition of the harsh realities of world politics. Perhaps most striking was the speed with which the issue subsided, for both governments were determined not to allow this episode to undermine their basic relationship.

President Kennedy and Ambassador Reischauer set off on a new path in Japanese-American relations in 1961. An extensive and systematic effort was undertaken to strengthen intergovernmental consultation, but more novel and bolder in conception were the binational programs intended to alter each country's public perception of the other. With governmental encouragement since 1962, the media, the educational systems, and the scientific communities have worked together toward better understanding. The momentum of these programs is such that today the magnitude of U.S. governmental and private contacts with Japan is comparable to those the United States has with the major European countries. Even so, Japan remains little known and poorly understood by the great majority of Americans. Indeed, the "insular" Japanese have a much greater knowledge of the United States than Americans—despite their world role—have of Japan.[3]

The Vietnam War created new strains in U.S.-Japanese relations. As had the Korean War earlier, it stimulated the Japanese economy. Unlike the Korean War, however, Vietnam darkened Japanese attitudes toward a United States caught up in racial turmoil and antiwar protests. The ambiguities and horrors of Vietnam raised Japanese doubts about American wisdom and strength. The years of America's involvement in Vietnam also saw the development of Japan's first trade surpluses with the United States. This development did not reduce Japan's dependence upon the United States, but together with reduced respect for its ally, created the first serious public discussions about the desirability of a more independent Japanese foreign policy.

Japanese have not been particularly rational or consistent in their attitudes toward their security ties with the United States. They generally recognized the need for American protection but wished to have it without American bases in Japan and without the risk of being involved in wars not of their choosing. The Japanese felt, often with good reason, that the Americans took them for granted. The American administration and many in Congress and the public often felt that Japan was benefiting from U.S. effort and sacrifice without making an adequate contribution, or even being particularly constructive in its comments.

Although Nixon's name will always be linked with "shocks" in Japan, it was the Nixon Administration which effectively resolved the last major bilateral issue remaining from World War II, the status of Okinawa. Given the prospects for an indefinite competition with the Soviet Union, the American decision to return Okinawa to Japanese control was a triumph for longer-run, more sophisticated thinking over attitudes that gave top priority to immediate security concerns. Japanese control would undoubtedly complicate the use of Okinawa as a base, but longer-run relations with Japan were deemed more important. The successful negotiation of Okinawa's reversion ironically may have contributed to the subsequent shocks by arousing in President Nixon unrequited expectations of Japanese compliance on other issues, such as curbing Japanese textile exports to the United States.

President Nixon and Henry Kissinger, in their passion for secrecy, made no exception for the Japanese. Concurrently, they needed to cope with an alarming deterioration in the U.S. balance of payments and strongly wished to open diplomatic contact with the People's Republic of China (P.R.C.) The Nixon shocks showed to the Japanese a less agreeable, less benign America. The textile shock and the dollar devaluation (which particularly aimed at. forcing a yen revaluation) signaled an American awareness that Japan had become so powerful economically its behavior had to be judged more than before in the cold light of American economic self-interest. The China shock was awkward for the government of Japan, but it also freed Tokyo to move rapidly toward normal diplomatic relations with the P.R.C., thereby ending a divisive issue in Japanese political life.

The world economic crisis that grew out of the 1973 war in the Middle East and the resulting disruption of oil flows was particularly severe for Japan. Its self-confidence was still fragile, and since virtually all of Japan's oil is imported—amounting to approximately 75 percent of all Japan's energy needs—its vulnerability to events beyond its control was made starkly clear. Since a large part of Japan's oil imports are handled by American corporations, the possibility existed for serious strains on Japanese-American relations. But the United States accepted Japan's tilt toward the Arabs, and Japan continued to receive a fair share of the reduced oil supply. A different American policy probably would have shaken confidence in the United States more deeply than did the U.S. military collapse in Vietnam two years later.

The tensions of the early 1970s gave way to the subsequent period of goodwill with amazing speed. President Ford selected Japan for his first foreign trip, and was the first incumbent president to travel there. Secretary Kissinger took pains to consult Japanese leaders frequently. In May 1974, Foreign Minister Ohira spoke of the existing good relations, and a year later Henry Kissinger asserted that relations between the two countries had never been better in three decades.[4] In 1975 the Emperor and Empress of Japan made their historic and successful visit to the United States.

Several points emerge from this brief survey of developments in Japanese-American relations from World War II until the mid-1970s. The basic nature of the relationship did not change, but it was flexible enough so that the two countries could make the necessary adjustments called for by changes in world affairs and by Japan's increasing strength relative to that of the United States. The two countries have a legacy of solving the problems that arise without letting them undermine the basic relationship. This provides valuable experience as well as reassurance to each country that its importance is recognized by the other. Past crises, however, have tended to be due to specific episodes—such as the 1960 security riots or Kissinger's secret visit to Peking—rather than to enduring or structural problems. Yet today Japan and the United States are so closely involved in each other's affairs that strains and differences are likely to be a normal aspect of their relations. (The United States now insists that Japan's economic growth rate is a legitimate American concern, and Tokyo maintains that U.S. energy policy is a legitimate Japanese concern.) Thus the management of relations will be a continuing rather than a periodic task for American leaders, and complacency arising from past successes is hardly warranted.

New Strains in an Old Relationship

At the start of the Carter Administration, relations between Japan and the United States appeared on the surface to have matured and deepened to the point where most issues could be dealt with amicably. No prior administration, thanks in part to the work of the Trilateral Commission, contained more individuals in high places with at least some knowledge of Japan.

Yet the calm in Japanese-American relations acclaimed in 1974 and 1975 by Ohira and Kissinger was brief. Early in the Carter Administration long-run developments abetted by well-intentioned but inadequately prepared policies of the new Administration in Washington combined to produce three major disputes. These can be labeled trade and the balance of payments, access to energy (and other resources), and security. Each dispute, as the succeeding chapters make clear,

[13]

arises from many complicated factors which are deeply embedded in the economics and policies of each country. In addition, important new developments within Asia, such as the Sino-Japanese and the Soviet-Vietnamese treaties, will complicate the task of keeping Japanese and American policies in harmony. Yet, as William Barnds indicates, difficult problems for the relationship could arise if either country ignores the needs of the other in dealing with key issues in Asian affairs.

The balance-of-payments issue combines multilateral, bilateral, and specific industry elements. It arises in part from sharply different rates of increase in productivity and real capital formation—Japan being a leader in both among the OECD countries and the United States a laggard. Further, Japanese officials and private businessmen have devoted themselves with much greater purpose to making their economy efficient, especially with an eye to export competition. Americans have pursued numerous worthy social goals, e.g., pollution control, safety for workers, anti-trust, with insufficient regard for their economic consequences, which has weakened the competitiveness of the United States in the international economy.

The sudden increase in world oil prices in 1973-74 produced gigantic balance-of-payments deficits for the oil importers, and efforts to cope with these pressures led to stagflation in the industrial world. Japan and Germany have been uniquely successful in converting their current account deficits into surpluses and bringing inflation under control. The Carter Administration sought to enlist the two nations, along with the United States, in the role of "locomotive economies" which would pull the world out of recession by pursuing expansionary economic policies at home and by running balance-of-payments deficits to offset OPEC surpluses. Considerable friction developed as both nations insisted

[14]

on pursuing more cautious courses lest inflation be rekindled. Yet the United States was reflating its economy, thereby further increasing the attractiveness of its market as Japan began another export drive. Tensions increased as Japan accumulated a trade surplus of about $17 billion in 1977—of which more than half was with the United States.[5] U.S. officials, businessmen, and journalists argued that Japan was acting in a narrow and short-sighted manner that ignored its international responsibilities. Moreover, specific industry problems, such as Japanese exports of color television sets and steel to the United States, threatened U.S. firms and jobs and heightened the tensions.

This led to a major U.S. government effort to influence Japanese economic policies, which is described by I.M. Destler in Chapter 5. This effort bought some time for the two countries to deal with their economic relations, but despite some favorable developments there is doubt that either nation is making the best use of that time. As Robert Feldman and William Rapp make clear in their description of the evolving strengths and weaknesses of the Japanese economy, the U.S. and Japanese economies are unlikely to achieve a stable relationship until the United States puts its own economic house in order. The United States needs to export more to Japan's growing market, but until American firms can compete more successfully with Japanese firms in the U.S. market their prospects for selling to Japan will not be bright.[6] Moreover, the Japanese are no longer willing to accept most of the responsibility for U.S.-Japanese economic strains. Japanese officials have begun openly to criticize the United States for failing to curb inflation, curtail oil imports, defend the dollar, and increase productivity more rapidly. Kiichi Miyazawa, then head of the Economic Planning Agency, insisted in July 1978 that Japan has been "doing its best under given circumstances

[15]

to behave well while none of the fundamentals are being touched in the United States." [7] Such public criticism by officials is still rare, but is widely echoed by Japanese in private conversations.

Secure access to raw materials is an issue that has been less in the public eye and has seemed less important to Americans, but the Japanese regard it as a central issue. A dangerous dispute over nuclear energy was created by the unilateral decision of the Carter Administration to alter the policy on nuclear fuel reprocessing. The Japanese had previously been encouraged by the United States to develop reprocessing capacity as a way of lessening their dependence on imported energy. However, the Carter Administration's efforts to retard the spread of capacity for nuclear weapons production led it to abruptly announce its opposition to reprocessing of spent fuel since with current technology this produced weapons-grade plutonium as a by-product. This change came shortly before the Japanese were preparing to activate their first reprocessing plant at Tokai Mura. A two-year agreement has postponed the problem, but unless new technology is developed in the interim, the problem will arise again in 1980. Given Japan's determination to reduce its dependence on oil imports, the potential for conflict is substantial.

The energy issue is but one type of problem arising from potential conflicts over access to resources. The brief, ill-conceived embargo on soybean exports in 1973 and the extension of U.S. jurisdiction over its coastal waters to two hundred miles are two cases where domestic supply needs were given priority. Congressional resistance to the sale of Alaskan oil to Japan and concern about selling West Coast lumber are other examples. Given Japan's dependence upon imported raw materials, such U.S. policies encourage Japan to diversify its sources of supply and reduce its reliance on U.S.

sources. At a time when U.S. officials are pressing Japan to increase the level of its imports from the United States such restrictions seriously weaken the American case.

The third important issue involves security affairs, but in a different way than was the case in the past. There is now widespread acceptance among Japanese of their country's security relationship with the United States, but there are growing doubts about future U.S. ability and willingness to assure Japan's security. These Japanese concerns stem partly from the gradual but steady growth of Soviet military power in Asia and the Western Pacific over the past ten years, although Japanese officials recognize that much of this is connected with the Sino-Soviet dispute. More worrisome is the decline of U.S. military power in the Western Pacific to levels below those that obtained before the U.S. involvement in Vietnam. Concern over these trends was reinforced by the proposal made by Carter as presidential candidate to withdraw U.S. ground combat forces from South Korea, a proposal which became U.S. policy after he was elected. In Chapter 4 Martin Weinstein describes the appraisals made by Japanese officials of these trends and discusses the circumstances which could lead to a major shift of Japanese policy in the directions of becoming a major military power.

* * *

There are common features in these cases. Each issue is of great importance to both nations, but in each the perspective is substantially different. The United States' view of these issues contains a larger concern for the world system than does the Japanese. The experience of a generation in leading a world coalition has conditioned American policy makers to a greater awareness of the needs of the free world's economic and security systems. The Japanese experience during this generation, in contrast, has been roughly analogous to that of the

United States during the nineteenth century: a foreign power provided a shield behind which the business of the nation could proceed in expanding its own economy.

Thus the United States is not only worried about the bilateral trade imbalance, but is also concerned about the strain Japan's large current account surplus places on the economies of all non-Communist oil importers. The United States feels that Japan should play a larger role in helping the other non-Communist nations to recover, even at the risk of greater inflation in Japan. Japan's traditional feeling of vulnerability and insecurity leads it to hesitate in moving much beyond its short-term self-interest. The risk of nuclear weapon proliferation is more apparent to the United States, while the Japanese are more concerned for a larger degree of control over their own energy supplies. U.S. policy makers are compelled to think in global security terms, including among other things the strategic balance, the one land front where Russian and American troops confront each other (Western Europe), and the protection of essential ocean supply lines. For Japan the regional balance in Northeast Asia (including Korea) inevitably looms as the first concern.

Each of these cases raises questions about the ability of the two nations to understand the interests and concerns of the other and to communicate in ways adequate for the depth of their mutual involvement, whether bilaterally, in Asian affairs, or in the world at large. Beyond the need for better understanding and communication lies the challenge of overcoming the strains due to the changing economic and strategic environment in a manner that facilitates the necessary adjustments in the respective roles of the two countries. Will American assertiveness and Japanese compliance be moderated enough to permit a mutually satisfactory relationship? Will understanding be followed by a willingness to incur the domestic political costs necessary to preserve the relationship?

As the following chapters describe, both regional and global issues of mutual concern to Japan and the United States will place great demands on their ability to cooperate effectively. Each nation can help the other. The United States can help Japan perceive its own self-interest in playing a larger role in the management of the free world's economic system since Japan's size makes it a major influence on the system. Japan, as the largest and economically most powerful of America's allies, has a unique opportunity to remind the United States as often as necessary that American interests and the interests of the free world are not synonymous. Effective Japanese-American relations will make an important contribution to a viable world; a serious weakening in this relationship could undermine the positions of both countries and destabilize much of East Asia.

Notes

1. For an appraisal of the occupation see Herbert Passin, *The Legacy of the Occupation in Japan.* (New York: East Asian Institute, Columbia University, 1968).

2. Diplomatic relations with the U.S.S.R. were resumed in 1956, but Soviet occupation of the Northern Territories continues to block a final peace treaty. Relations with the People's Republic of China were resumed in 1972, but a formal peace treaty was not signed until 1978.

3. Alan Miller, "The Information Imbalance," *The Japan Interpreter,* Vol. 12, No. 2 (Spring 1978), pp. 254-59.

4. Ohira's speech was published in *Japan Report,* Vol. XX, No. 12 (June 16, 1974), pp. 2-4. For Kissinger's speech, see

The Department of State Bulletin, Vol. LXXIII, No. 1880 (July 7, 1975), p. 3.

5. IMF, *International Financial Statistics,* October 1978; IMF, *Direction of Trade,* May 1978; Japan, Ministry of Finance, *Quarterly Bulletin of Financial Statistics.* September 1978, pp. 30-31. Exports and imports are on an f.o.b. basis. Japan's total trade surplus would be about $10 billion if imports were calculated on a c.i.f. basis and exports on an f.o.b. basis.

6. For a description of how the U.S. *share* of Japan's imports has declined, see James C. Abegglen and Thomas M. Hout, "Facing Up to the Trade Gap with Japan," *Foreign Affairs,* Vol 57, No. 1 (Fall 1978), pp. 146-68.

7. *The New York Times,* July 24, 1978.

[TWO]

Domestic Politics and
Japanese Foreign Policy

Gerald L. Curtis

This chapter is concerned with an analysis of Japanese
domestic political trends and their implications for foreign
policy. Is the Liberal Democratic party (LDP) likely to lose
power, and if so, what kind of government is likely to replace
single-party LDP rule? What are the foreign policy objectives
of those parties that are potential candidates for governmental
participation, and are those objectives in conflict with the
policies that have been pursued by Japan's conservative
governments? How are changes in the distribution of party
power likely to affect governmental decision-making processes,
including the processes of making foreign policy decisions? To
what extent do Japanese mass attitudes ("public opinion")
generate pressures on the political leadership to try to have
Japan assert a different and more positive role in international
affairs?

In discussing these and other questions, I emphasize the

formidable internal political pressures for continuity and stability in Japanese foreign policy. This is not to say that Japan will remain inflexibly wedded to the status quo and unable to change its policies should its external environment dramatically change. But the internal dynamics of Japanese foreign policy formation inhibit major new policy initiatives and encourage a foreign policy style that is essentially defensive and reactive and characterized by pragmatic responses to international developments as they unfold. For the foreseeable future Japanese political trends are likely to have the effect of reinforcing this foreign policy orientation.

Political Trends: The LDP

The Liberal Democratic party was formed in 1955 and has been in power ever since. In its first election, in 1958, it won 57.8% of the vote. The party's vote percentage has declined with each subsequent election, but it obtained over half of the popular vote until 1967, when its percentage dropped to 48.8% (see Table 1). In the 1972 election it obtained 46.9%, and in the December 1976 election, 41.8% of the vote. The party's two most serious losses were in 1967, when it suffered a decline of 5.9 percentage points, and in 1976, when the percentage point decline was 5.1. Both of these elections were conducted in the midst of major LDP scandals: the "black mist" scandal of 1967 and the Lockheed scandal of 1976.

Japan's electoral system has made it possible for the LDP to obtain a larger percentage of Diet seats than its percentage of the vote. In the elections of 1967, 1969, and 1972, with less than 50% of the popular vote, it took over half of the lower house seats with its officially endorsed party candidates. In addition, several conservative independents joined the party

TABLE 1

Party Performance, Lower House Elections 1958-76
(In percentage of popular vote and, in parentheses, number of seats)

	LDP	JSP	KMT	JCP	DSP	NLC	IND	Total
1958	57.80	32.94	—	2.55	—	—	6.71	100.00
	(287)	(166)		(1)			(13)	(467)
1960	57.56	27.56	—	2.93	8.77	—	3.18	100.00
	(296)	(145)		(3)	(17)		(6)	(467)
1963	54.67	29.03	—	4.01	7.37	—	4.92	100.00
	(283)	(144)		(5)	(23)		(12)	(467)
1967	48.80	27.89	5.38	4.76	7.40	—	5.77	100.00
	(277)	(140)	(25)	(5)	(30)		(9)	(486)
1969	47.63	21.44	10.91	6.81	7.74	—	5.47	100.00
	(288)	(90)	(47)	(14)	(31)		(16)	(486)
1972	46.85	21.90	8.46	10.49	6.98	—	5.32	100.00
	(271)	(118)	(29)	(38)	(19)		(16)	(491)
1976	41.78	20.69	10.91	10.38	6.28	4.18	5.78	100.00
	(249)	(123)	(55)	(17)	(29)	(17)	(21)	(511)

Notes:

LDP = Liberal Democratic Party
JSP = Japan Socialist Party
KMT = Komeito (Clean Government Party)
JCP = Japan Communist Party

DSP = Democratic Socialist Party
NLC = New Liberal Club
IND = Independent and minor party candidates

Sources:

for 1958-1969: Nishihira Shigeki, *Nihon no senkyo* [Japanese Elections] (Tokyo: Shiseidō, 1972), Chart 6-1, "Tōha-betsu Tokuhyō-Sū (Shūgin) [Number of votes cast by party–House of Representatives]," p. 265; and Chart 7-1, "Tōha-betsu gisekisū (Shūgin) [Number of Diet seats by party–House of Representatives]," p. 269.

for 1972-1976: Hans H. Baerwald and Nobuo Tomita, "Japan's 34th General Election: Cautious Change Amidst Incremental Instability," *Asian Survey* 22, no. 3 (March 1977), Table 2, "Results of the December 5, 1976, Election," p. 228.

[23]

after winning in the election. In the 1976 election, however, the LDP failed to return a majority with its own candidates, and was able to put together a bare majority only with the entry into the party of several successful independents.

Under the present Japanese election system, members of the lower house are elected in 130 districts, each of which selects from three to five members. To win a substantial number of seats (a majority requires 256), parties have to run more' than one candidate per district. But since the voter has only one vote, unique problems of candidate endorsement and campaign organization and strategy arise as parties try to contain intra-party competition while maximizing the party vote.[1] Where the LDP runs too many candidates, they can be defeated by opposition party politicians who obtain a smaller percentage of the popular vote than that represented by the combined LDP vote. To the extent the LDP overestimates the potential total party vote in a district and in instances where intra-party competition results in one candidate getting a particularly large vote at the expense of another LDP candidate, the system benefits the smaller opposition parties which, with the exception of the Japan Socialist party (JSP), run only one candidate per district.[2]

On the other hand, the system also can benefit the LDP. A three-member district, for example, may be contested by two LDP candidates and by one candidate from each of four opposition parties. Though the combined opposition percentage of the vote may total a majority, they may divide the vote in such a way that both LDP candidates win. To give a hypothetical example: if, in a three-member district, the JSP obtained 20% of the vote, the Komeito (KMT) and Democratic Socialist party (DSP) each 15%, the Communist party (JCP) 10% and each of two LDP candidates 20%, the combined vote for the opposition would be 60%, but the LDP,

[24]

with 40% of the vote, would take 67% of the seats (that is, two out of three) and the opposition parties (in this example, the JSP) would obtain just one seat.

Given the peculiar problems this system creates for both large and minor parties, it is little wonder that all of Japan's parties advocate some kind of revision. There is no agreement, however, on what should replace the present system which, with the exception of the wartime years and a short period immediately thereafter, has been in effect since 1925. The LDP has called for a single-member constituency system, and the opposition parties have proposed a variety of proportional representation schemes. A revision of the present system would upset predictions of future election outcomes, but, given the present balance of party power in the Diet, it is unlikely that either the LDP or the opposition will be able to revise the system to its liking, or that they will be able to agree on a compromise formula. Thus, my discussion proceeds on the assumption—an entirely safe one, I believe—that Japanese voters will continue to elect their leaders through the present complex and unique electoral system.

A number of features of LDP electoral performance over the past two decades are relevant to predictions about future trends. First, the downward trend in LDP support has been thus far irreversible: in no lower house election has the LDP been able to reverse earlier losses. Second, the decline has been slow, an average of 2.7% per election. Third, there is no evident correlation between economic performance or specific policy issues and the rate of LDP decline. Whether the economy grows fast or slow, whether the nation suffers "shocks" or enjoys tranquility, the slide in LDP support has continued on its slow, inexorable course.

LDP decline has been the consequence of broad and continuing social changes: e.g., the movement of population

[25]

from rural areas to the cities (and the urbanization of formerly rural areas), the expansion of higher education, and the emergence of an urban, young electorate not locked into the traditional social networks so important to conservative party techniques of mobilizing support. As the society becomes more urban, more affluent, and more middle class, it becomes increasingly difficult for any party, under the present Japanese electoral system, to maintain the support of a majority of the voting public.

The direction of Japanese social change offers little reason to believe that the LDP will be able to reverse substantially the downward trend in its electoral support and recover its erstwhile position of unchallengeable dominance. But other factors suggest that the party's decline may be bottoming out. In the short run, given the disarray in the opposition camp, the LDP even may be able to enjoy a modest, though I suspect temporary, increase in its number of lower house seats.

The LDP has suffered its major losses in densely populated metropolitan districts where the party finds it increasingly difficult to successfully run multiple candidates. But it still obtains a higher percentage of the metropolitan popular vote and a larger number of seats (see Table 2) than does any single opposition party. There are now few districts in this category in which the LDP runs more than one candidate and, with the consequent absence of intra-party competition, it is unlikely that the party will suffer major losses in seats in coming elections even though there be a continued slow erosion in the party's popular vote. Furthermore, despite repeated increases in the number of Diet seats in order to give urban voters greater Diet representation, the system is still heavily weighted in favor of the rural electorate. The LDP remains overwhelmingly strong in rural Japan in spite of recent advances by the opposition parties.

TABLE 2

Party Success in Number of Seats, 1976 Lower House Election,
in Metropolitan, Urban, Semi-Urban, and Rural Constituencies

	LDP	Conservative Independents	NLC	JSP	KMT	DSP	JCP	Progressive Independents
Metropolitan	29(+ 1)	3(+1)	7(+7)	17(−1)	23(+7)	9(±5)	10(−12)	2(+1)
Urban	64(− 5)	1(0)	7(+7)	32(+1)	18(+8)	10(+4)	3(− 8)	1(+1)
Semi-urban	100(−10)	6(+1)	2(+2)	53(+3)	12(+9)	9(+1)	3(− 1)	0(−2)
Rural	56(− 8)	8(+3)	1(+1)	21(+2)	2(+2)	1(0)	1(0)	0(0)

Notes: The numbers in parentheses indicate change from the 1972 election. According to the urbanization index designed by the Asahi Shinbun and used here, the country's 130 districts are classified into 25 metropolitan districts with 100 seats, 34 urban districts with 136 seats, 46 semi-urban districts with 185 seats, and 25 rural districts with 90 seats.

Source: Asahi Shinbun, December 7, 1976.

[27]

The LDP also may benefit from the fact that its majority has become so narrow. Until the 1974 upper house election, voters going to the polls, and politicans going to the stump, did so with the certainty that the LDP would emerge victorious. The era of one-party dominance was not simply one in which the LDP maintained a majority of Diet seats, but one in which its power was unchallenged. Opposition parties could promise things for which they knew they would not be held account-able, and voters critical of the LDP could vote for one opposition party or another, knowing they were registering a protest and not choosing a government. In 1974 the "reversal of the conservatives and the progressives" became both an opposition slogan and a real possibility for the first time.[3] As a consequence, voters were made aware that their votes could make a difference, not only in registering a protest against the party in power, but in determining what party or parties would be in power. This introduces a new element of choice for the Japanese voter which must inevitably affect his behavior. Polls suggest that a majority of Japanese voters desire either the continuation of LDP government or an LDP-centered coalition.[4] The prospect of LDP defeat may well bring back to support of the party voters who heretofore had perceived the LDP's dominant position as affording an oppor-tunity to register a safe protest. The LDP's success in returning its majority in the 1977 upper house election suggests that the LDP may already be benefiting from voter reluctance to bring other parties into power.

Finally, the LDP may be helped at least temporarily by the decline in growth rates and fears about continued economic recession. An inclination not to rock the boat politically when economic conditions are shaky, particularly in a society unaccustomed to the alternation of power among different political parties, serves as a potent conservatizing force.

Furthermore, recent local elections suggest that in times of financial stringency the public may more easily become discontented with "progressive" parties in power in local government than with conservative regimes because of the greater expectations for improved and expanded public services which these anti-LDP governments engender. Progressive candidates suffered a string of important defeats in a number of local governor and mayoral elections and in Diet by-elections following the lower house election at the end of 1976.

Limited economic resources also have created problems for the opposition by bringing to the surface conflicts between local progressive government leaders and their most important support groups. In Tokyo, for example, Governor Minobe found himself under intense pressure from citizen groups that had supported his election to refuse the demands for salary increases from the Tokyo municipal workers' union, one of the governor's major backers.[5] This conflict, which resulted in Minobe's decision to postpone the increase, proved particularly painful to the opposition camp, coming, as it did, in the middle of 1978 when the opposition parties were trying to organize their forces for the post-Minobe governor's race in 1979.

There is no certain answer to the question of whether or when the LDP will lose its majority position in the Diet. Even if the LDP maintains its narrow majority of seats, it will have to compromise with the opposition to keep the parliamentary process functioning. In that sense the crucial transition is already underway from a system of one-party dominance, and a peripheral opposition party role in policy-making, to a new multi-party system in which parties other then the LDP will be directly involved in policy formulation.

Furthermore, the composition of the government if the LDP loses its majority will largely depend on how great a loss

JAPAN AND THE UNITED STATES

the LDP suffers. Falling short of a majority by fifty or sixty seats suggests different possibilities than would arise if the LDP found itself ten or even twenty seats short of majority control of the lower house. Obviously, any prediction of LDP decline must be based on some assessment of the future performance of the opposition parties. The paradox of Japanese electoral trends is that declining support for the LDP has not directly benefited the opposition.

Political Trends: The Opposition Parties

Elections of course are zero-sum games in which one set of party gains is balanced by an equal number of party losses. But in a political sense recent Japanese elections have produced no winners, and all of Japan's ever-increasing number of political parties are apprehensive about their future possibilities.[6] The popular vote for the Japan Socialist party has declined steadily over the past decade at a rate comparable to that of the LDP. There is no sign this trend will be reversed. In the lower house election in 1976 the Komeito recouped the losses it suffered in the previous 1972 election, but there is little evidence that it is developing a broad base of support outside its supporting religious organization, the Soka Gakkai, and, consequently, little reason to believe that it will quickly increase its Diet representation much beyond its present strength. The Democratic Socialist party also recouped its 1972 losses in the 1976 election; it did so by running fewer candidates than ever before, and by concentrating its financial and organizational resources in the few districts in which its candidates stood. Its popular vote was the lowest ever, and it won fewer seats than in either the 1967 or 1969 elections. Although the Communist

[30]

party suffered no loss in its percentage of the national aggregate vote in 1976, it lost half its seats and substantial numbers of votes in urban constituencies where its support is concentrated. The New Liberal Club (NLC), on the other hand, unexpectedly captured 18 seats in its first national election. But enthusiasm for this new party quickly cooled, and in the 1977 upper house election it was able to elect only three of its 13 candidates.

In the December 1976 lower house election the LDP popular vote declined by 5.1 points from the previous 1972 election. The combined percentage point increase for the four parties characterized in Japanese as the "progressive parties"—the Socialist party, the Komeito, the DSP, and the Communists—was only 0.4! Virtually the entire loss in the LDP percentage of the popular vote could be accounted for by the vote for the New Liberal Club, a group founded in the spring of 1976 when six young LDP Diet members led by Yohei Kono, the son of a famous former LDP leader and a popular figure in his own right, bolted the party, and by conservative independents who joined the LDP as soon as being elected. Among the opposition parties only the KMT increased its percentage of the popular vote (from 8.5% in 1972 to 10.9% in 1976); the JSP, JCP, and DSP each suffered fractional declines.

The opposition did no better in the number of seats it won than it did in the popular vote. The percentage of total lower houses seats won by LDP candidates declined from 55.2% in 1972 to 48.7% in 1976, but the percentage of seats won by the combined opposition increased from 41.5% to only 43.8%. Between the elections of 1967 and 1976 the combined opposition gained just 2.8 percentage points (or 6.3%) in the popular vote while the LDP lost 7 percentage points (or

14.4%). During the period the LDP percentage of seats declined by 8.3 points (or 14.5%), but the opposition increase was only 2.7 points (or 6.5%).

Not only has the opposition failed to make gains proportional to LDP losses, but the trend of declining LDP support has been accompanied by the proliferation of opposition parties and the weakening of the Japan Socialist party. In the 1958 election the JSP obtained one-third of the popular vote and dominated the opposition to the ruling party. In the 1976 election its popular vote was 20.7%.

When JSP popularity was at its zenith, the party obtained considerable support from urban voters and white collar workers. Today JSP support comes primarily from members of government-enterprise unions affiliated with the Sohyo labor federation and from voters in small cities and semi-urban areas. JSP strength in these semi-urban areas stems from the fact that other opposition parties have concentrated their efforts in the more densely populated metropolitan districts, and that important JSP-supporting Sohyo unions such as the Japan Teachers Union *(Nikkyōsō)*, the Japan Prefectural and Municipal Workers' Union *(Jichirō)*, and the National Railway Workers' Union *(Kokurō)*, are often strong enough to mobilize considerable electoral support for JSP candidates in these relatively small districts. In the 1976 election the JSP won only 17% of the seats in metropolitan districts (the KMT won 23% and the LDP 29%) while winning 24% of the urban district seats, 29% of the seats in semi-urban districts, and 23% of rural district seats (see Table 2). Of the total of 123 JSP candidates elected in 1976, 43.1% were elected in semi-urban constituencies.[7] Only in the 1958 election did the JSP run more candidates than the number necessary to secure a Diet majority. The steady decline in its popular vote has forced it to reduce the number of endorsed party candidates, creating a

[32]

situation in which only the LDP runs enough candidates to obtain a Diet majority.

The JSP has been beset by a series of election defeats, factional battles, party defections and ideological struggles that have left it demoralized and in disarray. In the 1976 election the party's three major faction leaders—Saburo Eda, Seiichi Katsumata, and Kozo Sasaki—and several other senior party members lost their Diet seats. Shortly thereafter Saburo Eda, the leader of the party's right wing, left the party to form a new party called the Socialist Citizens League *(Shakai Shimin Rengo)* which sought to create an alliance between advocates of a British Labour type of social democracy and leaders of non-party-affiliated citizen movements. Eda's sudden and unexpected death shortly before the summer upper house election struck the fledgling party a devastating blow. But in September of the same year three more JSP members, led by Hideo Den, a member of the upper house and the only politician in Japanese electoral history to win the top vote in the upper house national constituency in two consecutive elections, left the party because of its inability or unwillingness to control the party's extreme left wing. The Den group and the Socialist Citizens League merged in March 1978 to form the Social Democratic League *(Shakai Minshu Rengo)*.

Following the poor JSP performance in the 1977 upper house election, the party's chairman and secretary-general declared their desire to resign their posts. This served to intensify factional and ideological battles for control of the party and, after an abortive attempt to choose new leaders at a raucous party congress in September 1977, the party finally agreed in December to make the popular mayor of Yokohama, Ichio Asukata, its new chairman.

Asukata's election to the top party post resulted in a kind of cease-fire among the various party groups contending for

[33]

control, but the basic internal divisions remain profound. The party is torn by two overlapping conflicts: one an ideological conflict between advocates of social democracy and defenders of a dogmatic "Marxist-Leninist" line; and the other a related struggle for power between long-time faction leaders and a group known as the Socialist Association *(Shakaishugi Kyokai;* usually referred to simply as the Kyokai) which has come to control much of the party's local organization and headquarters staff.

The Kyokai is a threat not only to the party's right wing, which sees it moving from below to capture the party organization and purge right-wing elements, but to all groups in the party, both left and right, with vested interests in maintaining traditional factional control over party posts. As a consequence, the left-wing Sasaki faction joined with right-wing groups to oppose the Kyokai. But this "anti-Kyokai alliance" could not agree on a new party line; and Asukata, in the negotiations leading to his election in December, deftly maneuvered himself into the position of party mediator, succeeding thereby in effectively breaking up the anti-Kyokai alliance and putting a lid on the party's internal struggles.

A split in the JSP along clear ideological lines is unlikely. For many members of both wings of the party, ideology is, above all, a convenient tool for intra-party power struggles. In addition, the great majority of right-wing JSP members are dependent on the Sohyo labor federation for financial and campaign support. Sohyo's leadership is anxious to prevent a major party split because of the reverberations that would inevitably be felt in the labor movement itself. Without the assurance of a strong union base, right-wing politicians are for the most part unwilling to force a break. Both Saburo Eda and Hideo Den were able to leave the party because neither was dependent on Sohyo support. Few other JSP members find themselves in a comparable position.

The JSP no longer entertains the hope of becoming a majority party, and it now defines for itself a role as the "linchpin" of the anti-LDP political forces. The party alternately portrays itself as the hub of a wheel whose spokes radiate out to all the other opposition parties, or as the "bridge" that will link the Communist party on one end and the Komeito and DSP on the other in an anti-LDP coalition. Although the KMT and DSP steadfastly refuse to consider cooperating with the JCP, the Socialist party remains wedded to a policy of an "anti-LDP united front of all opposition parties." There is nothing to indicate that this party, preoccupied as it is with internal power struggles, will be able to reverse the downward trend of its public support. Recent polls put JSP support at less than 15%.[8]

Much about JSP behavior suggests comparison with the Italian Socialists, a party that was once the leading opposition party in Italy. The Japan Socialist party may come to look increasingly like the PSI as it suffers further declines in popularity and generates splinter groups unable to mobilize mass support. Because of the strong inclination to manipulate ideological issues for purposes of striking a balance in factional power, the party is likely, on the one hand, to feel compelled to give lip service to a radical ideology that has little relevance to current Japanese problems while, on the other, advocating short-term policies that reflect a moderate, reformist stance. In 1960 it was hard to conceive of any alternative to LDP rule other than a Socialist-led government. In 1977 it is difficult to imagine a situation in which the JSP would be at the center of a coalition government. An LDP loss of its Diet majority could, perhaps, precipitate a major split in the JSP (and in

Sohyo), with some elements moving off to join other centrist groups in a new party or in a multi-party coalition. But the chance for the JSP to obtain a position in Japan comparable to the Social Democratic party in Germany has been irretrievably lost.

As a result of the 1976 election the Komeito, a party formed in 1964 as the political arm of Soka Gakkai, has become the only opposition party since 1955 other than the JSP to have more than the 50 seats necessary to submit budget-related legislation and motions of nonconfidence in the Diet. The KMT first ran candidates for the lower house in the 1967 election when 32 candidates stood for election and 25 won seats in the Diet. In the next election in 1969, the party put forward 76 candidates and almost doubled its representation in the lower house by capturing 47 seats. The party suffered a serious setback in the 1972 election when only 29 of its candidates were elected. This election followed on the heels of a scandal involving efforts by the KMT and the Soka Gakkai to prevent publication of a book critical of the Gakkai. The aftermath of that election saw a formal break between the Soka Gakkai and the KMT, the adoption of a new party program, and a concerted effort to build up the party organization. By 1976 the party felt confident that it could recoup the losses incurred in 1972. In the December election it ran a total of 84 candidates in the country's 130 districts, winning 55 seats and 10.9% of the popular vote. The party's percentage of the vote in 1976 was the same as it received in the 1969 election. It won eight more seats in 1976 than it had won in 1969, but the total number of lower house seats had been increased from 486 in 1969 to 511 in 1976. The KMT now holds 10.8% of lower house seats compared to 9.7% in 1969.

Although the KMT recouped the losses it suffered in 1972 and won more seats than in any previous race, these results do not suggest that the KMT is riding on a new wave of popularity or that it can look forward to a major increase in its Diet representation in the next lower house election. In the 1972 election KMT candidates in 24 districts lost with the highest vote among the losing candidates—what Japanese refer to as *jiten*.[9] In 1976 the party won seats in 22 of these 24 districts. Only eight of the 29 candidates who were defeated in 1976 were in the runner-up position and four of these eight lost by more than 10,000 votes to the candidates winning in last place. In all but two of the other districts in which the KMT lost, the vote differential between the KMT candidate and the last place winner was so great as to make KMT victories in the next election unlikely. In any event, now that the KMT has recouped its earlier losses, it will have a much more difficult time in the next election to increase significantly its number of seats. It is likely, in fact, to find itself on the defensive, trying to protect the seats it won in 1976 against the vigorous efforts of the 37 Communist party candidates who lost, as did the 24 KMT candidates in 1972, with the highest vote among the losers.[10]

Although the KMT declared its formal independence from the Gakkai at the June 1970 party congress, it continues to be made up almost exclusively of Soka Gakkai members and to recruit its candidates for public office from among Gakkai activists. All but one of the party's candidates in the 1976 Diet election were Gakkai members. This continuing close relationship with the Gakkai reflects both the party's strength and its limitations. Despite the formal split between party and religion, the KMT is able to mobilize for its election campaigns a religious organization that claims a membership of some seven million families. On the other hand, Soka Gakkai membership is largely confined to urban areas and is no longer increasing rapidly, and the KMT's efforts to transform itself into what Japanese call a "national party" *(kokumin seitō)*, as contrasted with a class or religious party, are at least in part the result of its having largely exhausted potential Gakkai-based support. The antipathy to the Komeito of voters unsympathetic to the Gakkai, however, remains strong, Polls indicate that more Japanese actively dislike the KMT than any other party save the Communists.[11]

The results of neither the 1976 lower house election nor the 1977 upper house contest (see Table 3) indicate that the KMT has yet moved far in the direction of becoming a broad-based national party. Nonetheless, it has firmly established for itself a position as an important participant in Japan's party politics. Initially rejected by other parties for its allegedly Poujadist-like qualities and its intimate relationship to a militant and proselytizing religious sect, the Komeito is now accepted, and increasingly treated as a potential ally, by both the LDP and the opposition. To a considerable degree it has supplanted the JSP as the "bridge" between the various non-Communist opposition parties and it has obtained an important role in the parliamentary decision-making process and in any potential bargaining over the composition of a coalition government. But, contrary to KMT hopes, it seems unlikely that the party will be able to become the nucleus for an alliance of centrist forces capable of taking power. Its base of support is too limited and its relationship to Soka Gakkai, despite the formal separation of the two organizations, too intense to permit the party rapid growth in the near future.

The Democratic Socialists claimed a victory in the 1976 election for their small party when it won 29 seats, 12 seats more than it obtained in the previous election. But this "victory" gave the DSP fewer seats than it won in the 1967 or 1969 elections. Furthermore, the party's percentage of the popular vote nationwide in 1976 was the lowest of the six

TABLE 3
Party Performance, Upper House Elections 1971-77

Parties	Constituencies	1971 % of Popular Vote	1971 No. of Seats	1974 % of Popular Vote	1974 No. of Seats	1977 % of Popular Vote	1977 No. of Seats
LDP	national	44.47	21	44.34	19	35.83	18
	local	44.02	41	39.50	43	39.46	45
JSP	national	21.27	11	15.18	10	17.37	10
	local	30.95	28	26.00	18	25.87	17
KMT	national	14.09	8	12.09	9	14.16	9
	local	3.42	2	12.58	5	6.19	5
JCP	national	8.06	5	9.37	8	8.41	3
	local	11.99	1	12.02	5	9.96	2
DSP	national	6.11	4	5.92	4	6.68	4
	local	4.71	2	4.40	1	4.47	2
NLC	national	——	—	——	—	3.86	1
	local	——	—	——	—	5.70	2
SCL	national	——	—	——	—	2.80	1
	local	——	—	——	—	1.18	0
IND	national	6.0	1	13.10	4	10.89	4
	local	4.91	1	5.50	4	7.17	3
TOTAL	national	100.00	50	100.00	54	100.00	50
	local	100.00	75	100.00	76	100.00	76

Notes:
SCL = Socialist Citizens League.
IND = Independent and minor party candidates.
The 252 members of the upper house are elected for six-year terms, with 152 being chosen in local prefectural constituencies and 100 through a national constituency system, i.e., with the entire country treated as one district. Half the membership is elected every three years, i.e., 76 in the local constituencies and 50 in the national constituency.

Sources:
for 1971 elections:
 local: *Mainichi Shimbun* (June 29, 1971), p. 2.
 national: *Mainichi Shimbun* (June 29, 1971, evening edition), p. 2.
for 1974 and 1977 elections:
 local: *Mainichi Shimbun* (July 12, 1977), p. 4.
 national: *Mainichi Shimbun* (July 12, 1977, evening edition), p. 2.

lower house elections it has contested. The DSP vote has declined with each election since the party's first contest in 1960 when it obtained 8.8% of the vote; in the 1976 election its vote was 6.3%.

By itself this decline in the party's nationwide aggregate vote is not particularly significant because the DSP, in an effort to mobilize its financial and human resources behind candidates who stood a credible chance of winning, ran fewer candidates in the 1976 election (51) than in any previous race, less than half the number it fielded in its first contest in 1960. It reduced its number of candidates, in effect, almost entirely to those districts that had large labor unions affiliated with the DSP-supporting Domei labor federation. As a result, there are no DSP Diet members in 30 of Japan's 47 prefectures. Of the 22 DSP candidates who lost in 1976, only two came in as *jiten*. There is little chance that many of the candidates who placed further down will be able to obtain the large increase in support necessary to win the next election.

Nonetheless, in contrast to the Komeito, the DSP is likely to increase the number of its party's candidates in the next election.[12] The party can count on the financial support of Domei and of business corporations that see the DSP as a potential participant in a conservative-centered coalition. Running a larger number of candidates will contribute to the party's efforts to rebuild its organization and will inflate its nationwide aggregate popular vote, thereby enabling it to claim another election "victory" even if its gains in seats are modest. A marked break with long-term electoral trends would be required, however, for the DSP to obtain a substantially larger number of seats in the next lower house election than it obtained in 1976. On the contrary, the party will be hard pressed to fight off the challenge of *jiten* candidates of other parties in at least the six districts in which DSP candidates came in last among the winning candidates.

The New Liberal Club has contested just one lower house and one upper house election, and it is too early to say anything definite about the party's future prospects. The party's leadership is young and primarily from urban constituencies. It tries to distinguish itself from other opposition parties by referring to itself as "centrist conservative" but it, like the "centrist progressive" parties, seeks to attract the unaligned, young, urban voter. The major element in its platform has been its advocacy of a new political style in which youthful vitality, "clean politics," and public participation in party affairs are emphasized. Consequently, it has devoted the greater part of its energies to building an organization that could survive without large-scale big business financial support, and that could appeal to an urban electorate unattracted by the established opposition parties and disenchanted with the LDP.

In the 1976 lower house election the NLC defied all predictions by capturing 18 seats. It won only 4.2% of the popular vote nationwide, but in the 25 districts where it ran candidates it earned 18.4% of the vote; the percentage of the vote in the 18 districts in which NLC candidates won was 22.4%. In the subsequent upper house election in July 1977, however, the party was not successful. Only one of the party's four national constituency candidates was elected, and of the nine candidates running in local constituencies just two were elected.

The NLC represents the first instance since 1955 of a new party emerging from within the conservative camp. There are many voters who favor policies associated with conservative positions, but who dislike the LDP for one reason or another. Until the NLC was created there was no second conservative party for such voters to vote for. Obviously, the party's future prospects are bright if it can convince conservative voters that it offers a viable alternative to the LDP, and if it can attract young urban voters as well. On the other hand, a considerable part of the NLC's initial appeal appears to have been its maverick image and its criticisms of the ways in which established parties operate. Consequently, the NLC may find it increasingly difficult to expand its support as it becomes more established itself and as the memory of the drama of its emergence fades. Some of the speculation about the NLC's future is reminiscent of predictions made about the DSP around 1960. In a poll taken in October 1959 some 10 percent of JSP supporters indicated support for the new Socialist Club formed by Suehiro Nishio and several other Diet members who left the JSP that year. By January 1961 this group, reconstituted as the DSP, had lost 80% of these early supporters.[13] One should, in short, be cautious about predicting rapid NLC growth in the near future. In the end, the NLC's most significant role may be in stimulating the LDP to undertake some meaningful party reforms.

The Japan Communist party has suffered electoral defeats in the mid-1970s as significant as its electoral triumphs of the early 1970s. In the 1976 election the JCP obtained a nationwide popular vote almost identical to that received in 1972 (10.4% in 1976; 10.5% in 1972), but it lost half its seats, going from 38 to 17. It suffered its most severe losses in its popular vote in those districts where it was a real contender for election, and made its biggest gains in those areas where its chances of victory were minimal. It gained about 600,000 more votes than in 1972 in semi-urban and rural districts, and lost about 300,000 votes in big cities, its losses being particularly heavy in Tokyo, Kanagawa, Osaka, Kyoto, and Hyogo.

The JCP percentage of the popular vote went down in 24 of 25 metropolitan districts. The party won ten seats in these districts whereas it had won 22 in the 1972 election. On the other hand, the party's vote increased in 65% of semi-urban districts and in 71% of rural districts. In these districts, however, which together send 175 members to the Diet, the JCP was able to win only four seats. Considerable numbers of voters in these rural and semi-rural areas, in other words, took the opportunity afforded by the certainty of JCP defeat to register a protest vote by voting for the party, an opportunity no longer available in the more politically competitive, highly urbanized districts.

Survey data indicate that Communist party supporters number less than 5 percent of the electorate,[14] and, in contrast to France and Italy where Communist elements dominate the major labor union federations, the Communist party in Japan exerts only a limited influence over the Japanese labor movement. With Sohyo supporting the JSP and Domei backing the DSP, there is no labor federation aligned with the Communist party. The influence the JCP does exert over organized labor comes through its control of some local branches of Sohyo-affiliated unions that on the national level support the JSP.[15]

It is possible that the JCP, with its large number of *jiten* candidates in the 1976 election, will make some gains in the next election. This would be entirely in keeping with the pattern of intra-opposition party swings characteristic of the past decade of Japanese elections. But the JCP seems destined to remain a minor actor in national politics and an improbable participant in government should the era of LDP single-party rule come to an end.

Political Trends: The Future

Given these secular electoral trends—a steady decline in LDP and JSP support, and a proliferation of parties that draw votes primarily from other opposition parties rather than from

[43]

the LDP—what kinds of scenarios can one reasonably construct concerning the composition of future Japanese governments?

The first scenario, obviously, is of continued LDP majority rule. Prime Minister Ohira may well put off an election until the latter part of 1979 or sometime in 1980. If the LDP retains its present Diet membership. (i.e., if there are no defections), it is possible that a careful endorsement policy to anticipate a further moderate decline in the party's popular vote, and the post-election absorption of conservative independents into the party, will enable it to retain exclusive control over the cabinet. Conceivably the following election might not be called until 1983 or 1984. In other words, one should not dismiss the possibility that LDP will hold on to power well into the 1980s.

Should the LDP be unable to put together a majority as a result of the next or succeeding lower house election, its shortfall is unlikely to be large—in all probability less than 10 and almost certainly not more than 20 or 25 seats. To forecast a greater decline than that requires a prediction of substantially increased support for one or another of the opposition parties, and an assumption that such an increase would come at the expense primarily of the LDP rather than at a cost to other opposition parties. Nothing is impossible, but if trends over the past 20 years provide a meaningful yardstick for measuring possible change over the next five to ten years, a sudden and large decline in the number of Diet seats controlled by the LDP is improbable.

In the event, therefore, that the LDP were to find itself short of a majority, it might try to entice one of the small moderate opposition parties to join the cabinet. The New Liberal Club might find it difficult to join such a government because of its newness and the need of its leaders to demonstrate to the public that their motives for leaving the

LDP were "sincere" and not just a gambit for power. The Democratic Socialist party, on the other hand, might be drawn into such a coalition, believing that it could gain public support by demonstrating a greater sense of "responsibility" than other progressive parties, and obtain for itself the role of a crucial swing party able to make or break the LDP-dominated government. In an opposition party coalition the DSP would be but one of several small parties, and its power might be less than what it could hope to exercise in an LDP-dominated cabinet dependent on the DSP's continued cooperation.

Another possibility is that the LDP would rule alone without a majority and with the support, albeit not the formal participation in the government, of one or more of the opposition parties. Japan's opposition parties remember well the disastrous experience of the Katayama and Ashida governments in the late 1940s, when the Socialist party agreed to enter cabinets in which it was outnumbered by conservative party members: The JSP suffered its worst defeat ever in the election that followed that unhappy experience in government. At least some senior members of the DSP, which traces its lineage back to Katayama and his associate Suehiro Nishio, and leaders of the JSP and other opposition parties are understandably reluctant to risk a similar debacle by participating in an LDP-dominated coalition. Support for a minority government from outside the cabinet would enable the supporting party to obtain specific concessions from the LDP while avoiding responsibility for the government's performance.

What scenarios can one construct that would bring power to the opposition parties and exclude the LDP from the government? The answer to that question is that, if the LDP remains unified, there is virtually no possibility that the parties in the opposition camp will replace it in government. Given our assumption that even in the event of a major defeat the

LDP would command at least 235 seats in the lower house (a majority is 256) and that the remaining seats would be controlled by a least six parties (the JSP, KMT, DSP, JCP, NLC and the Social Democratic League [SDL]), a scenario excluding the LDP from power would have to provide for a coalition encompassing virtually the entire opposition camp.

Although the JSP clings to a position of advocating a united front of all anti-LDP parties, a proposal for a coalition government including Communist participation is certain to be rejected by the other opposition parties. Despite its recently moderate and nationalistic line, the JCP's relations with the KMT and DSP and with the Socialist right wing could hardly be worse. The controversies are bitter, the fight for the disaffected floating voter is intense,[16] and the historical legacy of mutual distrust and suspicion between Communists and Socialists is deep and powerful. Even the JSP extreme left-wing group is less than completely enthusiastic about coopera-tion with the JCP because of an enmity that goes back to the 1920s when the Labor-Farmer faction (Rōnō-ha)—to which the Kyokai traces its lineage—broke away from the JCP in a bitter dispute concerning theory and tactics. The 1978 breakdown of the Socialist-Communist alliance in France only contributed to undercut further the already limited interest among the opposition parties in forming a broad-based anti-LDP united front.

In the unlikely event that the LDP were to be about 20 seats short of a majority and the JCP unable to recover its 1976 election losses, the remaining lower house members conceiv-ably could have a mathematical majority. But the possibility that all non-LDP and non-JCP Diet members—from the DSP and NLC on one end to the left-wing Socialists on the other—could constitute a majority and agree to work together is too far-fetched to merit serious consideration.

There is no opposition party that at present admits to a

willingness to join a government in which the LDP is a participant, and there is little possibility that a government which excludes the LDP could be formed. Obviously it would be foolish for an opposition party now to offer to enter a coalition with the LDP and forfeit its bargaining leverage; hence opposition party denials of any intention to participate in a government with the LDP should be treated with considerable skepticism. But all the opposition parties, including the JCP for that matter, while rejecting a sharing of power with the LDP, publicly favor the formation of a coalition government in which elements presently in the LDP would participate. The hope of the centrist parties—the KMT, DSP, NLC, and SDL—is that both the JSP and the LDP will suffer further splits and that a coalition could be put together that would include members of the JSP right wing and a substantial number of LDP members organized under a new party banner. Efforts by the Komeito to create an *Ekomin* alliance—a close relationship between the former Eda faction of the JSP (the "E"), the Komeito ("ko"), and the DSP ("min")—is part of an apparent Komeito strategy to split the JSP and obtain for itself a pivotal role among the center parties. The careful manner with which NLC leaders have sought to maintain close ties with former LDP associates who drew back from leaving the party with Kono attests to the NLC's hope to join together with some of these people at a later date. The DSP under Ryosaku Sasaki, who became party chairman in 1977, has intensified its efforts to create an alliance with the KMT and the NLC and to develop better relations with right-wing Socialists. It is conceivable that some of these centrist parties might at some point formally coalesce in a new party and that some LDP members might join it. Eventually some consolidation seems likely though there are few signs that significant movement in that direction will occur in the immediate future.

It is within the range of conceivable alternatives that a

[47]

coalition government will be formed composed of a number of centrist parties and including elements presently in the LDP. In the last months of 1976 when Prime Minister Miki was battling to hold on to office, a major split in the LDP seemed a real possibility. But the party at that time was caught in a peculiar balance with Miki being its president and his opponents constituting the party's Diet majority. Each claimed that it had legitimate authority and the right to the party label, headquarters, and financial assets in the event of a split. After walking to the brink of a formal division, the party's leaders stepped back and held the LDP together. This was not the first time the LDP threatened to divide (Ichiro Kono, the father of the NLC leader, threatened to split the party in the early 1960s), and it is not likely to be the last. If the glue which has held the LDP together all these years has been political power, an LDP loss of its Diet majority might encourage some LDP members to bolt the party and provide the numbers necessary to bring a centrist coalition (and themselves) to power. Because of the seniority system that regulates the recruitment of LDP Diet men into cabinet and high party positions, some younger members of the party might try to seize the opportunity provided by the LDP's loss of its Diet majority to move into high office quickly by joining in coalition with opposition groups. On the other hand, if its survival were at stake, the LDP well might modify its rules governing high governmental and party appointments to forestall defections. In any event, in the absence of a major electoral defeat for the LDP—or of a scandal even more wrenching than Lockheed—a split does not seem likely.

In summary, it is *probable* that the LDP will remain at the center of the government for the foreseeable future, either with a small Diet majority or with the cooperation of one or more of the small opposition parties. It is *conceivable* that the

LDP will split and a multi-party centrist coalition government will come to power with leaders currently in the LDP playing a central role. It is *improbable* that there will be a government formed by the LDP with a comfortable and secure Diet majority or one formed which completely excludes the participation of leaders presently in the ruling party.

Political Trends: Impact on the Policy Process

Commentators differ as to when to mark the end of what is referred to in Japanese as the "1955 structure"—the long era of one-party dominance inaugurated in 1955 with the establishment of the LDP and the reunification of Socialist parties. But there is little doubt that this structure now is being transformed into a more fluid and more competitive system in which there is neither a party of unchallengeable dominance nor one that dominates the opposition. In this new period, parties other than the LDP, even without formal governmental power, are able to exercise significant influence in the determination of government policy. With its narrow Diet majority, the LDP is unable to control all important Diet committees and must be responsive to at least some opposition demands to get its own legislative program through the Diet. Some of the consequences of this new opposition party power already are evident. In the 1977 Diet session, for example, the government was forced to accept a tax cut and the amendment of an unprecedentedly large number of cabinet bills.[17]

The decline of the LDP, in effect, has resulted in an increase in the number of legitimate participatants in the policy-making process. In earlier years the LDP might have taken opposition views into consideration in the formulation of policy, but it was not necessary to involve opposition parties

[49]

directly in arriving at a consensus view. Since the Japanese decision-making process emphasizes consultation, accommodation, and face-saving, the need to consult more fully with the opposition will, in all probability, contribute to further slowing down and complicating a decision-making process already well known for these characteristics.

This tendency toward a more protracted decision-making process will be further reinforced by the increase in the number of bureaucratic actors in decision-making, particularly in regard to foreign economic policy. Bureaucratic in-fighting among the Foreign Ministry, MITI, and the Ministry of Finance has long characterized the making of Japanese foreign economic policy but, increasingly, ministries and agencies not formerly directly involved in foreign policy are coming to play important decision-making roles. The Environmental Agency's role in setting pollution control standards, the Welfare Ministry's prerogatives to set health standards, and the Construction Ministry's power to regulate plant construction, for example, will complicate inter-ministry coordination and the formulation of government policy. It also is possible that ad hoc alliance will be created between different political parties and particular bureaucratic agencies or sub-units for purposes of influencing the decision-making process.

Although they are able to exercise a new influence on government policy-making, Japan's opposition parties, as indicated earlier, are apprehensive about their future and looking for new sources of electoral support. The search for new support is likely to be manifested in the policy-making arena in intensified efforts to obtain particular benefits for important domestic constituencies. This may involve a new role for groups that had limited influence during the period of LDP dominance, such as organized labor, and an increase in opposition party efforts to court groups whose interest heretofore have been primarily articulated by the LDP, such as farmers and small businessmen.

Opposition party efforts in this regard already have begun to bring them into direct competition with the LDP on issues of foreign relations, propelling further than in the past domestic political competition into the debate on concrete, substantive issues of foreign policy. Foreign affairs have always been a crucial issue-area in domestic Japanese politics, but in the past the opposition has concentrated on generalized attacks on the U.S.-Japan security treaty, on demands for "unarmed neutrality," and on other broad issues. Now anxious to demonstrate to various domestic constituencies that they can be effective in representing their interests, opposition parties have rallied to the defense of farmers and small businessmen and others apprehensive about the impact of measures aimed at making Japan more accessible to the foreign investor and exporter. There is a tendency particularly strong among Japanese politicians to articulate, rather than aggregate, various organized interests; i.e., an inclination to act as intra-parliamentary lobbyists for specific pressure groups. Opposition party politicians exhibit this pattern as strongly as do LDP Diet members. By being the party in power the LDP has had to seek a balance between satisfying domestic demands and responding to bureaucratic and external pressures. It is not so easy for a government to resist the demands of parties it does not control.

Together, domestic political trends are likely to complicate decision-making processes, creating both a degree of political immobilism and a greater "domestication" of foreign economic issues as parties compete to obtain "victories" for interest groups that are sources of present or potential support. Given Japanese approaches to decision-making, and the increase in the number of participants in the policy process, Japan's political leadership is likely to experience considerable difficulty in implementing policies that reflect an appropriately balanced response to external and domestic pressures. Criticized by other countries for not moving fast enough to stimulate world-wide economic growth or for not taking adequate measures to restrain its exporters, and attacked by the opposition for buckling under to foreign pressure and sacrificing Japanese interests, the Japanese government will be hard pressed to construct a set of policies that are internationally responsible at the same time that they are rational in domestic political terms.

Domestic Policy Orientations

Along with increased political competition between the LDP and its opponents to service various domestic constituencies, one of the most salient features of the recent political scene in Japan has been the relative absence of major disagreement between the ruling party and the opposition on fundamental policy issues. Much of the opposition's attacks on the LDP has been attacks on its behavior, not on government policies. The NLC's appeal, as mentioned earlier, was not that it offered policy alternatives but that it raised hopes for a new kind of politics. All of Japan's opposition parties, acutely aware of their limited bases of support and endeavoring to become more broadly based "catch-all" parties, tend to be reluctant to advocate policies that might incur the opposition of any substantial sector of the voting public, and anxious to push policies that will gain new support. As a consequence, opposition parties generally have been moving closer to the LDP in their broad policy orientations at the same time that they have intensified their efforts to compete with the LDP in seeking to satisfy a variety of demands emanating from the public at large, and from a variety of specific interest groups.

On domestic policies—the issue-area Japanese voters, like voters everywhere, are most concerned about—the opposition has concentrated on attacking the LDP's pro-big-business policies and in calling for increases in governmental social welfare programs. An anti-big-business orientation is somewhat stronger in the JSP and the KMT than in the DSP and NLC, but each of these parties, though differing on specifics, has called for a strengthening of anti-monopoly legislation and for special government programs to assist small and medium-sized business firms. Attacks on LDP-big business ties, however, are moderated by repeated affirmation of a commitment to a mixed welfare state economy by all opposition groups but the Communists and left-wing Socialists, by a willingness on the part of all opposition parties except the Communist party to accept political contributions from business, and by a reluctance to offer specific proposals aimed at controlling business activities. With the final adoption in the 1976 Diet of a watered-down anti-monopoly law, and the passage in the 1975 Diet of a law restricting business political contributions, the opposition lacks, for the moment at least, specific policies to give substance to its verbal attacks on big business.

Japanese national government expenditures amount to about 20% of GNP, a figure considerably lower than that of other economically advanced countries. A defense budget that takes less than 1% of GNP (and 6% of the national budget) is a major reason for this low level of government spending, but comparatively low social welfare expenditures also contribute to Japan's ability to keep its budget relatively small.

The government, however, has in the past several years taken measures to meet increasing public demands for expanded social welfare programs. In 1973 the Diet passed a number of laws that substantially reformed health insurance and social security programs. Of particular importance were revisions of the laws regulating pension insurance schemes, revisions which immediately raised the level of benefits two and a half times and which introduced a "price slide system" whereby benefits are increased automatically to compensate for rises in the consumer price index.

As a result of these reforms social security expenditures have risen substantially—from 15.6% of total expenditures in the government general accounts budget in 1971 to 20% in 1977—and currently constitute the single largest category of expenditures in the budget. Expressed as a percentage of national income, Japanese government expenditures related to social security are still low compared to Western European countries. Although they reached a new high level of 10.1% of national income in 1976, this compares with figures (for 1974) of 25.2% for West Germany, 21.8% for France and 16.1% for Britain (the figure for the United States was 14%). But comparatively low social security expenditures are in part due to the relatively small ratio of the population over 65 to the total population, a figure of 8% in Japan compared to an average of over 14% in Western Europe. It is projected, however, that Japan's over-65 population will double in numbers between 1975 and 2000 and reach a ratio to total population of 14.2%, comparable to the European average. As a consequence of this demographic shift and as a direct result of the 1973 reforms, the Health and Welfare Ministry now projects that social security related expenditures will account for 19.3% of national income at the end of the century without any further expansion of welfare programs.[18]

Although opposition parties emphasize the need for expanded state activities in the area of social welfare and for improvements in what Japanese refer to as "quality of life" issues—such as pollution control, improved roads and sewerage systems, increases in the number of parks and recreational facilities, and government housing programs—they, for the most part, have not advocated a major reordering of government priorities to pay for new welfare related programs. The opposition used to call for a reduction in defense spending as a means of providing revenue for other government programs, but even the Socialist party today supports the maintenance of the self-defense forces at about their present level.

Unwilling to advocate policies of redistribution, and to pay the political costs involved in holding back expenditures for some programs in order to increase them for others, opposition party proposals for upgrading Japan's inadequate social services essentially depend on policies aimed at expanding the size of the budget. Increases in corporate taxes is seen as one means to this end, but the inclination to avoid proposing programs that might alienate any important sector of present or potential support has led the opposition, despite its earlier criticisms of the government's high growth policies and its calls for "stable growth," to itself press for policies aimed at making the economy grow faster. Although they differ with the LDP—and among themselves[19]—on how to accomplish this goal, they share with the LDP a desire to have economic expansion obviate the need for redividing in any far-reaching way the government's allocation of its share of the economic pie. Accordingly, there is today no substantial difference in the growth rate targets advocated by the LDP and the opposition parties. The Komeito, in fact, which stresses its commitment to the goal of greater government social welfare expenditures, in a lengthy (581-page) five-year social welfare plan published in October 1976, was impelled to project a five-year annual growth rate (1975-80) of 7.2%, higher than the official government target of 6%, to find the money to pay for its programs.[20]

The issue of constitutional revision deserves mention because it, along with party policies on the U.S.-Japan security treaty discussed in the following section, best symbolize the weakening of the ideological bipolarity that for so long characterized postwar Japanese politics.

When the LDP was formed in 1955, its platform called for the revision of the constitution. The Socialist party, on the other hand, claimed the defense of the constitution as its overriding objective. Throughout the 1950s and into the 1960s, constitutional revision was a major political issue, and parties could be classified as being either progressive or conservative according to the position they took on the constitution and on the security treaty issue.

Today constitutional revision has lost much of its earlier political significance, and the distinction between conservative and progressive has lost much of its earlier relevance. There still are individuals in the LDP who would like to see the constitution revised and aspirants to party leadership who raise the issue as a way to make themselves acceptable to the party's right wing. LDP faction leader and party presidential candidate Nakasone's well publicized statements [21] in the spring of 1978 calling for a revision of Article 9 are best understood in the context of the LDP's intra-party politics and Nakasone's personal political ambitions.

But revisionists, no matter how irate at having to live with the "MacArthur constitution," recognize that the balance of political power makes the amending of the constitution a practical impossibility.[22] The Socialist party, for its part, finds it increasingly difficult to rally support in the name of defending the "peace constitution" which the Japanese public, if not its political leadership, now takes largely for granted.

This basic law, drafted just thirty years ago under the guidance of American Occupation authorities, is now so widely accepted by the public as setting the legitimate and appropriate framework for conducting the nation's affairs that it is not possible for politicians to rally support for either side of the revisionist issue.

Broad public acceptance of the constitution, and of the legitimacy of the institutions and processes which it sanctions, symbolize and contribute to the stability of the contemporary political system. One should not confuse evidence of new patterns of political competition and flux, if not confusion, in party politics, with political instability. These patterns reflect the growing responsiveness of Japan's political elite to public demands for party programs that reflect contemporary rather than past concerns. There is an essential stability to the Japanese political system that results from the absence of the kind of wrenching social cleavages with which Western democracies are only too familiar, from public skepticism that another type of political system would bring greater security and prosperity than the present one, and from a broadly based belief that the constitution, as it has evolved over the past three decades, posits norms, and provides for institutions and processes, that are incompatible neither with Japanese traditions nor with Japanese interests.

In coming years there will no doubt be many specific issues where the LDP will find itself in conflict with the opposition and forced to make compromises. Public pressures on the government to increase its expenditures can only become stronger; competition among parties, and between parties and bureaucratic groups, will become more intense; and the decision-making process will become more complex and contentious. The domestic policies advocated by the opposition in the short- and mid-term, however, are not fundamentally incompatible with LDP policies. The search for power has moved the opposition to the right, and the determination to hold on to power has forced the LDP somewhat to the left, making domestic policy differences between them less susceptible than in earlier years to easy categorization.

Foreign Policy Orientations

In foreign policy as well as in the domestic area the present political situation is characterized by the absence of deep divisions. This is an extraordinary circumstance, given the fact that the foreign policy orientations of Japan's postwar parties were in fundamental conflict: the conservatives advocating a policy of alliance with the United States, and the opposition calling for a position of unarmed neutrality. Today there is a remarkable lack of sharp controversy on most issues.

On some issues, such as the northern islands dispute with the Soviet Union, there are no discernible significant differences between the opposition parties and the LDP. On issues such as the Fukuda government's emphasis on strengthening ties with ASEAN, opposition parties (and the mass media) have said either nothing or have offered implicit support. International economic issues and the acquisition of adequate energy and raw materials are a major source of malaise but, given the intractability and complexity of many of these issues, attacks on the government have rarely been accompanied by specific proposals for alternative measures.

China policy has long been a divisive issue in postwar Japanese politics. But with normalization of relations between the PRC and Japan in 1973, the subsequent steady deepening of relations, and the conclusion of a peace and friendship treaty in August 1978, China has ceased to be a source of major political controversy. Disagreements within the LDP in the months preceding conclusion of the friendship treaty over the so-called "hegemony" clause were replicated in other parties. And the incident involving the disputed Senkaku islands in April 1978, in which Chinese fishing vessels massed to give concrete expression to Peking's assertions of sovereignty over the islands, resulted in a nationalist reaction that spread across the Japanese political spectrum. But all party groups, including the "cautious" faction in the LDP, were in favor of a China treaty in principle and its signing in August 1978 was accomplished without generating any significant domestic political controversy.

On the contrary, Teng Hsiao-ping's statements on the importance of maintaining the U.S.-Japan security treaty and the need for Japan to strengthen its self-defense capabilities made during his visit to Tokyo in October 1978 to ratify the treaty proved to be a great embarrassment to the Japanese left, particularly to the JSP, whose opposition to the security treaty and support for unarmed neutrality for so long had been linked to its strongly pro-PRC position. In terms of its impact on domestic Japanese politics, the treaty, and Teng's visit especially, served to reinforce the impression that the Socialists were wed to an outmoded and irrelevant foreign policy line.

Teng's remarks also added additional fuel to the so-called Japanese "defense debate." For years domestic political controversy over defense policy in Japan revolved around the question of whether Japan should maintain any defense force at all. Today, although the Socialist party remains formally committed to a position of unarmed neutrality, the question of whether Japan should maintain defense forces is no longer a live issue. Rather the question now being posed is how much more defense—in terms of gross expenditures, new weapons systems, domestic production of armaments, strategic planning and the like—is necessary. This debate, however, is taking place in an environment in which there is widespread public support for maintaining defense forces at approximately present levels. Many recent proposals for strengthening Japanese defense forces are, in effect, trial balloons intended to test the limits of this consensus; ironically, they have put much of the political opposition in the position of defending the status quo.

Broad public support for present Japanese defense policy is evident in a variety of recent public opinion polls. In a 1976 nationwide opinion poll, for example, some 54% of the respondents expressed support for a security system based on the U.S.-Japan security treaty and the maintenance of the self-defense forces "as they presently exist." [23] This support was naturally highest among voters for the LDP (67%), but 53% of JSP, and even 33% of Communist party, supporters expressed support for the treaty and the self-defense forces.

In a 1977 poll commissioned by the defense agency,[24] some 83% of respondents indicated support for the maintenance of the self-defense forces at their present level. There was little expressed support for a major effort to develop a greatly increased defense capability and almost no support for the Socialist alternative of unarmed neutrality.

Significantly, increasing public approval of the security treaty and of current levels of defense expenditures has been accompanied by growing opposition to the revision of Article 9 of the constitution. In an *Asahi Shinbun* poll published on November 1, 1978, 57% of the respondents expressed support for maintaining defense forces at their present level and 19% thought they should be strengthened. In contrast, only 11% supported a reduction, and 5% the total abolition, of the defense forces. (Other opinions and "don't knows" account for the remaining 8%.) In the same poll, however, only 15% of the respondents expressed support for amending Article 9. This contrasts with support for revising the constitution's no-war article by 26% of the respondents when the *Asahi* asked the same question in a poll in 1962. When taken together, these responses reflect the broad public support that currently exists for maintaining the status quo in defense policy.

On many issues related to defense, however, a large percentage of Japanese questioned in opinion surveys tend to give a "don't know" response. In an April 1978 *Yomiuri* poll, for example, 46.6% of the respondents said "don't know" to the question whether Japan should strengthen its self-defense forces "to cope with America's separation from Asia, such as the planned withdrawal of U.S. ground forces from the Republic of Korea." Some 31.1% supported an increase and 22.3% were opposed to it. In the same poll 52.5% of the respondents replied "don't know" to the question whether they agreed with the Defense Agency's view that the definition of what constitutes "war potential" as prohibited by Article 9 of the constitution depends on the international situation and the state of military technology. The Defense Agency's view was supported by 23.4% and opposed by 24.1% of the respondents.[25]

These kinds of responses compound the difficulty of measuring current public attitudes on defense and security matters. But, on the whole, the data indicate that agreement is widespread that the government's present security policies are sensible responses to the perceived constraints and opportunities created by Japan's external environment. They do not reveal broad support for any policies markedly different from those currently being pursued.

The defense question has entered a new stage in Japan in terms of the issues being debated. But a greater willingness than in the past to discuss defense and to debate the merits of increasing the nation's military power is not likely, in the short run at least, to lead to significantly new departures in defense policy. Proposals for substantially increasing defense capability not only attract little support; they continue to generate considerable and emphatic opposition. Furthermore, even conservative proponents of a greater defense role argue for relatively modest increases in the Defense Agency's share of the budget, and few challenge present government policy banning the deployment of troops overseas, conscription, or the acquisition of nuclear weapons.[26] The Defense Agency itself, while stressing in recent White Papers the seriousness of the Soviet threat and the declining power of the United States, remains committed to a policy that emphasizes the qualitative improvement of logistics, communications and existing weapons systems rather than the redefinition of the Self Defense Forces' mission or major changes in force structure.

The defense budget for fiscal year 1979 is slightly over $10 billion (2,094,489 million yen), an increase of 10.2% over the previous year's budget. However, in terms of its percentage of GNP, Japan's 1979 defense budget accounted for the same 0.9% as in 1978. In the absence of major changes in Japan's external environment it is unlikely that this percentage will be significantly increased.

Despite growing attention to defense issues, public pressures on the government's budget are for greater expenditures for housing, social services, improved social security pensions and the like, and not for increased defense spending. In contrast to the 10.2% increase in the defense budget, expenditures for housing in the 1979 budget increased 22%, public works expenditures were up 20%, and spending on environmental and sanitation projects, such as the construction of modern sewer systems, increased by a full 30% over 1978.[27]

In absolute sums, of course, Japan's defense expenditures are expected to increase considerably over the next decade. If defense spending remains pegged approximately at 0.9% of GNP, an annual growth rate rate for the economy of 7% will mean the doubling of defense expenditures to over $20 billion in ten years. Given our assessment of public and leadership attitudes, our projections of future party support, and our assumption of relative stability in Japan's external environment, it is highly improbable that there will be a government in power in the foreseeable future that will attempt to adjust substantially upward the spending on defense. A careful reading of the defense debate provides very little evidence to support those observers who argue that Japan is on the verge of inititiating a major defense buildup or that it is in the process of reconsidering in a fundamental way its basic defense policies.

The declining importance of major foreign policy issues in the domestic political debate is best symbolized by opposition party statements on the U.S.-Japan security treaty—which itself symbolizes for Japanese the basic orientations of postwar Japanese foreign policy. In postwar Japan to be "progressive" meant, more than anything else, to advocate the "defense of the constitution" and the termination of the security treaty. In 1960 the combined progressive forces were able to turn out masses of people to protest the treaty and the continuation of Japan's close alliance with the United States. It would have been difficult at that time to imagine a situation in which an increase in opposition party influence over government policy would be combined with the virtual shelving by the opposition itself of the treaty issue. Yet that is precisely what has happened. No matter what configuration a Japanese government coalition may take in coming years, the security treaty is likely to be at the bottom of its agenda.

Within the opposition camp the DSP advocates the most conservative position on the treaty, its position now being virtually indistinguishable from that of the LDP. Until 1975 the party maintained a mildly revisionist policy in calling for a "security treaty without bases." The party's stated goal was to maintain a security relationship with the United States while revising the security treaty itself so as to eliminate the presence of American troops on Japanese soil. In its 1975 congress the party adopted a new position calling' for the retention of the treaty in its present form. During the 1976 lower house campaign, party chairman Kasuga demanded JSP acceptance of the treaty as an essential condition for cooperation between the two parties.[28]

The Komeito's position on the treaty has swung in the past few years from demands for immediate abrogation to tacit acceptance. In the party's first program in 1964 it called for the treaty's abrogation but took a position to the right of the JSP and the JCP by cautioning against "immediate" abrogation. In 1967 the party position was that the treaty relationship should be gradually dissolved in the coming ten to twenty years. For a brief period following the party's defeat in the 1972 lower house election, the Komeito moved into close alliance with the JSP. At its 1974 party congress, it fell in line with the JSP position on the treaty, adopting a policy plank calling for its "immediate" termination. The party was not long, however, in retreating from this position. In 1975 it adopted its current position of treaty abrogation "through diplomatic negotiations." The party has not spelled out what kind of negotiating process it envisages, but its position seems to suggest support for treaty termination at some unspecified future time when it could be accomplished without harming U.S.-Japan relations and without compromising Japanese security. The "vision" published in 1976 by the Society to Think about a New Japan, an organization created to bring together KMT, DSP, and right-wing JSP leaders, includes a statement on the security treaty that probably comes closest to describing the KMT position: "to make diplomatic efforts to create an environment in which military alliances will be unnecessary so that the security treaty can be dissolved." [29] By putting the emphasis on creating a peaceful environment before abolishing the treaty, this formulation represents a complete reversal of the view long held by the Japanese left that the treaty itself is a cause of international tension, and its abolition an essential step in creating a peaceful international environment. This approach is rather symbolic of the general Komeito approach to foreign policy. Given a different world, the party seems to say, a Komeito government would implement a different foreign policy.[30]

The Socialist party has long been committed to a policy of demanding the treaty's immediate abrogation and reaffirms this position at each year's party congress. In reality, however, the party's position is considerably more ambiguous. Party leaders now suggest that "immediate" does not mean termination immediately upon coming to power but immediately upon the realization of conditions that would insure continued close ties with the United States. During the 1976 election campaign, party chairman Narita indicated that if the Socialist party came to power, the security treaty "would be dissolved through a process of diplomatic negotiation." [31] This statement received front-page coverage in the press, suggesting, as it did in its use of the Komeito phraseology, a marked JSP retreat from the "immediate abrogation" position with which it has long been identified.

The Communist party in its official ideology claims that Japan is a semi-colony of the United States and that the security treaty provides the mechanism by which the United States holds Japan in a subjugated state. Central to its nationalistic appeal is the demand that Japan recover full

[65]

independence and autonomy by abrogating the treaty. None-theless, even the Communist party has moderated its public position on the treaty. After Narita's statement during the 1976 election campaign, JCP chairman Miyamoto announced that if a broad-based coalition government with Communist participation were to be formed, the JCP would support the shelving of the treaty issue. The party apparently wished to demonstrate with this campaign postion its willingness to subordinate its own policies for the greater good of creating a united front capable of ousting the LDP from power. But the fact that the JCP saw tactical advantage in making somewhat more ambiguous its public statements on the treaty also is indicative of the extent to which it believes that a strong anti-treaty stance has become a political liability.

As was evident in policies enunciated during the 1976 lower house election campaign, Japan's opposition parties are seeking to reassure the voters that, were they to participate in government, the abrogation of the security treaty would not be an immediate goal. But eventual abrogation of the treaty remains a central objective in the official programs of the JSP and KMT as well as the Communist party. This objective, muted though it has been in election campaigning and in the general drive for broader public support, finds expression in other contexts. The suggestion of DSP chairman Sasaki that an alliance of the DSP, KMT, NLC, and SDL might be formed on the basis of support for the security treaty drew an immediate denial from KMT secretary-general Yano.[32] A joint communiqué issued by JSP chairman Asukata and the North Korean Workers Party, in addition to declaring virtually complete Socialist party support for the North Korean position on "the unification and democratization of the motherland," declared that the North Koreans fully support "the JSP demand for the abolition of the security treaty and the removal of all American bases and American military personnel from every part of Japan including Okinawa." [33]

Thus, the treaty issue remains as a potential source of political controversy should the international situation evolve— or rather deteriorate—in such a way as to convince political groups that an aggressively anti-treaty stance would have new popular appeal. It is likely, however, that present trends will continue to undermine treaty opposition in Japan and make more ambiguous and muted the opposition that persists. The argument that the treaty might involve Japan in a war of American making increasingly rings hollow in the context of American withdrawal from Asia following the Vietnam war. Chinese support for the treaty has robbed anti-treaty forces of the argument that the treaty places Japan in a position of hostility to this large Communist neighbor. And, ironically, decreasing confidence in the United States has led many political leaders to recognize, and occasionally to say so publicly, that the treaty has become a positive factor in securing a relationship that is, above all others, crucial to Japan's prosperity and security.

Korea

Relations with the two regimes on the Korean peninsula provide one of the few issues in the current domestic politics of Japanese foreign policy where fundamental differences persist. The existence of a Korean community in Japan divided in its loyalties to South and North Korea and a history of colonial rule before, and of extensive economic influence after, the Second World War contribute to make Korea an extremely complex issue in Japanese politics. The opposition protested the 1964 normalization agreement with South Korea and, with

[67]

the exception of the DSP which maintains close relations with the South, it has called for an improvement of relations with North Korea, and a withdrawal of American troops from the South. The bilateral tensions sparked by the kidnapping of Kim Dae Jung from a Tokyo hotel in 1973, the development of the Koreagate scandal in the United States and allegations of extensive corruption between South Korea and the Japanese "Korean lobby," and the Carter Administration's decision to withdraw ground troops from South Korea, have had the effect in Japan of further exacerbating an already divisive issue in Japanese domestic politics and foreign policy.

The Korean issue, perhaps more than any other, tends to polarize Japanese opinion, and it is not clear what positions will be evolved by self-defined centrist parties in regard to Korean relations. American troop withdrawals from Korea are widely interpreted in Japan as being part of a more general American disengagement from Asian affairs, and one gets the sense that demands for a complete American pullout are much less forcefully stated and more qualified now that withdrawals have actually begun. Nonetheless, despite apprehensions about the impact of withdrawal on regional security, parties and politicians who have been calling for the improving of relations with North Korea and for the complete withdrawal of American troops from the South are not likely to retreat suddenly from these well-known positions.

Depending on developments in U.S.-South Korean relations, and the pace of the U.S. military withdrawal, opposition elements, as well as some groups within the LDP, might believe that they would have a fairly popular issue in arguing that Japan should not be left as the only major power totally committed to support for the Park regime. Again depending on the evolution of U.S. policy, political leaders both in the LDP and among the opposition might be able to argue with a degree of credibility which results from recent experience that Japan should move quickly to normalize its relations with the North to avoid incurring the "shock" of U.S. moves to go "over the head" *(atamagoshi)* of Japan to engage in direct negotiations with the North Koreans. As far-fetched as this concern may seem, some Japanese already worry out loud that the Carter Administration may be contemplating initiatives toward the North without informing, much less consulting, the Japanese. Japanese press reports that Yugoslav President Tito carried a message from President Carter to Kim Il-sung during his August 1977 trip to North Korea are symptomatic of Japanese nervousness on this issue. In addition, of course, there is the possibility that Japan will become embroiled in its own version of Koreagate. Tokyo has long been rife with speculation of corrupt dealings between South Korea and Japanese politicans and business leaders, but no concrete evidence has been produced to prove these allegations. Should there be revelations of widespread kickbacks and other forms of corruption, the scandal could have consequences much more profound than those produced by the Lockheed incident. Depending on the personalities involved, it could precipitate the breaking up of one or more of Japan's political parties and bring intense pressure to bear on the government to change the course of its Korea policy.

Public Opinion

Japanese public opinion, in the sense of the opinion that is attentive to foreign affairs—particularly the opinion of the mass media and of foreign affairs commentators and scholars—and Japan's political leadership are strikingly unified in their perceptions of the external constraints imposed on Japanese

[69]

foreign policy. Although a verbal emphasis on an "autonomous foreign policy" *(jishu gaikō)* is characteristic of the foreign policy rhetoric of both the conservative and the opposition parties and appears in a great deal of the public discussion of foreign policy, Japanese elite groups of virtually all political persuasions tend to be keenly aware of the constraints on policy imposed by recent changes in the world situation. Deterioration in relations with the United States and international economic and political uncertainties reinforce a Japanese sense of vulnerability and a perception of Japan as a country buffeted by the winds of change and unable to do much more than make pragmatic adjustments to situations created by others more powerful. The image evoked by former Prime Minister Fukuda of his being captain of the ship *Nippon Maru* strikes a responsive chord in Japan. Foreign policy is seen as a problem of moving Japan between the Scylla and Charybdis of international political and economic affairs, with success being dependent on a combination of skill, fortitude, and luck. This pyschological orientation is not conducive either to bold initiatives or to grand strategy; it contributes to a proclivity toward policies that emphasize the minimizing of risks rather than the maximizing of opportunities, and to behavior that is reactive and defensive.

The upshot of these attitudes is a consensus on foreign policy that can best be described as a kind of consensus by default. It results from an inability to articulate alternatives to present policy, which, in turn, is the consequence of a widely shared perception of Japanese vulnerability and of the limited range of foreign policy choice.

Japanese intellectuals have for years been writing about the need for Japan to define a new role, a concern that recently has become intensified as a result of Japan's emergence as one of the world's great economic powers, increasing foreign demands that Japan play a more activist role in dealing with important international issues and, most important of all, a widespread perception in Japan of rapidly declining American power and prestige. But there is little evidence to support the view that Japanese believe, as many foreigners think they must believe, that Japan should play a politically and possibly militarily more assertive role in world affairs, much less that Japan currently is characterized by a widespread and irrepressible desire for greater world power. Obviously, Japanese would like their country to attain a position of prestige in the international community commensurate with Japan's economic power. Naturally, Japanese would like to be in a position to be able to resist the often heavy-handed pressures put on them by the United States and others. But there is little to suggest that Japanese are willing, much less anxious, to pay the political price that comes with power and leadership.

There is much talk, to be sure, about how Japanese recently are more willing to express their views on international issues. The younger generation of Japanese business leaders and government bureaucrats and, to a lesser extent, politicians are, on the whole, more skillful in English, and they are more willing to speak out on issues of concern to Japan. The attainment of positions of increasing influence by this postwar generation should have some impact on Japan's foreign policy style; at the least, it should help alleviate those problems in Japan's international relations created by a severe language barrier and misunderstandings rooted in cultural differences.

But the significance of a generational shift in Japanese leadership should not be exaggerated. Perceptions of the constraints on Japanese policy cut across generations. Japan cannot easily adjust the rhetoric of its foreign policy away from a traditional postwar "low posture" without generating further demands abroad on Japan to do more in areas where it is reluctant to play an active role. Since stimulating such demands runs counter to the risk-minimization orientation of Japanese foreign policy, it is likely to be checked, particularly as the younger generation gets older and finds itself playing more central policy-making roles.

In addition, one should not underestimate the extent to which Japanese continue to see the national purpose as being the achievement of higher levels of affluence. The notion that Japanese have taken satisfaction in having achieved their goal of catching up with the West economically and that they must now move on to pursue new goals is premature at best. Lower economic growth is not popular, and most of the salient issues in contemporary Japanese politics revolve around public demands for improved living conditions. Japan is not a society bored with the pursuit of wealth. It remains a strongly conservative society: one in which values associated with economic growth remain powerful, and in which perceptions of Japan as being resource-poor and vulnerable to outside forces beyond its control remain widespread.

Furthermore, it is unlikely that Japanese patterns of leadership recruitment will permit the emergence of a leadership which would actively seek to define new national goals and a different foreign policy. In 1978 the LDP revised the rules governing the election of the party president who, as long as the LDP remains the majority party, becomes premier. This reform and the Diet's passage in 1975 of a bill revising the law regulating political funding were intended ostensibly to weaken the role of factions in choosing the party's leadership and to constrain the competition between them for political funds.

The first election under the new LDP system was held in December 1978 and resulted in the victory of Masayoshi Ohira over the incumbent Prime Minister Takeo Fukuda. The new system provides for a two-tiered election process which for the first time gives all LDP members an opportunity to play a role in choosing the party leaders. In the first round of balloting, party members vote for one of the party's declared candidates. Votes are tallied in each prefecture according to a complicated formula that distributes the votes of all the candidates among the two top-placed ones. The two candidates who then come out with the highest votes nationwide go before a convention of the Diet members of the LDP, which chooses one to be the party president. In the December 1978 election the candidates were the incumbent Prime Minister Fukuda, secretary general Ohira, MITI minister Komoto, and LDP executive council chairman Nakasone. Although the rules state that any LDP Diet member who obtains the support of at least twenty other LDP Diet members may run in the election, all of the candidates in 1978 were faction leaders with the exception of Komoto, who is the senior member and heir apparent of the faction led by former Prime Minister Miki. In the first round of balloting Ohira, to the surprise of most observers, won a solid victory. Thereupon Fukuda withdrew from the race, knowing that he would not be able to reverse the decision in the Diet members' party convention and recognizing that a fight in the convention might split the party.

This system is still too new to permit definitive judgments as to its long-term impact on the LDP but, in the short run at least, the consequences of the system have been, ironically enough, to strengthen certain patterns of organization it was supposedly intended to weaken. In the past the party president was selected by the members of the Diet in the LDP (along with one representative from each of the party's prefectural chapters), the successful candidate being the one who could put together a winning coalition of factions with which LDP Diet members were affiliated. The new system, rather than

[73]

weakening factions, has had the effect of pushing the factions to extend *their* organization down to the grass roots in order to mobilize the votes of party members in the primary. Since there are relatively few people who are militant activists for the "party," party members have been recruited largely through the personal organizations of individual Dietmen who tended to encourage the registration as party members of as many of their personal supporters as necessary to maintain a balance with other LDP Diet members in their election district. A large number of party members voting in the presidential first round balloting, therefore, tended to be concerned with serving the interests of the individual Diet member whom they support, interests defined largely in terms of the position taken by the faction to which the Diet member belongs. Ohira's success was not due to his being personally popular among large numbers of party members but, rather, because he had put together a winning coalition of factions, the support of the faction loyal to former Prime Minister Tanaka being particularly crucial.

The change in the system for selecting the party president has not only failed so far to weaken the role of factions in choosing the party's leader. It also has failed to reduce the large amounts of money consumed in the Japanese political process. Although the support of many party members can be mobilized by individual Dietmen for their faction's candidate for LDP president, making sure that they understand what is at stake and what choice at the polls will best serve the interests of the Dietmen they support requires extensive campaigning. To prepare for the new primary system, the LDP initiated a major membership drive in 1978 in which it registered some one-and-a-half million members in time for the December election. Consequently, in the weeks leading up to the election, LDP Diet members engaged in a major election campaign, returning to their districts to meet with local party members and to explain whom they were supporting and why, a range of activities that costs money not provided by membership dues which, in any event, go to the party headquarters and not to the effective campaign organizations—the individual Diet member's machine and the party factions.

The decision to change the system for choosing the party president was spurred largely by a feeling among the party's leaders that, in the aftermath of the Lockheed scandal, they had to do something to demonstrate to the electorate that they were seriously committed to party reform. At the same time they were unwilling to institute a reform that would fundamentally upset long-established patterns for recruiting the top leadership of the party and that might threaten their own position in the party. Although the incumbent prime minister was defeated in the December 1978 election, this was not due, as I have argued, so much to the new element of a party-wide primary as it was to the ability of the challenger, Ohira, to put together a winning factional coalition among LDP Diet members.

In the long run, however, the reform may have a significant impact on the party's choice of its president. The LDP currently is committed to doubling the party membership to three million. The larger the membership becomes, the larger becomes the number of party members on the margin who are either not locked into an individual Diet member's support organization or who refuse for one reason or another to vote for the presidential candidate endorsed by the Diet member they do support. In addition, the larger the number of members, the more difficult and expensive campaigning becomes. There probably is a size threshold which, once passed, might enable a fairly small inner-party "floating" vote in a close contest to swing the election in favor of a candidate who is not the strongest in terms of his factional support. The questions this raises of course is whether the party in the second round of balloting would be able politically to reverse the decision made by the party's mass membership in the first round, and, if it did so, whether the defeated candidate, having demonstrated his support among the party members, would not be tempted to split the party.

In any event, for the foreseeable future, factional structures will continue to mediate the recruitment of political leadership and to give the edge to politicians who are skillful in attracting loyalty from inner-party groups, and who project their role as representing the views of those groups, rather than to politicians who achieve broad public popularity and overtly demonstrate individual initiative and personal leadership. Even in a situation where the latter type of politician might obtain power, social values and organizational arrangements would continue to impose considerable constraints on the exercise of personal and dynamic leadership. Moreover, with increased opposition party influence, and particularly in the event of coalition government, one may well see an even greater leadership role than in the past for the technocratic element in the LDP. Many of these former government bureaucrats, particularly among the younger generation of LDP politicians, are regarded by the opposition as more ideologically neutral than other LDP leaders, and they possess expertise in policy matters that the opposition largely lacks. These technocrats do not have the attributes, however, that one usually associates with dynamic leadership, and there is little evidence that their perceptions of the constraints impinging on Japanese foreign policy are markedly different from the present generation of political leaders.

Furthermore, mass opinion, though its impact on foreign

policy decision-making is no less indirect in Japan than elsewhere, serves an essentially constraining role.

Conclusion

The picture I have drawn here places in sharp relief factors that contribute to stability in Japan's basic foreign policy orientations and to a foreign policy approach that emphasizes pragmatic responses to external events as they unfold. I have not maintained that these factors compel an inflexible adherence to the status quo, but I have argued that they strongly militate against major departures in Japan's foreign policies. I also have suggested that political trends will complicate decision-making processes, creating both a degree of immobilism and a greater "domestication" of foreign economic issues as parties compete to obtain "victories" for interest groups that are sources of present or potential support.

These trends do not portend well for Japan's role in international society. They do not create pressures in the direction of encouraging the Japanese government to take initiatives to try to resolve important international problems but, if anything, act as a counterbalance to pressures from abroad on Japan to take a greater leadership role in international affairs. Whether the issue be tariff-reduction talks in the GATT, economic assistance to less developed countries, or whatever, the Japanese reaction is likely to continue to be belated moves to keep in step, as one so often hears in Japan, with the "trend of the times."

The notion so widespread in Japan that the nation's survival depends on a correct reading of, and response to, the "trend of the times," however, also provides opportunities for the

[77]

government to justify new actions as unavoidable, given changed world conditions. Accordingly, if major changes are to occur in Japanese foreign policy, they are likely to come about, and be justified, as defensive reactions to new external circumstances rather than as the result of government strategy or as the consequence of political pressures generated in the domestic environment. We are not likely to see a Japanese de Gaulle emerge to lead the Japanese people to assert their nation's power in the world. Should Japan set off on a new course in its foreign relations, it will in all probability be led there by men who claim to be taking defensive measures made inevitable by world conditions and Japan's vulnerable position. In this sense, the important question for the future is not only whether a government with different foreign policy orientations will come to power, but whether external events will encourage and enable the government to mobilize broad support for a departure in policy characterized as a necessary defensive move to meet a threatening and hostile situation. It is this quality of defensive responsiveness that imparts to Japanese foreign policy both its resistance to change and its considerable flexibilty.

The breakdown of the rigid bipolarity that characterized postwar Japanese politics and foreign policy conceivably could make it easier for the government to respond with new policies to a dramatic change in Japan's external environment. The weakening of political forces that "oppose for opposition's sake" and the increased strength of centrist parties that hold ambiguous and vague foreign policy positions could enable the government, given a radical change in Japan's foreign relations, more easily to mobilize a consensus in favor of a new policy line than has been possible in the past. In contrast to Western societies where the challenge to political stability comes in the form of centrifugal forces created by class conflict and racial, ethnic, linguistic, or geographical cleavage, Japanese society is marked by a relative lack of class-based antagonism and a virtual absence of conflict rooted in racial or linguistic or geographical differences.[34] Should the stability of the Japanese political system be challenged, the threat is likely to come not, as one would expect in the United States, in the form of social disintegration, but in the call for an all-encompassing social integration in the name of national survival. It is not inconceivable that a Japanese government, particularly if it were a broad-based coalition, in the context of a marked deterioration in Japan's external environment, could push to the fringes of the political system what would be left of the political opposition and move off in new policy directions.

I would not exaggerate this possibility. The Japanese political system, by any comparative measure, is remarkably stable; the ideological cleavage that characterized earlier years is being replaced by a political pluralism that is now fairly deeply rooted; and the conservatizing pressures on the making of Japanese foreign policy are extremely strong. We know that dramatic changes in international political and economic relationships and shifts in the global distribution of power in the past decade impelled the Japanese to reaffirm their adherence to basic policies formulated in an earlier era. The world situation one would have to posit as possibly undermining Japanese democracy would have to be so cataclysmic that it would in all likelihood have a similar impact on other democracies.

But leaving aside such apocalyptic developments, one must consider what changes in international political and economic relationships might occur that would enable Japan's political leadership to rally a broad-based consensus on behalf of substantial departures from current foreign policy orientations: The adoption of extensive protectionist measures by the

United States and Western Europe and a drastic deterioration in Japan's relations with these countries? A worsening of Japan's relations with the Soviet Union? A massive arms race on the Korean peninsula and a South Korean development of a nuclear weapons capability? A new oil boycott that would effectively prevent supplies from reaching Japan's shores?

Some of these issues are discussed in other chapters of this book and, in any event, a detailed discussion of them goes beyond the scope of this article. The point to be made here is that the pragmatic, reactive, and essentially defensive qualities of Japan's approach to foreign relations make Japan particularly sensitive and responsive to perceived changes in the policies, both toward Japan and toward other states, of those countries with which Japanese interests are most deeply intertwined. These countries, and the United States above all, can try to encourage the development of Japanese policies that would lead to a more direct and positive Japanese role in the resolution of pressing world problems, or they can continue, as in the present fashion, to deal with Japan on an issue-by-issue basis without any long-term goals, leaving it to the Japanese to improvise policies to respond to perceived, and misperceived, pressures. In any event, many of the crucial variables in projecting Japan's future foreign policy course lie outside of Japan and, as Japanese to some extent rightly assume, beyond Japanese control.

NOTES

1. For a discussion of these issues see Gerald L. Curtis, *Election Campaigning Japanese Style* (New York: Columbia University Press, 1971).

2.   The Socialist party is the only opposition party consistently to run more than one candidate in a large number of districts. Because of its declining support, however, it has steadily reduced the number of districts in which it runs two or more candidates. In the 1976 election, the party ran two candidates in only 31 districts and elected both in just 13.

3.   For an analysis of the 1974 upper house election, see the articles by M. Blaker, G. Curtis, and H. Passin in *Japan At The Polls: The House of Councillors Election of 1974,* edited by Michael K. Blaker (Washington: American Enterprise Institute, 1976).

4.   In a *Yomiuri Shinbun* poll published a month before the 1976 election, 44.2% of the respondents indicated support for a coalition government comprised of the LDP and various opposition parties (15.5% in favor of an LDP-NLC coalition and 28.7% in favor of an LDP-NLC-JSP-KMT-DSP "grand" coalition), and 16.1% indicated support for continued LDP rule. Only 10.2% favored an opposition party coalition, and 29.5% expressed no opinion. Support for an LDP-opposition party "grand" coalition was highest among DSP supporters (56%) and JSP supporters (42%) and lowest among LDP supporters (22%) and JCP supporters (16%). See *Yomiuri Shinbun,* November 11, 1976.

   The response to a May 1978 *Mainichi Shinbun* poll was similar, some 16% favoring LDP rule, 18% an LDP-NLC coalition, 32% a coalition involving the LDP and various opposition parties, and 12% a coalition excluding the LDP. The remaining 22% expressed no opinion. See *Mainichi Shinbun,* May 1, 1978.

5.   See *Asahi Shinbun,* April 12, 1978.

6.   For an extended analysis of the recent electoral performance of Japan's opposition parties, see Gerald L. Curtis, "The Opposition," in Herbert Passin, ed., *A Season of Voting: The Japanese Elections of 1976 and 1977* (Washington: American Enterprise Institute, 1979).

7. *A May 1978 Mainichi Shinbun* poll indicated that Socialist party support was highest in semi-urban areas (16%) and lowest in metropolitan cities (10%). Fourteen percent of the respondents in medium-sized cities and in rural areas support the party. See *Mainichi Shinbun*, May 1, 1978.

8. Support for the JSP was 13% in an April 1978 nationwide *Yomiuri* poll and 14% in a *Mainichi* poll conducted the following month. See *Yomiuri Shinbun*, April 14, 1978 and *Mainichi Shinbun*, May 1, 1978.

9. *Jiten* is a term that refers to the candidate who places first among the losers, i.e., fourth in a three-member district, fifth in a four-member district or sixth in a five-member district. A *jiten* candidate automatically obtains a Diet seat should one of the successful candidates in his district vacate his seat within three months of the election.

10. In May 1978 *Asahi Shinbun* reported that the Komeito was planning to concentrate its resources on the campaign of its incumbents in the next lower house contest and that it would *reduce* the number of party candidates from the 84 who ran 1976 to about 70. See *Asahi Shinbun*, May 8, 1978.

11. See, for example, the poll in *Asahi Shinbun*, December 1, 1976.

12. DSP chairman Ryosaku Sasaki announced in June 1978 that the party hoped to run more than 70, and elect more than 40, candidates in the next lower house election. See *Asahi Shinbun*, June 2, 1978.

13. See Kiyoshi Karube, "Nihonjin wa dono yō ni shite shiji seitō okimeru ka," in Nihonjin Kenkyūkai, *Nihonjin Kenkyū 2, Shiji Seitō Betsu Nihonjin Shūdan* (Tokyo, 1975), pp. 78-79.

14. The April 1978 *Yomiuri* poll cited in note 8 above recorded JCP support at 2.6%.

15.   Estimates of JCP strength in the organized labor movement are based on the percentage of delegates to Sohyo conventions who vote for a motion demanding the "freedom of party support." This is a catch phrase for ending Sohyo support of the JSP and is regularly submitted by Communist labor leaders. Voting on this motion at the 1976 convention suggests that the JCP is able to control somewhat under one-third of Sohyo convention delegates. This figure has remained constant for the past decade.

16.   Public opinion polls indicate that between a quarter and a third of the electorate support no political party. This percentage has risen steadily for the past decade. "No party supporters" are particularly conspicuous among urban and young voters. In a nationwide *Yomiuri Shinbun* poll published on November 2, 1976, for example, 28.6% of the respondents supported no party; the percentage for voters in their twenties was 43.4%. In the May 1, 1978, *Mainichi Shinbun* poll, 31% of the respondents indicated that they supported no political party; the LDP was supported by 35% and the JSP by 14% of the respondents. The other parties each received 5% or less support (KMT-5%, NLC-5%, DSP-4%, JCP-2%, SDL-1%, no answer-3%). In the ten largest cities non-party supporters formed the single largest group, comprising 36% of respondents; LDP support was 31%, and the JSP obtained only 10%. The figures for the other parties were: KMT-6%, NLC-6%, DSP-4%, JCP-3%, SDL-1%, others and no answer-3%.

17.   Of 76 bills submitted by the government, 65 (85.5%) were passed but of these 21 (32.3%) were amended in Diet committees. This contrasts with the amendment of only 10% of cabinet bills passed in the 1970 Diet when the LDP majority was larger. See *Asahi Shinbun,* June 10, 1977.

18.   Based on figures issued by the Statistics Bureau, Prime Minister's Office, and cited in Ministry of Health and Welfare, *Health and Welfare Services in Japan* (Tokyo, 1977), Kōseisho, *Kōsei Hakusho 1973* (Tokyo, 1974), and *Asahi Shinbun,* July 25, 1978.

19.   On the whole, opposition parties have not produced detailed economic programs. The Komeito study mentioned in the next note is a conspicuous exception. In general, all opposition parties place heavy emphasis on large cuts in personal taxes to stimulate consumer demand, and they successfully pressed the government, over the strenuous objections of the Ministry of Finance, to institute a modest tax cut in 1977. But they differ significantly on the issue of increased government spending through greater borrowing. Interestingly, the Socialist party takes the most conservative view on fiscal policy and opposed the government's decision to break through the 30% ceiling in deficit financing in the 1978 fiscal year budget.

20.   See Komeito Sōgō Seisaku Kenkyū Iinkai, *Fukushi Shakai Tōtaru Puranu* (Tokyo, 1976). The "mid-term economic plan" issued by the DSP in 1978 called for a growth rate target of 6.2%; the Communist party calls for a rate of 5.8%. Other opposition parties have not cited specific figures but their policies on growth do not diverge significantly from these other parties. For a summary analysis of the opposition parties' economic programs, see *Asahi Shinbun,* May 8, 1978.

21.   See for example *Asahi Shinbun,* April 23 and May 28, 1978. Article 9 is the famous "no war" provision of the constitution.

22.   Revision of the constitution requires a two-thirds vote of all members of the Diet and a majority of valid votes in a national referendum.

23.   Cited in Seiichiro Ohnishi, "A Recollection and Perspective of the Buildup of Japan's Defense Capabilities" (mimeo, July 16, 1977).

24.   Japan Defense Agency, "Opinion Survey For Analyzing Public Relations," *Defense Bulletin,* Vol. I. No. 4 (January 1978).

25.   See *Yomiuri Shinbun,* April 17, 1978. It should be noted that Japanese polls are characterized generally by a rather high "don't know" response rate.

26. For a detailed analysis of the nuclear weapons issues in Japan, see Herbert Passin, "Nuclear Arms and Japan," in *Asia's Nuclear Future,* ed. William H. Overholt (Boulder, Colo.: Westview Press, 1977), pp. 67-132.

27. See *Nihon no bōei* (Tokyo: Bōeichō, July 1977). The main points in the white paper and figures on defense spending are cited in International Institute for Strategic Studies, *Strategic Survey 1977* (London, 1978), pp. 85-89.

28. See his statement as reported in *Asahi Shinbun,* December 1, 1976.

29. Atarashii Nihon o Kangaeru Kai, "Ashita No Nihon No Tame Ni" (mimeo, 1976). p. 12.

30. Komeito's description of its foreign policy positions is included in the party's "action policy" submitted to the 1978 national party convention. See the party's English language pamphlet, *The 15th National Convention, January 11-13, 1978* (Tokyo, 1978).

31. See *Asahi Shinbun,* December 2, 1976.

32. See *Asahi Shinbun,* June 2, 1978.

33. See *Asahi Shinbun,* May 17, 1978. The communiqué, however, did not use the word "immediate" in calling for treaty abolition.

34. The issue of the integration into society of the *burakumin,* the group formerly treated as Japan's "untouchables," is an important political issue in some local areas, particularly in Kansai (the Osaka-Kyoto-Kobe region), but it does not have major influence on national politics.

[85]

[THREE]

Japan's Economic Strategy and Prospects

William V. Rapp
Robert A. Feldman

INTRODUCTION

Japan's impressive economic growth since World War II has had two important consequences. First, growth has lifted the Japanese people from poverty to affluence in a single generation. With real growth averaging 9.5% annually between 1949 and 1973, the Japanese economy became the world's third largest. Even though real growth since the oil crisis in 1973 has averaged only 3.0% annually, Japan's 1978 GNP was $1,100 billion; per capita income, $9,483; and exports, $96 billion.[1]

The second, and less widely recognized, consequence has been some structural rigidity. Many of the sources of rapid growth are now so firmly rooted that they have become

[86]

sources of inflexibility and international friction in the different economic environment of the 1970s. Analyses of Japan's postwar growth are many,[2] and a full one will not be repeated here. However, certain key variables will be reviewed because their changes explain Japan's present condition and indicate its future prospects. By highlighting these structural issues and the policy reactions they require, the direction and magnitude of various changes become clearer, and related policy considerations can be examined. This is the purpose of the historical perspective outlined in the next few pages and examined more thoroughly in the first two sections. Specifically, we shall consider how Japan's remarkable progress occurred; where the economy is now; the outlook for rapid growth in the future; the likely evolution of Japan's economic structure; and how its economy will affect and interact with the rest of the world.

Success and Its Legacy

Soon after World War II the Japanese government embarked on a growth strategy that concentrated on renewed and rapid industrialization in the private sector. A very high investment rate (averaging 28.2% of GNP between 1949 and 1973)[3] combined with the high savings of individuals, businesses, and even government to permit both high economic growth and wholesale and export price stability. Continued high investment rates were then encouraged by the resulting increased productivity and greater price competitiveness brought about by investment for growing domestic and world markets. Investment was also fostered by Japan's labor structure, the availability of cheap bank financing, and a generally benevolent government attitude toward an economy focused on business expansion. Expansion was helped by growing personal consumption levels and the Ministry of

Finance's conservative fiscal policies whereby adequate resources were available for the private sector. These internal factors combined with expanding and liberalized world trade to develop a business-investment-led economy. Capacity expanded in anticipation of demand and in turn contributed to that demand, helping to justify the investments. In effect, public and private growth strategies evolved which systemically became self-fulfilling.

High growth rates, rising investment levels, increased wages, incomes and consumption, and expanding exports led to rapid shifts in industrial structure which emphasized capital intensive and higher technology industries. The relative importance of light industries in total product and in exports declined remarkably, while that of heavy industries rose. This shift in competitiveness and industrial structure is illustrated by the steel industry and its synergism with a Japanese-induced revolution in ocean transportation.

Steel has been the key industry upon which Japan built its postwar development. In 1949, the industry was not particularly efficient, and access to raw materials was a serious problem. By 1958 it was exporting, and since the late 1960s it has accounted for about 50% of world trade in steel. The industry has been assisted in this remarkable development by easy access to debt capital, major technological changes, and a willingness to invest in bigger and bigger furnaces. The readiness to invest has been due to that fact that construction and material costs of larger furnaces (related to surface area) have not risen as rapidly as the greater production volume (related to cubic area) made possible, so that bigger plants have always been more cost efficient. Today Japan has 37 basic oxygen furnaces of over 2,000 cubic meters capacity, whereas the United States has only five.[4] At the same time, expanded capacity created demand for more raw materials and bigger ships to carry them. Ships are subject to the same cost/volume relationship as blast furnaces. As bigger ships were built, raw material carrying costs dropped dramatically, making Japanese port-based steel more competitive due both to cheaper inputs and to lower export costs. This then created more demand for steel and for ships. More and bigger ships created a greater demand for steel, and cheaper steel lowered ship costs and thus transportation costs. Therefore, the two industries interacted dynamically to raise demand for each other's output and to make each other increasingly competitive. Automobiles and specialized ship carriers have added to this overall effect, and steel, ships and autos together accounted for 39% of Japanese exports in 1976.[5]

The net result of this and similar industrial developments has been rapid but somewhat imbalanced industrial and GNP growth. Pollution levels increased, and the government sector remained relatively small (less than 20% of GNP until 1971). Social welfare programs and public investments have been inadequate. Although by 1971 Japan had caught up with the Western industrialized countries in GNP, industrial structure, and per capita income, it remained weak in social services, infrastructure, and quality of life. This situation led to rising dissatisfactions that are clearly indicated in various public opinion surveys and in the gradual success of opposition parties (as a group) at the polls.

In the 1970s, however, domestic and international demand for the output of Japan's major industries, particularly heavy industries like steel, shipbuilding, and chemicals began leveling off. This natural maturation of demand has been hastened in turn by the yen appreciation since 1971, the oil crisis, the 1973-74 inflation, the 1974-75 recession, and the current stagnation. These special events have combined with normal slowing at this stage of industrial development to dampen business expectations and shift Japan from an investment-led economy to a demand-led one. Businessmen are no longer investing in anticipation of demand, except in a few high-growth, knowledge-intensive industries that are not capital-using.

The industrial structure, though, remains concentrated in industries like steel, chemicals, shipbuilding, nonferrous metals, machinery, automobiles, and power. These industries have to invest if the private sector is to use the high savings still generated by business and by individuals (well over 20% of disposable income is still saved). Yet, as noted above, heavy industry is now waiting for demand to materialize before investing. Thus, if savings are not to be deflationary, the government, through its own investment and consumption, must become the main generator of recovery and continued economic growth.

The government can either act to lower the aggregate savings rate by increasing its own current consumption, by transferring resources to those with high propensities to consume, and by decreasing the uncertainties that contribute to a high savings rate. Or it can act to increase total gross investment by spending more on infrastructure development. Due to the large imbalances of Japan's rapid postwar development, both infrastructure investment and social services are needed and appropriate.

However, the government's past policy of keeping the public sector small and of favoring private business and industrial development is limiting how fast it can expand its direct contribution to the economy. In fact, public debt at the end of FY 1977 was up 103% in only a two-year period.[6] This was a creditable job of deficit spending and debt financing, but it was insufficient to take up the total slack between savings and private investment. Further, the government has a limited number of personnel who can generate and monitor new projects, whether for domestic infrastructure or foreign aid, and it is reluctant to introduce new expenditure programs which may reduce future fiscal flexibility. These constraints are particularly important as the current fiscal program is focused more on spurring public works and investment than on attempts to decrease savings. Yet both approaches are needed. In fact, excess savings are currently being transferred abroad via a large export surplus and the accumulation of excess foreign exchange reserves. This hardly benefits the Japanese people's standard of living.

While the government is struggling with this dilemma, the built-in efficiency of Japan's heavy industry prolongs Japanese export competitiveness across a narrow product range. Even with textiles and ship exports hurt seriously by world stagnation, shifting comparative advantage, and yen appreciation, exports grew 20% in 1977 and 22% in 1978 (in dollar terms), based mostly on autos and precision machinery. The development of new industries would broaden the export base, but this has been frustrated by the greater competitiveness of foreign producers in new knowledge-intensive industries, by a stronger yen that makes catching up difficult, and by Japan's liberalized foreign investment policies in these industries.

At the same time, Japan's export concentration in basic industries, where other countries' unemployment is currently high, is creating major international tensions and pressures for protectionism. Orderly marketing arrangements are a possible solution, but these decrease potential business investment, thus exacerbating Japan's recovery problem and increasing the requirement for greater government expenditures. Such agreements also will increase the need to redirect heavy industrial firms' growth. Such an economic restructuring, however, will take at least four or five more years, particularly with slower growth. Will other countries be willing to wait this long for Japan to become a locomotive economy again and to reduce competitive trade pressures? The forces at work forming Japan's long-run industrial and economic evolution seem clear enough and will be discussed in more detail. But major domestic and international economic policy difficulties will emerge as Japan tries to alleviate its immediate and near-term internal tensions successfully enough to allow sensible longer-term restructuring.

We now turn to a consideration of some of the key mechanisms of the postwar period, the persistence or dilution of which will bear heavily on the nation's economic future.

JAPAN'S POSTWAR INDUSTRIAL GROWTH STRATEGY

Emergence of the Postwar Industrial Growth Strategy

Japan's economy was shattered by the Second World War, but the worst time came in the immediate postwar period with famine, dislocations caused by destruction of productive capacity, and the return of troops and emigrants. Morever, Occupation authorities soon began an economic deconcentration program, disbanding large industrial groups, retiring prominent businessmen, and encouraging labor unions. The economy languished, and even in 1949 industrial output was still only three-quarters of the mid-1930s level.

The cold war radically altered this situation. U.S. authorities felt that a strong Japan was needed to defend against communism in East Asia, particularly after the Communist victory in China. The vision of an agricultural Japan, founded on the fear of resurgent militarism, gave way to a vision of an industrial Japan, and the Korean War provided a vital spur to Japan's industrial demand. U.S. military procurements were almost two-thirds of total exports by 1953,[7] while the share of agriculture in total output fell to 16% from 23% in 1949.[8] And the boom continued after the armistice, due to the pent-up domestic demand for all goods, the need to rebuild industrial plant, and the willingness of the United States to absorb increasing manufactured exports. Further, GATT, the Bretton Woods Agreement, and the Marshall Plan had created the basis for an expanding world economy—one particularly favorable to trade.

There were, however, important constraints. Capital and foreign exchange were scarce, and industrial funds were mostly debt. Priorities had to be set. During the Korean War, over 80% of new funds came from private financial institutions, which in turn relied on rediscounting with the Bank of Japan. Strict foreign exchange controls were established to discourage non-essential imports. These exchange constraints remained until the late 1960s, as foreign exchange reserves typically covered only three months' imports. The power, fertilizer, shipping, coal, and steel industries were favored in the allocation of credit and foreign exchange. As an overall development strategy evolved, new industries were substituted or added, such as automobiles, chemicals and petrochemicals. These infant industries were also favored by such tax benefits as rapid depreciation and special reserves that promoted growth, investment, and improved competitiveness. Tariff restrictions and restraints on foreign investment were also part of this overall industrial promotion.

The international political situation and Japan's industrial potential combined with the basic constraints to put the economy on a new course. This course was set by policy planners, who established three basic goals: (1) dynamically efficient capital allocation to foster growth and to relieve long-run capital scarcity, (2) increased industrialization and international competitiveness, and (3) preservation of foreign exchange reserves. At times, these goals were bound to conflict; initially, promoting industrialization and capital growth would require substantial imports of both raw materials and advanced machinery.

The challenge of the 1950s was to create a policy that could achieve all goals. In the long run, though, efficient industrialization would achieve greater growth and greater export competitiveness, thus eliminating the exchange constraint. Efficient capital allocation through the financial and fiscal system to high-growth industries attracted labor and other resources, though the goverment sector tended to get short-changed by resulting under-budgeting and tax reductions. What in effect occurred was the evolution of a dynamic self-reinforcing system that promoted rapid growth and survival of the most efficient and competitive. Rationalization was encouraged by restrained application of anti-trust laws, and government-sponsored mergers.

Fostering Investment: Government Policy, Industry's Financial Structure, and Capital Scarcity

The guidelines for industrial development were the industrial plans of the Ministry of International Trade and Industry (MITI), particularly its Heavy Industry Bureau. Planning was on an industry basis, after continuous consultation with the companies involved. Investment allocation for plant and equipment among producers was the objective in strategic or key industries. Allocations within established industries were most often based on a firm's past share of the market. But the plans were not legally binding, and businessmen had every incentive to invest more, particularly in new high-growth industries where gaining a larger market share would both improve competitive position and help gain a better position in the next plan. Also, MITI and business did not always agree on how much investment was appropriate. Thus, competition developed among producers over who could invest the most. This process was encouraged by readily available bank financing and a tax structure that gave favorable treatment to interest costs, depreciation, and investment reserves, thus lowering capital costs. In addition, experience showed that new investment resulted in improved productivity, allowing greater price competitiveness and expanded demand, justifying the investment.

The government could control investment and credit rationing via monetary policy, providing an essential policy tool to restrain excessive growth. As bank loans were the prime source of funds for new investment, any rediscount tightening by the Bank of Japan had great impact on the ability of banks to lend, and thus on investment. In this way, the Bank of Japan discount rate became the symbol of the government's investment expansion policies. In turn, the Ministry of Finance (MOF) allocated loan limits among the major city banks, so-called "window guidance," according to what it considered appropriate expansion, and according to bank size. When foreign exchange reserves were adequate, the discount rate was lowered and banks allowed to expand loans. Business in turn invested aggressively. When reserves started to dwindle, the Bank of Japan (a creature of the MOF) raised the discount rate and enforced window guidance, so credit became scarce. Investment then cooled momentarily while exchange reserves rose to a safe level. Then the process was repeated. Thus, credit scarcity was the pressure point through which the government attempted to guide economic and industrial progress with an eye to the balance-of-payments constraint. But this reliance on monetary policy was only

[95]

successful because business investment was the engine of growth and because there were intense competitive pressures on firms to operate at high capacity in order to cover high fixed costs, interest, and wages, and to invest for future market-share and productivity increases.

Given competition, capital scarcity, and periodic credit squeezes, many firms needed a loan source they could depend on when money was tight. In time, guaranteed availability became more important than price. Thus it was natural for firms to attach themselves to certain banks that in turn became the financial hubs for groups of companies. The main banks were more than lenders, however, since they provided investment opportunity information, coordinated group activities, and helped negotiate with MITI and MOF on expansion plans. They thus reduced business risk by providing credit and information to their client firms. As the economy boomed, these banks became more important. They provided about a third of the new industrial funds in the mid-1950s, 45% in 1965, and over 50% in 1971, while the stock market's share declined from around 15% to 5% over the same period.[9] (Most of the remainder came from smaller financial institutions and government banks.) The result for most firms was increasing leverage, particularly for capital-intensive heavy industry, the banks themselves, and trading companies. Long-term debt as a percentage of net worth for the 500 leading firms grew from 35% in the first half of 1954 to 98% in the first half of 1970 in an environment of high growth and large capital requirements.[10] As already noted, this leverage made the system quite responsive to monetary policy. Firms became more dependent on their banks and banks more dependent on the MOF and the Bank of Japan. Interest rate fluctuations bore directly on costs. In addition to capital available from the Bank of Japan, funds were supplied to banks from declining

[96]

industries like agriculture, fishing, textiles, and handicrafts, whose expansion needs were minimal, as well as from high personal savings and fiscal surpluses. Tight fiscal policy made monetary policy more effective by denying any fiscal expenditure cushion when money was scarce.

With private investment the growth engine during this period, a concomitant was a small government sector. Total government expenditures averaged slightly under 20% of GNP during the era of high growth. The government was a net saver in most years, both undershooting expenditures and collecting more taxes than anticipated. Among general account expenditures, public works increased in share, along with social security payments (though social security was still not a significant percentage of GNP), while the percentage for defense declined. Special accounts, e.g., post office, railways, hospitals, telephone and telegraph, were budgeted for an amount usually 75%-100% greater than the total general account,[11] but undershooting expenditure was prominent here as well. With small budgets, even smaller actual expenditures, and frequent surpluses, government debt was negligible. Small amounts were floated for specific purposes, but in 1970 total debt outstanding was less than 9% of GNP, and less than a year's tax receipts.

Investment, Structural Evolution, and Savings

Investment was the main force behind Japan's growth in the postwar period. In 1953 gross fixed capital formation was already over 20% of GNP, rising to 30% by 1960 and 35% by 1970.[12] Between one-half and two-thirds of this was plant and equipment investment, with the rest as private dwellings, government investment, and inventories. By industry, investment was heavily concentrated in iron and steel, chemicals, and machinery—not a surprise given their capital intensity. Investment in turn translated quickly into income multiplier effects for the economy, even before the impact of price cuts based on increased productivity.

Given high growth and high investment rates, factor proportions changed significantly over the period, favoring capital intensity. Initially, such capital intensity may not have seemed appropriate, given Japan's relative labor abundance. But firms realized that their competitive position depended on the incorporation of new technology through investment to avoid rising labor costs. This was especially true for large firms facing the permanent employment system, in which workers are hired directly from school for life, and in which wages rise on the basis of seniority. Hence, factor proportions in actuality developed to fit the dynamic conditions of an expanding market.

The product mix within and between industries shifted toward products with higher value added. In 1950, metals, machinery, and chemicals accounted for about 40% of value added in manufacturing; the figure rose to 60% in 1960 and 62% in 1970.[13] The competitive process reinforced this evolution. Increased capital availability, declining capital costs, and increasing wage rates all combined with government policies and incentives and with rising domestic demand to stimulate a shift toward higher-technology, capital-intensive products with more value added and more processing per unit of output. At the same time, however, productivity increases brought about by capital investment and technical progress combined with pressures to gain a larger share of the market to push for lower value added (and hence lower prices) on particular established products. This freed resources to move to new product lines. Moreover, additional productivity gains have usually been more available in technologically more advanced products with higher value added per unit, a fact which reinforced the cycle. Thus, there occurred together a decrease in value added per unit in specific products and an overall shift to products with higher value added per unit, which, on balance, resulted in higher value added per unit of output for industry as a whole.

In the aggregate, these trends had three important implications. First, export competitiveness grew, particularly in the capital-intensive industries. Second, effective tariff protection on domestic value added rose sharply, especially as most raw materials came in at little or no duty. And third, on goods exported the value added per unit rose relative to the imported raw material input. All this, combined with a favorable shift in the terms of trade and a higher proportion of exports in raw-material-intensive industries, meant a narrowing trade deficit and finally a growing surplus.

Since investment in technologically superior plant (particularly in heavy industry) was the basis for structural shift, economies of scale played an important role. This required larger and larger projects so that average firm size also grew. While firms of over 1,000 employees had a slightly declining share of total employment,[14] they had an increasing share of output, due to large productivity increases relative to the rest of the economy. The persistence of small firms (less than 300 employees) seems concentrated in the nonmanufacturing industries or as subcontractors in those manufacturing sectors where average firm size is large. Concomitant with this change has been the large firms' increasingly dominant share of exports, particularly in fields like steel, transportation equipment, electrical machinery, and chemicals.

But investment alone was not sufficient to cause high growth with relative price stability. Savings were needed as

[99]

well, and in this Japan was fortunate. The population-age structure in the early postwar period was concentrated in young-adult and lower-middle-age brackets, which favored savings for big-ticket consumption items and housing. Lack of pensions or social security also encouraged saving for retirement. The bonus system was an additional savings impetus since workers typically receive extra large paychecks twice a year, in June and December. While normal household expenditures have been tied to base income, bonus income has been saved and used for long-term purchases, e.g., houses, cars, or TVs. Moreover, between closing the books and paying bonuses (typically three months), firms have had the use of bonus wages, thus reducing working capital requirements.

Depreciation allowances were an important and growing source of gross savings for the economy. Starting at only 5% of GNP in 1949, depreciation grew to 10% of GNP in 1960 and 13.5% in 1970. Household savings stabilized at about 12% of GNP in 1960, and government savings ran between 5% and 8%.[15]

The financial system itself both impelled and made productive use of rising savings rates, as private banks aggressively gathered savings from the public, particularly at bonus time. These funds were then lent to growing businesses which needed to finance further development. The government's postal savings system was also a major collector of small deposits, the proceeds of which were held by the Trust Funds Bureau of the MOF. These funds were invested in national bonds, special bank debentures, local government securities, and other securities that were used to finance public works or were lent to firms in priority industries.

Virtuous Cycles

The postwar growth and investment orientation gave rise to two important virtuous cycles. The first was productivity growth leading to price stability (or even price declines), improved competitiveness, expanded domestic and international markets, more profits, more investment, even higher productivity, and so on. By the 1960s, productivity in manufacturing as measured by output per man-day was growing an average of 10% per year, and some years saw it rise by over 15%. In contrast, real wages rose less quickly (though not slowly) at 5.4% per year.[16] In no year did real wages rise faster than productivity, thus leaving a substantial surplus for businesses to invest or pass along in lower prices. These effects are reflected in the wholesale price index. The aggregate index was quite stable, with rates of increase often less than 1% per year. The aggregate index, however, understates a key phenomenon: growing industries like machinery, iron and steel, and chemicals showed actual price declines in most years, while more labor-intensive industries, not able to invest massively in new equipment to improve productivity, raised prices. The contrast between wholesale and consumer prices corroborates the point. Consumer prices, in which the services and direct labor content is higher than in wholesale prices, rose an average of 5.5% per year in the 1960s once the labor market began to tighten. Conversely, the export price index, which became more heavily weighted with goods like steel, chemicals, machinery, electronics, and automobiles, showed even greater stability than wholesale prices and sometimes even declined, indicating both the importance of investment, productivity, and price competitiveness in certain

[101]

industries and the differences in product-weighting between particular indices and markets.[17]

The second major virtuous cycle involved wages, income, and consumption. Although productivity gains were higher, real wage increases of 5.4% per year are quite high by most standards. Given the large wage-earning work force, the resulting personal income gains were also large. The net effect was a consumption boom that went from one durable good to the next. In urban households the saturation ratio for radios, sewing machines, and bicycles passed 50% before 1955 and for television sets by 1960. By 1965, the 50% mark was passed for cameras, washing machines, and refrigerators, and by 1970 for vacuum cleaners, while passenger cars and color televisions passed 20%.[18] The consumption boom fed on itself, creating new industries which invested rapidly and paid higher wages, creating more demand for new products and industries. But the Japanese did not spend too fast; despite the large growth in consumption, incremental savings rates averaged about 20% during the high-growth era.

Export Growth and the Balance-of-Payments Constraint

Exports were an improtant source and support to growth in the postwar era. In volume terms, export markets provided the sales prospects to justify continued large capital equipment expenditures once an industry was established domestically. Firms expanded into foreign markets and increased their competitiveness through additional investment, higher productivity, and more sales, which at the same time lowered domestic prices and bolstered demand at home. Export dynamics thus represented a logical extension of domestic competition. As domestic markets developed first, Japan's shifting industrial structure translated with some lag into a shifting export structure. This phenomenon is sometimes called product cycle evolution. For example, steel exports (and steel prices were stable or declining during the period) rose only 50% between 1955 and 1960, but grew 230% in the next five years, and another 120% by 1970.[19] Ships followed a similar pattern, as did television, automobiles, and other products. Each industry increased both its own share of total exports and the proportion of exports in its own total output (see Table 1). Product specialization, too, was often an important characteristic of these exports, as exporters concentrated on specific market segments where competitors were weak and they were strong, e.g., small cars, small-screen TVs, tankers, and so on. But in basic commodities like steel, Japanese firms were more competitive across the board. As a result of industry's structural change, exports came increasingly from large firms as the plants necessary to produce the new products efficiently and competitively grew so large that smaller firms were not competitive even domestically, much less internationally. The top 200 manufacturing firms accounted for over 50% of exports in the 1960s.[20]

The import structure evolved in tandem with that of industry and exports (see Table 2). As international competitiveness rose in more products, fewer finished and semi-finished imports were needed. Raw materials and fuel took their place. Metal ores, for example, rose from 7.5% of imports in 1955 to 15% in 1960, while mineral fuels jumped from 12% to 17% in the same years.[21] As a result the share of manufactured imports provided by industrial countries declined. However, as Japan became more competitive in capital- and technology-intensive industries, it became less competitive in labor-intensive commodities. Exports of textiles and handicrafts fell and, later, imports from the LDCs rose, though often produced by firms using Japanese equipment and often with some Japanese investment. These trade trends combined

[103]

TABLE 1

Japanese Exports: Commodity Composition, and By Destination
(In US$ millions, and percentage)

	1955		1960	
	US$ mil.	%	US$ mil.	%
TOTAL	2,011	100	4,055	100
Commodity Composition				
Food	126	6.3	256	6.3
Textiles	749	37.2	1,223	30.4
Chemicals	103	5.1	181	4.5
Metals	387	19.2	568	14.0
Iron & steel	259	12.9	388	9.6
Machinery	249	12.4	1,035	25.5
Motor vehicles	6	0.3	78	5.8
Scientific & optical	—	—	92	2.3
TV	—	—	3	0.1
Radio	1	0.0	145	3.6
Vessels	78	3.9	288	7.1
Other	397	17.7	792	19.5
By Destination				
Asia	841	41.8	1,458	36.0
Europe	207	10.3	538	13.3
North America	539	26.8	1,345	33.2
United States	456	22.7	1,102	27.2
South America	149	7.4	180	4.4
Africa	206	10.2	352	8.7
Oceania	69	3.4	182	4.5
Communist Bloc	39	1.9	73	1.8
Southeast Asia	727	36.2	1,307	32.2
Middle East	105	5.2	178	4.4

Sources:
Bank of Japan Statistics Department, *Economic Statistics Annual.*
Bureau of Statistics, Office of the Prime Minister, *Japan Statistical Yearbook.*

to increase the concentration of Japanese exports in a few selected capital-intensive industries. Japan has virtually no agricultural and raw materials exports, and few very high

1965		1970		1975	
US$ mil.	%	US$ mil.	%	US$ mil.	%
8,452	100	19,318	100	55,753	100
344	4.1	648	3.4	760	1.4
1,582	18.7	2,407	12.5	3,719	6.7
547	6.5	1,234	6.4	3,889	7.0
1,718	20.3	3,805	19.7	12,517	22.5
1,290	15.3	2,844	14.7	10,176	18.7
2,975	35.2	8,941	46.3	30,004	53.8
237	2.8	1,337	6.9	6,190	11.1
217	2.6	498	2.6	1,368	2.5
85	1.0	384	2.0	783	1.4
216	2.6	695	3.6	1,324	2.4
748	8.8	1,410	7.3	5,998	10.8
1,286	15.2	2,283	11.8	4,864	8.7
2,747	32.5	6,033	31.2	20,488	36.7
1,297	15.3	3,363	17.4	10,346	18.6
2,933	34.7	7,095	36.7	14,697	26.4
2,479	29.3	5,940	30.7	11,149	20.0
248	2.9	596	3.1	2,368	4.2
818	9.7	1,423	7.4	5,556	10.0
404	4.8	802	4.2	2,295	4.1
478	5.6	1,045	5.4	4,683	8.4
2,195	25.7	4,902	25.4	12,543	22.5
356	4.2	634	3.3	6,075	10.9

technology exports. Imports have been composed mostly of raw materials, foodstuffs, and fuels, with a few labor-intensive goods from LDCs and some very high technology commodities from the United States and Europe.

These evolutionary trends finally lifted the balance-of-payments constraint on growth. With higher aggregate domestic value added, higher value added per unit of output, and higher productivity in industry, the import content of exports declined, and the value added to raw materials processed and exported increased, yielding improved foreign exchange earnings. Exports exceeded imports (c.i.f.) for the first time in 1965, symbolizing this major change in postwar economic history. These developments continued through the late 1960s and Japan achieved larger and larger trade surpluses. At the same time, the concentration of Japan's growing export competitiveness in a few basic industries combined with an expanding trade surplus and few manufactured imports to sow the seeds of serious tensions between Japan on the one hand and the United States and Europeans on the other.

Emerging Problems of Growth

Growth skewed toward plant and equipment investment has created problems. By the late 1960s some external effects began to emerge as serious causes of concern, and public opinion started to rethink the desirability of continued high growth. The nation's industry was packed between Tokyo and Osaka, aggravating pollution and population density. Several cases of deleterious effluents ignored by polluters became widely publicized. The urbanized and now more affluent population also became conscious of insufficient social facilities such as parks, roads, sewers, and highways. In 1971, Tokyo had only 1.15 square meters of park area per capita, compared with New York's 19 or Munich's 20. Only 25% of the total roads were paved versus 80% in the U.S. Only 17%

of the houses had indoor flush toilets,[22] and garbage disposal wars between prefectures were common.

Unfulfilled welfare, medical, and social security needs were another problem. The percentage of population over retirement age (55) reached 15% in 1970,[23] while urbanization and rising land prices reinforced the trend to smaller houses and nuclear families, making the inadequate pension systems a greater burden on the aged. The situation was particularly difficult for those who had relied on savings accounts or postal savings as a cushion, since consumer price inflation had eroded their value.

Furthermore, housing was insufficient. The Japanese had less than one room per capita in 1968, versus one-and-a-half in the United States, and Japanese rooms were smaller to boot. In addition, housing was difficult to get, as land costs had risen so rapidly. The price index of urban residential land rose an average of 17.7% *per year* between 1955 and 1970.[24] If time deposits, the main money source for home-building, are deflated by this, the real ability to purchase land barely increased over the entire period despite the rapid rise in real wages. Moreover, when housing was available, it was increasingly far from work, markedly lengthening commuting times.

Nor were the adverse externalities of growth solely domestic. As already noted, bilateral trade surpluses and tensions with the United States increased in the late 1960s. The United States was the chief export market on which many Japanese firms had based investment plans, while raw materials came increasingly from others. Some U.S. industries—particularly steel, textiles and electronics—began to ask for protection, citing Japanese firms as the source of injury. The result was orderly marketing agreements in which Japanese producers agreed to limit shipments for a specified period. These

TABLE 2

Japanese Imports: Commodity Composition, and By Origin
(In US$ millions, and percentage)

	1955		1960	
	US$ mil.	%	US$ mil.	%
TOTAL	2,471	100	4,491	100
Commodity Composition				
Food	625	25.3	548	12.2
Textile Materials	586	23.7	762	17.0
Metal Ores	186	7.5	673	15.0
Raw Materials	491	19.9	774	17.2
Mineral Fuels	289	11.7	742	16.5
Chemicals	112	4.5	265	5.9
Machinery	132	5.3	435	9.7
Other	50	2.0	293	6.5
By Origin				
Asia	902	36.5	1,367	30.4
Europe	177	7.2	488	10.9
North America	1,022	41.4	1,923	42.8
United States	774	31.3	1,554	34.6
South America	104	4.2	145	3.2
Africa	63	2.5	164	3.7
Oceania	203	8.2	404	9.0
Communist Bloc	89	3.6	125	2.8
Southeast Asia	663	26.8	915	20.4
Middle East	189	7.6	449	10.0

Sources:
Bank of Japan Statistics Department, *Economic Statistics Annual.*
Bureau of Statistics, Office of the Prime Minister, *Japan Statistical Yearbook.*

agreements were not always costly to Japanese producers as a whole, since, for example, exports to the United States were only about 4% of output for Japan's textile and apparel industries in the early 1970s. Nor were they always helpful to the U.S. industry, since, for example, textile imports from Japan were only 1.2% of U.S. textile production in the same period.[25] But the textile issue was the first major expression of bitterness over the bilateral imbalance, and was later followed by disputes over steel. At the same time, it should be

1965		1970		1975	
US$ mil.	%	US$ mil.	%	US$ mil.	%
8,169	100	18,881	100	57,863	100
1,470	18.0	2,547	13.5	8,814	15.2
847	10.4	963	5.1	1,524	2.6
1,019	12.5	2,696	14.3	4,416	7.6
1,354	16.6	3,017	16.0	5,718	9.9
1,626	19.9	3,905	20.7	25,640	44.3
408	5.0	1,000	5.3	2,057	3.6
760	9.3	2,298	12.2	4,286	7.4
684	8.4	2,427	12.9	5,404	9.3
2,731	33.4	5,553	29.4	28,345	49.0
1,002	12.3	2,555	13.5	5,778	10.0
3,040	37.2	6,886	36.5	14,929	25.8
2,366	29.0	5,560	29.4	11,608	20.1
391	4.8	976	5.2	1,701	2.9
353	4.3	1,099	5.8	2,320	4.0
654	8.0	1,812	9.6	4,788	8.3
524	6.4	887	4.7	3,006	5.2
1,406	17.2	3,013	16.0	10,586	18.3
1,112	13.6	2,337	12.4	16,447	28.4

recognized that for particular U.S. market outlets and commodities within certain industries, the share of Japanese products was relatively large and important to certain Japanese producers. Thus, orderly marketing arrangements were not easily negotiated or enforced on the Japanese side. Further, many U.S. industries were not aided at all, and some, such as ballbearings, suffered greatly.

The U.S. response to this imbalance on a policy level was

the so-called Nixon shock forcing both yen revaluation and a simultaneous devaluation of the dollar, a net 17% appreciation of the yen. U.S. authorities hoped that this revaluation would slow the growth of Japanese exports to the United States through the price mechanism, but this did not occur. Japan's exports to the United States rose 18% in 1972.[26] Psychologically, however, the Nixon shock was a jolt to Japan which, when combined with the subsequent oil crisis, led to a re-evaluation of policies involving trade, growth, and investment, their roles in the economy, and their effects on other countries.

Thus, after two decades of successful growth, there emerged both internal and external imbalances that required new plans and a new economic strategy. What had occurred during the 1949-71 period was the development of an economic system dedicated to the competitive growth of private manufacturing, particularly in heavy industry and by large internationally competitive firms. All elements of the economy played their mutually supportive and interactive roles, leading to an efficient re-allocation of resources from low- to high-growth industries. But like any successful system, the Japanese economy has developed a strong inertia and an internal logic that are difficult to alter even after various shocks. Yet in the last few years Japan has experienced major changes in basic economic parameters which have brought a transition period. One can already see slower growth rates, lower investment levels, different fiscal and monetary policies, more Japanese foreign investment, yen revaluations, declining business confidence, increased international tensions, and emerging popular dissatisfactions. Still, many characteristics of the high-growth era continue, such as generally high financial leverage, business's export orientation, export concentration, price competitiveness, the employment system, the cooperative government-business-labor relationship, the push into new technologies, and the import structure's emphasis on fuel and raw materials. The interplays between these changing and unchanging factors began to develop more quickly after 1971 and continue to the present. Their examination in the current context is thus critical to developing an outlook for Japan's economic future.

THE RECENT AND CURRENT ECONOMIC ENVIRONMENT

A Turning Point

Several events and emerging trends in the early 1970s proved conclusively that the postwar era, as Japan had known it, was over. These were the appreciation of the yen, the maturation of several important industries, potential scarcities of energy and raw materials, the shift in national economic priorities, and the impact of a prolonged recession.

Pressure on the yen became quite strong in the summer of 1971, but the Bank of Japan defended the long-standing ¥ 360/ US$ rate by buying dollars. However, this intervention was not sufficient, and the yen broke away from the rate in September. Even the setting of the Smithsonian rate of ¥308/ US$ did not remove all pressure, and when the Smithsonian agreement collapsed in February 1973, the yen rose again. The Bank could not resist market forces, and the yen averaged ¥265/US$ from March through October of 1973.[27]

The government's attitude toward a stronger yen was not implacable resistance. Despite attempts by the Bank of Japan to postpone and smooth appreciation, the government generally realized a stronger yen was inevitable. Rather than try to suppress the rate, the government adopted adjustment policies to aid marginal exporters and those exporters who had already accumulated long-term dollar assets, both having been harmed by appreciation. Ship-builders and major equipment suppliers were permitted to borrow dollars and convert them prior to major currency moves. The government also began dismantling exchange controls, liberalizing access to capital markets, and encouraging Japanese investment abroad. Because the yen rise came when demand and profits were generally good, business was able to absorb much of appreciation's effects, and the possible disruptions from a 35% appreciation in two years were largely offset by strong demand. Further, as most exports are by large firms rather than small, the impact fell most heavily on those best able to adapt.

Nevertheless, yen appreication did hasten the natural decline of simple labor-intensive industries such as handicrafts, textiles, and apparel. Imports of such products from LDCs increased correspondingly, often based on Japanese investments. At the same time, many of Japan's basic growth industries, such as steel, chemicals, shipbuilding, machinery, electronics, and automobiles, were experiencing maturing demand. Existing plant and equipment seemed adequate. As saturation ratios for appliances passed higher levels, industries had to be content with replacement demand or try to find new products. This situation in turn encouraged all industries to rationalize, and also encouraged large, internationally competitive firms to export more and/or invest abroad. In the long run this reaction promoted larger trade surpluses.

Pressure on the yen was largely relieved by the rise in raw materials prices, starting late in 1972 and culminating in the oil crisis in the fall of 1973. During the postwar era, Japan had been able to buy all the raw materials it needed from the cheapest sources. But raw materials prices began to rise in late 1972, signaling shortages and potential supply problems. Great fears of vulnerability hit when President Nixon embargoed soybean exports, allegedly to counter inflationary speculation. Raw materials inflation and shortages then spilled over into consumer goods, with shortages of paper products, detergent, and other items. Japan was now a very large economy, both affecting and affected by the world market.

Japan became an active foreign investor in the early 1970s, as economic incentives changed and foreign exchange laws were liberalized. Foreign investment both provided an important outlet for foreign exchange accumulated from trade, and dovetailed with needs for secure supplies of raw materials, for market access in case of trade restrictions, for easier industrial siting, and for cheaper labor for declining domestic industries. Thus corporate incentives and strategies corresponded with national objectives. Long-term capital outflow rose to $1,591 million in 1970, hit $4,487 million in 1972, then more than doubled to $9,750 million in 1973.[28] Of the total, direct investment was a small part (20% in 1973) while the bulk was acquisition of equity and debt instruments. But these data somewhat understate the impact of direct investment, due to the leverage involved. In the United States, for example, Japanese direct investment accounts for only about 3% of the equity, but over 22% of the assets of foreign-owned companies. By sector, investments in manufacturing industries took about half the total by 1973, with banking, insurance, and commerce together taking about a quarter. By region, investments in Asia took the largest share in 1973, with North America not far behind, and Latin America a close third. But the oil crisis dramatically reduced pressure to invest abroad, left a large deficit in Japan's current account in 1974, and dampened discussion of Tokyo becoming a major international money center. In effect, foreign investment policies were actually just another instrument of the MOF's foreign exchange adjustment policy. Thus by 1974 there was some divergence between government policies and the long-term strategies of major Japanese corporations.

Political debate in the early 1970s centered on shifts in national priorities. People worried not about how to grow, but about how to live better, given a largely mature industrial structure without a mature public sector. Pollution was a major scandal, and auto emission standards were adopted that were both stronger than U.S. standards and postponed less often. Pollution standards for plants became so strict that, by 1976, 20% of steel industry investment went for pollution abatement equipment.[29] Health care and care for the elderly were also major issues, along with expenditures for parks, roads, and sewers. Recent discussions on how to spend reflationary funds focus primarily on public works projects, reflecting the new priorities.

The final indicator of a changed economic environment was the 1974-75 recession. Other postwar recessions had simply reduced the rate of growth, but this recession saw decline in real output, and it continued for well over a year and a half. It was also accompanied by severe inflation, record high interest rates, and little plant and equipment investment despite various countercyclical policies. Late 1973 was the turning point from boom to bust. The raw materials and product shortages spawned very large investments in plant and equipment in 1973, but when OPEC announced its oil price hikes, business expectations shifted 180 degrees. By mid-1974, industrial production was below 1973 levels, and unemployment was rising. But with wholesale prices rising 23% and consumer prices 22% in 1974, [30] the government's chief policy goal was not maintaining demand but containing inflation.

Interest rates were raised, with the discount rate going from 5.5% in June 1973 to 9.0% in December of that year. Through this and other restrictive measures, the year-to-year growth of money supply (M1, i.e., currency in circulation and demand deposits) was brought down from 30% in June 1973 to 10% in September 1974.[31] In contrast to other recessions, when monetary restraint was used to suppress real investment and reduce trade deficits, this recession saw monetary policy used to fight inflation, as done in other countries. This was a totally new kind of recession for Japan, not induced by monetary policy and the balance-of-payments constraint. Moreover, endogenous demand for plant and equipment investment was not ready to bring a new round of expansion, and massive fiscal expansion would be required to generate demand growth.

From an Investment-Led Economy to a Demand-Led Economy

Investment's failure to bounce back has been the distinguishing characteristic of the post-oil-crisis economy. Private nondwelling capital formation fell 11% in real terms in 1974, and a further 13% in 1975 (see Table 3). The reasons include uncertainty over the existence of markets for ouput of new capacity, domestic inflation, recession, and slow growth abroad. Meanwhile, personal savings are rising, due to similar uncertainties, creating a further deflationary impact.

It is not clear when Japan's adjustments will be complete or when the various changes in the world economy brought by the oil crisis will subside. But until the outlook is clearer, businessmen will proceed cautiously and will not invest in anticipation of demand, especially since many companies continue to carry high inventories.

With continuing weak investment, GNP growth depends on consumption, government expenditures, and international payments surplus. Consumption growth has been moderate,

[115]

averaging 3.8% in 1976 and 1977.[32] Wage increases have slightly outpaced inflation, leaving some increases in real income to underpin demand. However, uncertainty suppresses consumption as well as investment since households save more, regardless of inflation. With unemployment and bankruptcies continuing, it will be difficult to induce consumers to save less. This leads to a vicious cycle of tepid real consumption depressing markets and keeping production flat, which in turn holds down income, further lowering consumption. Some change in savings behavior is necessary before consumption can be a greater source of growth. Logically, Japan appears to be in a liquidity trap where additions to income are saved, and money is not borrowed despite lower interest rates. Indeed, Japan seems to be switching from a classical to a Keynesian style economy.

Government expenditures have been a major source of new

TABLE 3
Japanese GNP Growth 1974-1977
(Real; in percent)

	1974	1975	1976	1977	1974-77
Private Consumption	1.5	6.2	4.4	3.2	3.8
Government Consumption	4.4	7.4	3.7	3.6	4.7
Government Investment	−6.7	11.5	1.7	10.1	3.8
Private Plant and Equipment Investment	−10.8	−13.1	3.4	2.9	−4.8
Private Housing	−12.8	7.3	6.9	−0.2	−0.1
Exports	21.3	4.4	16.8	10.4	12.3
Imports	12.4	−8.1	8.0	2.0	3.2
GNP	−1.3	2.5	6.0	5.1	3.0

Source:
Bank of Japan Statistics Department, *Economic Statistics Monthly.*

demand since the oil crisis. While real GNP fell 1.3% in 1974, real government consumption expenditures rose 4.4% and in 1975, 7.4%. In 1975 government capital outlays also began to bolster growth, with real expenditures rising 11.5%.[33] Government investment has continued growing and has apparently become the preferred means to support demand, partly because the government's special budget accounts, under which many such expenditures are made, can finance part of the increase themselves. Supplementary budgets have also been an expansionary tool, though they often appear more potent than they are. Large portions of the supplementary packages are not direct expenditures, but rather monies made available for loans to small business, etc., so their economic impact has lagged considerably. Further, the MOF has tried to follow a "rule" that no more than 30% of general account expenditures can be supported by government bonds in any one year. Opposition to this, an artifact of the 1930s, has been rising in all sectors, but fiscal conservatives have not yet abandoned it even though it has absolutely no analytical foundation or justification. In short, the Japanese government is at war with itself over expenditure policy; it knows it must spend vigorously to really support the economy, but it also tends to continue the fiscal conservatism so successful in the high-growth era. The current consensus seems to be that deficits are acceptable if money is used for specific public works projects of demonstrated benefit. The government is not yet willing to use deficits to finance short-term public service jobs, substantial income support programs, or transfer payments programs, such as improved or expanded social security, unemployment benefits, and medical care. Meanwhile exports continued to expand the most rapidly while excess savings de facto ended up as an excess investment in foreign exchange reserves by the Bank of Japan. However, the increased money supply thus made available was merely absorbed by the system and did not result in investment growth.

International Tensions

Increased rancor over international economic issues involving Japan has been common in the 1970s. U.S. criticism has focused on Japan's dependence on export markets for continued growth, without reciprocally providing a market for manufactured goods from the United States and other industrialized nations. Japan's export dependence is often minimized as being a small percentage of GNP, but this misses the point; exports are almost exclusively manufactures (about 96%) and represent 30% or more of production for certain key industries like steel, shipbuilding, and automobiles.[34] Indeed, exports in the high-growth era may have grown only slightly faster than GNP, but from 1974 to 1977 exports grew four times faster. Still, the rancor and tensions are not due so much to the aggregate export level but rather to export concentration in a few products. Theoretically, comparative advantage dictates that nations should specialize, but adjustment costs—of employment particularly—have been high in recipient countries as comparative advantage shifted to Japan. Moreover, factor endowments dictate that raw materials be the largest part of Japanese imports (only 20% are manufactures),[35] so Japan's trade structure naturally leads to specific adjustment problems and bilateral imbalances. Trade imbalances have become political problems chiefly due to unemployment, as highly unionized basic industries in the United States and Europe have lost markets at home and in third countries.

Japan's preferred approach to solving such problems has been to establish trade cartels, voluntary quotas, orderly marketing agreements, etc. There is little worry over potential losses to oligopoly, since recession cartels have been long accepted as appropriate to tide industries over short-term difficulties. The U.S. approach is different, concentrating on price effects through exchange rate adjustments, primarily to shrink the total bilateral imbalance. U.S. policy though has been implemented with little concern for the broad effects yen appreciation has on Japan, and this has raised frustration with the United States. Nor has the United States assessed the long-term competitive implications of increased rationalization by Japanese firms in key industries, or of foreign investment by such firms. Appreciation eliminates marginal producers, thus increasing the market share and long-run competitiveness of leading producers and exporters. Further, investments in the United States and elsewhere will be leveraged, using parent company guarantees. Thus such investments will reduce capital costs while geographically diversifying trade competitiveness and sales—in effect multilateralizing the competitive issue.

The 1977-78 steel controversy provides an excellent case in point. Japan's steel industry has long recognized the U.S. steel industry's import problem. Beginning in the 1960s, as weak steel demand and strikes squeezed U.S. firms' profits and product availability, U.S. domestic prices were raised. U.S. buyers began substituting imports for American steel, further pinching profits and raising dumping protests. In response, the Japanese negotiated an orderly marketing agreement from 1969 to 1974. The 1977-78 crisis has been similar, but has been exacerbated by weak domestic demand in Japan and Europe. This increased pressures to export to a reflated U.S. economy. The Japanese response to protests was the same as in 1969, the suggestion of voluntary restraints; but the U.S. government preferred to encourage anti-dumping suits.

However, when the highly restrictive implications of fully enforcing U.S. trade laws became clear, a reference or trigger price mechanism for steel imports was proposed. Though there has been expanded demand for U.S.-produced steel, it is still not clear this mechanism will solve the problem. The U.S. industry's profits may not rise sufficiently nor steel markets expand enough to justify needed investment in more modern plant and equipment. Neither will a reference price give the consumer the benefits of more efficient steel production through lower prices or promote efficiency at home. Meanwhile, obvious dumping by European firms has combined with yen appreciation to reduce Japanese sales in the United States anyway.

The American attitude toward solving trade problems has concentrated on finding the right mechanism (e.g., orderly marketing agreements, dumping law enforcement, or reference prices) and then has trusted the mechanism to create the "right" solution. There is no awareness that U.S. trade policy must be formed in the context of an overall industrial policy: e.g., what kind of steel industry does the United States want, and how should trade policy be formulated to foster this goal? The issue is how best to make U.S. industry more competitive and productive at home and abroad. Promoting competitiveness, investment, and productivity in key industries is the most constructive way to promote exports, reduce imports, improve employment, and strengthen the dollar. Although the United States is bad enough in this regard, Europeans seem even more phobic and unresponsive to Japanese trade competition, blatantly restricting access to their markets.

Until recently, Japan has not worried about the overall size of the trade surplus, rather viewing it as the natural outgrowth of a successful industrial policy. This is understandable, given the traditional balance-of-payments constraint and apparent willingness to finance the surplus by accepting increased reserves, thus transferring some excess savings abroad. But the record surpluses of 1977 and 1978 have again afforded critics a powerful argument that the yen has been undervalued, and several sharp appreciations have shocked the economy, though the net effect of appreciation is still unclear. Some will certainly gain from appreciation. Import-intensive firms and industries with relatively low domestic value added may actually gain over the long run through lower input costs and a consequent ability to cut prices. But less import-intensive firms and industries, such as autos and computers, will have to improve non-price competitiveness and production efficiency. Further, as already noted, the impact is not uniform among firms or industries, but rather hurts primarily the marginal firms in weak industries. But as no one really knows the long-run aggregate price elasticity of exports vs. imports, the overall net effect of appreciation on the trade surplus remains to be seen.

In 1978 despite substantial revaluation (¥240 to ¥189), export volume was down only 3%-5% while the value of exports was up 22%, indicating rather inelastic demand. When one further allows for the tendency for export adjustment to lag considerably behind exchange-rate changes, the probable trend appears to be a relatively constant export volume but a rising export value and continued trade surplus. Micro-economic pressures on leading firms to maintain at least current operating volumes also support this conclusion.

Still, appreciation has set off another vicious cycle in the economy. Profits have been reduced when general demand is already weak, which in turn further depresses plant and equipment investment, drives down bonuses, affects wage increases, and lowers government tax receipts. This chain reaction intensifies debate on how much the government can

[121]

afford to support the economy, while increasing the need for such support. In 1978, profits started to rise again. But for heavy and traditional industries, this primarily reflects declining interest rates, lower depreciation allowances, and foreign exchange gains on dollar debt. As such, they indicate no real change in final product or investment demand, thus continuing the government's dilemma. Responding to appreciation, the government has implemented a plan of emergency imports, lowered tariffs, and enlarged some agricultural import quotas, while fiscal expansion is being pursued through public works and housing programs. But thus far, primarily due to MOF resistance, these measures are insufficient. Also, many impediments to imports remain out of reach of government policy, .such as the complex distribution system with its frequent high markups on imports and substantial financing requirements. Yet there are areas of guidance amenable to change, such as for high technology industries (which still strongly promote local licensing and inputs), or restraints on foreign banks from entering consumer finance and rediscounting with the Bank of Japan (which restricts their ability to help finance imports through the distribution system). Given these many complexities, the U.S. bilateral imbalance will not shrink quickly.

Though trade relations with advanced countries are experiencing difficulties, those with Southeast Asia are going rather well. Japan continues to be a supplier of high-grade machinery, plant, and basic fabricated materials to Southeast Asia, as well as an important investor and aid source. Japan is committed to financing major development projects in the ASEAN nations. Relations with Australia have been somewhat bumpy, but Japanese investment in resource development there over the next few years is potentially great, depending on continued Japanese liquidity and world raw materials demand.

Trade with Communist nations will also provide an important opportunity for Japan. The long-term trade pact with China, signed early in 1978, outlines substantial provision of industrial plant and technology by Japan to China in return for raw materials. The problems with China trade for Japan are basically two: the quality of raw materials used as payments, and financing. China needs Japanese products quickly; however, the value of Chinese oil, a major part of the trade potential between the two countries, is reduced by its high paraffin content. China is not expected to be able to earn enough foreign exchange from other exports in the next few years to be able to pay for what it wants from Japan now. Thus, if trade is to expand, the Japanese will have to give credit to China to finance shipments. There is little doubt among Japanese that China will be able to pay off eventually, but it may be a long wait.

Trade with the Soviet Union will also bring Japan opportunities. Siberian development—which is essential to the Soviets if they are to earn the foreign exchange they need—will require substantial quantities of heavy industrial products that are too costly to ship from the western republics. Japanese suppliers are the logical answer. Oil exploration off Sakhalin has shown promising signs as well, and this could be used as partial payment for Japanese shipments to Siberia. Furthermore, assuming some Soviet success in exporting, Japan is a prime candidate to provide consumer goods to the Soviet Union should Soviet authorities allow more leeway for satisfaction of consumer demand. Moreover, the Soviets appear increasingly eager for trade with Japan, as seen in the unexpected concessions given in the Russo-Japanese fishing agreement of 1978. Of course, the difficulties are at least as great as the potential. The U.S. alliance with Japan and the continued stationing of U.S. troops in Japan cannot but give the Soviets second thoughts about Japan's intentions, just as

[123]

the U.S.S.R.'s military buildup in East Asia gives the Japanese pause. Also, continuation of the Sino-Soviet dispute will require of Japan a great sense of balance in determining the appropriate levels of participation in Siberian development.

A final consideration in Japan's current international economic relations is pressure to be a locomotive economy for the world as a whole. Considering the basic import structure, prospects appear dim relative to other developed nations. Reflation and revaluation will chiefly affect imports of raw materials or simple manufactured goods from LDCs. To reduce U.S. and European bilateral surpluses, tariffs must come down and various administrative trade impediments must be eased. Equally important, foreign firms must commit themselves to selling in Japan. Many Japanese are critical of what they feel is a lazy attitude toward their market. Many foreign firms expect to make profits too quickly without adapting policies or products to local conditions. Too many U.S. firms also separate the world into domestic and international operations only, treating all foreign markets equally and feeling all should be responsive to U.S. marketing and organizational methods. The Japanese government has made efforts to spread information on how to sell in Japan, but U.S. and European governments have not been particularly helpful to their corporations. Yet this cannot be the whole story, given the government's reluctance to truly liberalize incoming investment and imports. Administrative guidance still restricts foreign competition when it is really competitive, e.g., the Dow case.[36] Nor can the laziness of the majority explain the frustrations of those who have made or are willing to make a commitment to the Japanese market over a period of years, often successfully. Both sides must improve if Japan is again to have a locomotive rather than a deflationary impact on the world economy.

[124]

Continuing versus Non-continuing Elements of Competitive Growth

Japan clearly entered a transitional stage after 1971, and many aspects of the previous high-growth stage changed. Yen appreciation, maturing demand, depressed investment, changing social attitudes, and external pressures have continued. Nevertheless, the trade surplus has grown, overcoming even the quintupling of fuel and energy costs, and basic industries have improved competitiveness and comparative advantage since 1973. This is due to the continuation of many basic corporate attitudes, behavior patterns, and incentives formed during the high-growth era. While firms generally no longer invest in anticipation of demand, they are still investing and modernizing relative to foreign competition, and Japan will maintain technological advances and productivity gains relative to that competiton. Japanese have also adopted very long-term strategies to begin to produce higher value-added products, including plant and equipment exports related to foreign aid investment. Lower technology goods will be produced in and exported from Japanese-built plants abroad. Lower capital costs, the permanent employment system, and the compulsion for full capacity operation all contribute to this trend to keep improving. As Japan moves into the next decade, therefore, the large corporation will remain on the cutting edge of Japan's economic evolution and international competitiveness. It is the exploration of some of these trends, including new industry development, Japanese multinational corporations, existing industry's technological and product innovations, evolving trade patterns, foreign investment, and an expanded government sector, to which we now turn.

[125]

Japan's Economic Prospects 1978-1985

The need for further structural change in Japan has been recognized throughout the 1970s, but specific events—raw materials shortages, capacity constraints, the oil crisis, recession, high inflation, the Lockheed scandal—have sometimes diverted attention from the basic issues. Now, however, these events have either faded or have merged with older, continuing problems. Outstanding questions are: How will Japan's economic structure evolve to relieve the payments surplus, rising unemployment, excess savings, slower growth, and inadequate social capital? Will corporations adapt to growth not skewed toward investment in capital equipment? Will financial institutions adjust to a borrower's market? Will labor develop new skills needed for new industries, yet preserve the permanent employment system within the larger firms where it predominates? Can international problems be solved with a minimum of rancor, while gains from trade, technological progress, economies of scale, and the international division of labor continue?

MITI's Vision

A revised view of the long-range evolution of Japan's industrial structure was published by MITI in 1971, with a fundamental revision in 1975.[37] The latest view outlines both generally and specifically which industries and which products MITI feels will lead the next stage of development, and the country's basic goals are redefined. Previously, emphasis was on industrial development, investment, exports, and aggregate income. Now, emphasis has shifted to surety of raw materials supply, better housing, better medical care, more social capital, and less pollution. Therefore inputs are to shift from basic industries that are raw material intensive, such as steel and chemicals, to high technology industries where design and research are a larger share of value added. So-called "knowledge-intensive" industries will develop to replace Japan's present leading industries. Marketable goods' share of output will fall as public and semipublic sectors such as public housing grow. Given decreased production of low-technology and labor-intensive goods, imports of these items will rise, reducing raw materials imports and decreasing exports of certain manufactured goods. Thus, the economy will become more knowledge intensive and information oriented as the proportion of value added contributed by technology rises.

This scenario implies low growth or even decline for the basic industries and corporations that underpinned postwar development. Steel, chemicals, petrochemicals, aluminum, nonferrous metals, and low-grade machinery all face mature demand, difficult plant siting, pollution control problems, and shifting comparative advantage. Foreign investment is of course one outlet, as new plants can be located abroad, closer to growing markets, with extra capacity used to supply Japan's incremental needs. In aluminum, for example, high energy usage and exhaustion of Japan's hydroelectric potential will force rationalization and major investment abroad, as Mitsui has already done with Amax in the United States. MITI foresees 49% of Japan's aluminum needs imported by 1985. Basic industries tend to be energy and petroleum intensive, so that shifting abroad will also help ease the nation's precarious energy situation.

Prospective growth industries include high grade general and electric machinery, transportation equipment, precision

[127]

machinery, prefabricated housing, plants, and engineering. With labor costs rising, capital and technology substitution will become increasingly necessary across a broad range of industries. New machinery will have to be developed to prevent wage-cost inflation and to preserve competitiveness. Greater research and development related to these new industries will itself create demand for scientific instruments and computing equipment. Among the many new products forecast will be anti-pollution equipment, industrial robots, biomechanic sensors, large-output lasers, Chinese-character recognition equipment, seabed development machinery, and automobile anti-skid systems.

The plan is logical, but there is some question as to where the new knowledge will come from and how it will be developed. Japan is certainly capable of research and development (R & D), particularly in process engineering, but the firms best able to produce new techniques are in established industries. Many new products which MITI envisions have never been produced before, even abroad, so that much basic research will be needed along with innovation and adaptations to production processes. This would be a new technological thrust for Japan. Further, given past experience, Western innovators are less likely to sell technology to potential Japanese competitors. Indeed, many like IBM and Texas Instruments are successfully competing in Japan. Therefore the most likely source for Japan's new knowledge-intensive products, particularly in the three-to-five-year range, is not from new industry but rather from an upgrading of existing basic industries. Steel companies and similar firms will export plant, equipment, engineering, and pollution control devices, while improving technology and upgrading domestic products. These firms have the cash and incentives to do this, and can thus both maintain competitive positions and raise employment and wages. In addition, many are already at the technological frontier in their industries and are quite competitive. There is no need to catch up, as the very high technology industries must do. Moreover, upgrading basic industry will not be competitively frustrated by yen appreciation or the liberalization of imports and investment. Thus intra-industry knowledge-intensive development is a more likely scenario than MITI's projected inter-industry evolution, and in fact corresponds to the countervision proposed by Keindanren (the Federation of Economic Organizations).[38]

And there are other problems with the MITI plan. First, the government's influence on industrial development has fallen, due to high bank and firm liquidity. Banks no longer rely so heavily on the Bank of Japan for credit, so this critical pressure point is gone. Further, R & D is too risky to make bank financing appropriate, which further lowers the government's ability to influence industrial development except via direct subsidies. Another problem is how research benefits will be shared. The scientific and engineering talent available in private firms may not be made available to competitors or to the public. But if technology is spread among too many producers, no one may become truly competitive, a common liability of publicly sponsored research made available to all. Finally, bureaucratic responsibilities for many new products like medical equipment, for housing, time-sharing, and transportation are not lodged in MITI but in other ministries, making coordinated development plans difficult to construct and implement, compared to the past.

Fiscal Policy and the Government's Expanding Economic Role

Even if the MITI plan is not completely accurate on the form of evolution of the industrial structure, employment upgrading will occur to justify higher wages and living

[129]

standards. Similarly, on a sectoral basis MITI properly emphasizes greater investment in social overhead capital and higher government expenditures as essential to a successful structural evolution. This is readily apparent with the economy facing recession and continued high savings. But it is also a logical development, given Japan's transition from a classical to a Keynesian economy, and the public sector deficiencies generated by imbalanced postwar growth. Some changes have been made, but more remains to be done. While budget increases were about 17% and 20% in FY 1977 and FY 1978, respectively,[39] the economy still needs additional stimulus. With proposed public works projects of ¥240 trillion over a decade, plus the needed overhauling and funding of larger national health and unemployment insurance schemes, annual expenditures of at least ¥39-40 trillion (1978 yen) will be required. But at most ¥23.5 trillion in revenues is available, even including possible extra crude oil levies and public monopoly profits, leaving a deficit financing gap of over 40%, far higher than MOF conservatives will accept.

Since a cabinet reorganization was necessary to get a budget for FY 1978 of ¥34.3 trillion with an actual debt ratio of 37%, prospects do not appear bright for quickly bringing expenditures to a level needed for real economic restructuring. The persistent conservatism of the MOF, despite continuous pummeling by all economic sectors, particularly MITI and business, is the major stumbling block. The nature of Japanese decision-making supports the MOF position, since lack of a consensus forces default in MOF's favor. Still, the slimness of the LDP's majority plus continued pressures on the yen will aid the pro-reflation forces. Momentum in this conflict is growing, and the expansionists seem to be winning the battles, e.g., larger rather than smaller supplementary budgets and breaking the 30% debt ceiling for the FY 1978 budget. Still,

[130]

expenditures are not at the required levels, and two or three more years may be needed before the final, full consensus emerges. Therefore, the FY 1979 budget deficit should continue at about a 35% to 40% debt-ratio level. Correspondingly, Japan's growth prospects, with little or no growth in export volume anticipated, should then be in the range of 5.5%. Even without MOF opposition, project lead-times would delay increases in expenditure. There is a large backlog of projects, but most are small scale·and local. Such projects do help employment, particularly where small industry has been hurt, but major national projects are also needed to redress structural imbalance. Extension of high-speed rail lines and major highways are two areas often cited, but both are affected by land costs and sunshine rights, as is infrastructure for new residential areas. Thus, some land-use planning or even land price "guidance" may be necessary to avoid speculation, as occurred in 1973-74, and to allow stable and appropriate long-term land-use decisions. Housing projects face a similar dilemma, whether sponsored directly or via government or government-stimulated expenditures. In short, the structural evolution foreseen by MITI based on social capital spending does not appear likely to be in full swing before the end of 1979, though the commitment, once made, should last well into the 1980s.

Capital Surplus and Corporate Strategy

Even with successful government stimulus, average real growth per year until 1980 is not likely to exceed 5.5%, and after that for the next few years probably will not exceed 6.5%. However, savings are expected to continue at high

[131]

high levels. Thus, given lower capital requirements in a lower-growth economy, the savings surplus might continue for some time. Over the long term the propensity to save may well be lowered by an aging population structure, changing attitudes, higher unemployment benefits, more available housing, and improved social security. On the other hand, profits and continued high depreciation in efficient basic industries, which are planning little new domestic investment, will add to net savings, offsetting some of the above effects. The results will be continued high liquidity and low domestic interest rates.

Excess savings will bring major changes in the country's financial structure, particularly given past assumptions of capital scarcity. Competition among financial institutions for good credits will be fierce, which could either accentuate traditional group relationships or detract from group solidarity. Confusion over main bank relationships may result and lead to more and larger bankruptcies. The large, international city banks will then feel more pressure to work with clients abroad and on foreign projects. But as smaller banks cannot do this, some consolidation in banking is likely, and the MOF is encouraging such thinking. There will also be diversification of services and roles, such as bank activity in underwriting and direct sales of government bonds to the public.

The effects on firms will be equally pronounced, and probably beneficial. Rollovers will be easier as banks seek to maintain loan volume and relationships. (Some banks are now refusing repayments.) Current high raw-materials inventories and future reserves will be easier for firms to finance. Lower capital costs will help offset higher wages and other cost pressures, thereby maintaining price competitiveness, particularly in mature capital-intensive heavy industries. Finally, greater cash flows and the logic of corporate growth will push investment overseas, shifting savings to countries where higher returns are available. This trend dovetails with pressures on financial institutions, the need to upgrade employment, and the excess of savings over domestic investment demand.

Japanese corporate strategies will be formed in this context. Basically, firms will continue to grow and compete, if not domestically then overseas, both to keep workers employed and to keep their financial conditions sound. Yen appreciation will promote industrial rationalization, with marginal firms in the least competitive industries suffering most. Their markets, particularly export markets, will be absorbed by larger firms, thus improving the latter's competitive position and putting further pressure on the yen. This situation also coincides with overseas investment strategies, domestic intra-industry development, and R & D activities. The long-term result will be emergence of profitable, strong, and highly competitive Japanese multinational corporations. This could accentuate and complicate existing trade tensions and problems if Japanese multinationals either export from the LDCs or establish competititive operations in the United States and in European Common Market countries, using low-cost debt capital from Japanese banks, trading companies, and/or corporate parents. Market access would remain while the competitive strength of Japan's basic industries and corporations improves.

Raw materials access, improved value added, and lower labor costs can all be achieved in these ways. However, multinationalization will present new problems for the Japanese managers in negotiation, project finance, communication with personnel, and political relations with local governments, which many firms still have shown difficulty solving. But in the past, business pressures and realities have proved effective spurs, and it would be short-sighted to assume the likelihood of retreat or failure. Yet, more participation by the government and large corporations in international forums and negotiations will be essential to contain possible frictions resulting from the rapid rise of the worldwide activities of Japanese multinationals.

Population and Energy

Two other elements will be important in Japan's economic future. The first is population dynamics; the second is energy. Some commentators worry that the labor force that was young and saving in the 1950s is now aging and retiring. In firms with a strict seniority wage system, this might imply a higher wage bill with no necessary net increase of productivity, though this situation can be largely offset by lower annual raises or smaller bonuses, such as actually occurred in 1977 and 1978. The lower savings rates of older people could imply less money available for financing the investment needed to offset rising wage costs, though again the economy is currently suffering from too much savings. Moreover, these critics claim that general aging implies fewer manual workers available for basic industries and hence cost-push pressures that could lower world competitiveness. Trends in education that emphasize university as the only route to success also have deepened the supply problem of manual labor. Some commentators thus feel that aging in itself will also bring an actual decline in productivity. On the fiscal side, more retirements just when demands are rising for improved social security will certainly impose a burden on the public treasury at precisely the time when the MOF is trying to hold down expenditures, thus increasing existing budgetary conflicts.

These points may seem threatening at first glance, but in the context of the structural evolution of the economy it appears that population dynamics should in fact improve the

[134]

nation's economic health. First, the lower savings rates implied by an aging population are really no threat at all; indeed, as previously noted, one of Japan's worst current problems is the deflation due to excess savings. To the extent that aging of the population lowers savings it will also contribute to economic balance. Second, the industries hit hardest by higher wage bills from aging labor forces tend to be those industries that are themselves older and either have lost or are rapidly losing comparative advantage. Higher wage costs in old industries provide only another incentive to develop new industries or upgrade existing ones, just as the MITI plan advocates. Third, the shortage of manual workers or excess of university graduates means increased availability of the very type of workers needed for knowledge-intensive industry. Such an abundance of workers for knowledge-intensive industries will of course lower the cost burden of developing such industries. At the same time, as a disproportionate number of older and retiring people are in agriculture and distribution, this trend will help to rationalize these sectors and raise imports. Of course, the social adjustment costs to the new population structure will be substantial. But it is more rational and beneficial to adjust and use some of the surplus of the more productive evolving industries to pay for the adjustment than to resist them, sacrificing both output and improved overall employment in a futile effort to preserve old, uncompetitive industries.

Energy too is one of Japan's most serious economic issues. Japan currently relies on foreign sources for virtually all its energy, and the bulk of this comes from the Middle East. In the five-to-ten-year range, there is no way to correct the overall dependence on foreign sources. Thus Japan's medium-term energy strategy is to diversify sources of fossil fuels. Through such diversification the consequences of disruption in

[135]

any one area, e.g., another OPEC embargo or a disaster in the Straits of Malacca, would be minimized. Oil from China, offshore wells in the Yellow and China Seas, and off Sakhalin, along with natural gas from Siberia and the western continental shelf of Australia, and coal from the United States and Australia are prime possibilities for diversification. Developing these fossil fuel resources is not only essential for reducing excessive dependence on a few sources, but also desirable as an outlet for excessive domestic savings and as an opportunity for capital outflow, and to generate more imports to offset trade surpluses.

Japan's longer run (1985-2025) energy future is inescapably nuclear. Diversified dependence may be better than concentrated dependence, but only nuclear power will afford Japan a measure of independence. Japan has made much progress in developing nuclear plant technology, and Hitachi has even signed an agreement with General Electric to exchange (not just obtain) reactor technology.

Even in nuclear energy Japan faces severe constraints. Capacity utilization rates of current reactors in Japan—as elsewhere—are abysmal, and expanded R & D is needed to correct this. But the worst problems are political. The United States has placed strict conditions on Japanese use and disposal of enriched uranium and the technology it has provided. World agreements on nuclear trade and waste disposal are not likely to be susceptible to much influence by Japan. Ironically, research in Japan aimed at improving nuclear technology is not always welcomed since it further complicates proliferation, processing, and waste disposal. But the rest of the world must realize that Japan has no choice but to obtain and use improved light water and breeder technology. If its legitimate needs are not accommodated within international accords, then Japan will be forced to develop nuclear capabilities outside their provisions. Avoiding the political instability inherent in such an unfortunate turn of events is worth much to the rest of the world, and concessions to Japan in nuclear agreements, particularly from the United States will be essential in securing Japan's cooperation.

International Issues and the "Balance of Payments Problem"

Japan faces some of its most troublesome problems internationally not only because of the consensus decision-making process, but also because of the power and logic of its competitive development. Japanese trade in particular faces two short-term issues. The first is the need for policy coordination with other governments, in which economic policy targets are taken seriously and are fulfilled as the quid pro quo for the similar efforts of others. Domestic goals and political constituencies may have to be sacrificed in this regard, and problems abroad must be anticipated before they reach crisis proportions. The second short-term problem will be disorderly markets brought about by competition in excess of what foreign economies can adapt to at normal speeds. Disorderly markets—in currencies, manufactured goods, or commodities—interfere with the ability to make efficient decisions on long-run resource allocation and depress business expectations through uncertainty. Japan is too big an economy to discount any longer its significant impact on the rest of the world.

At the same time, policy coordination and controlling market excesses both require a firm grasp on long-run economic trends and issues. The most important of these is a concept of dynamic, competitive economic evolution. While Japan has a relatively firm idea of how its economy should evolve, many other nations, particularly the United States, do not. This presents Japan with a dilemma. Should Japan frustrate its own efficient and logical development because of poor U.S. or E.E.C. competitive responses? Or should Japan proceed despite the risk of increased political and economic tensions? Japan will have to create a framework for deciding when and where adjustments are needed. When nations and large corporations choose a development course over time, long-term comparative advantage changes worldwide. Therefore, given Japan's economic size and the growing importance of Japanese multinationals, the consequences of its emerging economic structure are much larger than is generally appreciated for world economic relations and for trade patterns.

These long-term dynamics are often discussed in terms of the world's balance-of-payments structure, but in fact the "balance of payments" issue is many issues interwoven. Unemployment, union power, political leverage, consumer protection, inflation, factor endowments, technological capacities, and many other considerations combine to create a global, evolving structure of multilateral relationships. Wise policy on all sides requires a proper assessment of these complexities.

For example, a major current policy problem is the effect of Japanese exports on U.S. unemployment. According to one U.S. viewpoint, Japan is making products Americans could make—even if somewhat less efficiently—and thus is creating U.S. unemployment. The most virulent critics are well-organized, politically powerful unions with Congressional leverage. The struggle for jobs has, in effect, politicized the bilateral trade issue. Nevertheless, real adjustment burdens should not be taken lightly, and Japan needs to recognize this more and more. It needs to understand the real costs to a country of underutilized social infrastructure resulting from plant closings or regional decline. Japan's eagerness to conclude orderly marketing agreements indicates some under-standing of the problems involved, but its reluctance to reflate the economy shows the need for additional thought. On the other hand, the United States needs foreign products to increase its domestic growth potential through cheaper inputs, industrial rationalization, and efficient resource allocation. Foreign products help protect domestic consumer interests by providing higher living standards at lower prices. However, consumer groups are usually less well organized and more dispersed than unions or business. Plant closings that affect particular locations are highly visible and political events. The same situation exists in Japan in products such as beef, silk, textiles, and handicrafts, so perhaps Japan can now empathize more with foreign policy-makers.

Japanese imports are the other side of the trade coin.[40] The United States and the E.E.C. might be less upset if they appeared to have easy access to Japanese markets. Japan has been widely criticized for protecting its market through administrative guidance, tariffs, and quotas, all abetted by a complex distribution system which seems especially difficult for foreigners to penetrate. Japan did restrict imports in the initial postwar period to protect its weak industrial base. Now, however, it is the competitive power of Japanese industries combined with some residual protectionist attitudes and a lack of real commitment by foreigners which exclude foreign manufactures. A common indicator of this lack of access is manufactured imports' low proportion of total imports relative to other industrial countries. But here it is important to remember Japan's factor endowments, for, unlike the United States, Japan has virtually no domestic oil, iron ore, natural gas, uranium, and so on, and agricultural land is sparse. Thus, even if Japan had an industrial output structure identical to that of the United States, raw materials would have to be a higher

[139]

proportion of imports. Nevertheless, more can and should be done to promote manufactured and other imports.

For Japan the agricultural import issue is similar to the U.S. unemployment/import issue. A powerful lobby with votes essential to the ruling party is skewing policy to its advantage, but to the detriment of foreign suppliers and domestic consumers. More is at issue, however, than just beef and citrus fruit; rather, the LDP perceives its very life is at stake if major rural constituencies so essential to its political base are sacrificed. If the government fosters beef and citrus imports at the expense of the farmers, it sees the political consequences as dire. Similarly, the rice market is heavily protected through a price support system, and a setback for any rural constituency is an implicit threat to the price system for rice, and hence to virtually every farmer. An income subsidy might replace quotas and the price supports, but the LDP feels it simply cannot afford an erosion of the rural vote. Over the next ten years, though, this problem will ease as many farmers retire or find non-farm jobs. Further, as pointed out by Professor Curtis in Chapter 2, the actual political impact of changes in agricultural policy are not likely to be nearly as significant as the LDP suggests.

As for manufactured imports, an important aspect is that the high technology manufactures Japan could import from the United States and the E.E.C. to reduce bilateral imbalances are precisely those MITI's industrial plan wants to encourage. On balance, the government thus far has decided that smooth external relations are worth some sacrifice, but there remains significant resistance to full reliance on international specialization and comparative advantage in these industries. Imports and investments have been liberalized for these products, with some research subsidies granted as a palliative to domestic producers. Yet, as noted above, this approach is not likely to result in the quick, effective, internationally competitive development of these industries in Japan, given the strength of foreign competition and continued yen appreciation.

Japan's trade surpluses are often cited as "the problem" in economic relations, but in fact are a proxy for the other issues discussed above. As long as Japan finances the imbalance through absorption of reserves, savings are transferred overseas at no cost to foreigners. Indeed, this would be beneficial if foreign countries were operating close to full employment. One aspect of the surplus that does cause difficulties, however, is its impact on exchange markets. The exchange rate is a potent lever to force policy change and stimulus, but, as such, should be used with great caution, and only to smooth temporary disequilibria to prevent the mis-allocation of re-sources usually generated by disorderly markets. It is not a substitute or cure for basic structural difficulties. Still, with a probable two-year lag for the real impact of changes in government expenditure patterns to take hold, given the trade surplus, more pressure on the yen is likely into 1979 with the consequences examined above.

The increasing complexity and multilateralization of inter-national economic problems will require more negotiation among all parties. Japan's success in such cooperative agree-ments will in turn be affected by foreign conceptions about Japan's economy and about what is "fair." New rules to guide the adjustment of payments imbalances seem necessary since the current imbalances of both Japan and the United States are built into their economic structures which exchange rate adjustments are not sufficient to handle alone. A classical or neo-classical prescription would emphasize raising or lowering the level of domestic activity to correct imbalances through higher or lower imports and exports. But this approach ignores important political constraints. Furthermore, the product

[141]

composition of trade tends to be stable in the short to medium term, so that even strong stimulus would not necessarily move the balance of payments, particularly bilateral balances, toward equilibrium. The persistent inflation even in a recessionary environment also constrains the effectiveness of the classical and neo-classical payments adjustment policies.

Exchange rate adjustment as a way of changing major imbalances also leaves much to be desired. Not only do its rapid and fluctuating redistributive effects and its disruption of price allocative mechanism cause serious problems, but exchange rates as an adjustment mechanism presuppose a high degree of price elasticity of demand as well as quick and easy entry for new producers. In a world where products are often specialized and complex, where exchange adjustments tend to reflect past competitive differences, and where there is pressure on producers to modernize and maintain sales levels, these two suppositions are in serious question. Moreover, exchange rate changes can stimulate inflation in the devaluing country, particularly if the degree of concentration among producers is high enough to allow domestic price hikes in sympathy with now more expensive foreign products, and particularly if the domestic producers were initially higher cost. This has actually happened in the United States, e.g., in steel and autos.

The real solution to structural problems in the balance of payments seems to be rather a redirection of growth toward different sectors, and a reconstruction of domestic tax, fiscal, and credit incentives structures in such a way as to promote greater balance. In Japan's case this means larger growth for the government sector and domestic consumption sector at the expense of the export sector. This meshes well with the MITI and Keidanren plans as well as with the general tenor of the consensus that seems to be emerging in favor of more public works, expanded welfare and income support, and more housing. Indeed, the capacity of these plans to bring payments adjustment is one of their most compelling, if least recognized, attractions.

But more straightforward trade policies are needed too, such as quota relaxations and tariff cuts. Japan must recognize that despite recent liberalization, foreign firms have been denied access to its markets for many years, while Japanese firms gained experience and organization in foreign markets, particularly in the United States. In addition, Japan is an extremely difficult and complex place to operate due to linguistic, cultural, and regulatory differences. Training people to work there takes time and local assistance. From this perspective it is reasonable for Japan to help foreign firms with the difficulties of selling in Japan, perhaps to the extent of compensatory advantages in terms of credit, taxes, training, and information. Japan cannot afford the tensions and disruptions that will result from continued large surpluses during the ten years or more that foreign firms will need to develop the necessary experience and organization to sell in Japan in quantity.

At the same time the United States too must shift its economic structure to bring about a payments adjustment. The U.S. government should offer improved assistance and incentives to export. Rather than viewing such programs as "windfalls" for business, it should see the benefits to the U.S. economy of greater productivity, more employment, and a stronger dollar. After all, it was from similar policies of export encouragement that Japan benefited so greatly in the postwar period. However, export policy is far from the whole answer. The entire microeconomic framework in the United States must be rationalized to improve competitiveness not only in export markets but at home as well. Japan's sales in the United

States are concentrated in products that U.S. makers actually pioneered, but which, through a combination of poor investment plans, excessive wage hikes, excess government regulation, sleepy marketing, and other factors have been lost to more dynamic rivals. *The U.S. trade problem is more an import problem than an export problem.* If the United States cannot compete effectively with Japan in the U.S. market, how can it do so in third countries or in Japan itself?

The United States now needs substantial investment incentives so that competitive advantage can be maintained in very high technology industries, such as computers and nuclear equipment, and recouped in basic industries where its worldwide market share has fallen. Firms should be also given compensation for the burden that environmental and other regulations place on them. The strictness of regulations is another matter; no rational observer is against clean air and safe jobs. But the public must bear its share of these costs of regulation one way or another. Currently the public's share is paid through unemployment and higher prices springing from cost-push inflation induced by regulation and mandated expenditures. Safety and environmental investments now amount to more than 10% of total U.S. investment, but are disproportionately concentrated in a few industries, particularly power, energy, and basic commodities.[41] This regulation-induced inflation robs U.S. industry of competitiveness and gives markets to foreign producers, and the effects are greatest in those industries generally feeling the direct cost impact. Further, such structural inflation induces U.S. monetary authorities to raise interest rates, choking off the very investment that could improve competitiveness. It would be much more rational—and much less costly—for the public to pay its share of regulation costs in the form of offset payments through tax, fiscal and credit policies to the regulated; output would

[144]

then not be lost to inflation and foreign competition. Such offsets would also be fairer, since the current unemployment induced through the regulatory mechanism is not spread evenly across the economy, so that some people pay grievously while others not at all. All benefit from the externalities of a cleaner and safer environment, and thus it is only fair that these charges be made against general revenues.

The basic idea of the offset-payment approach is to move the supply curve for U.S. goods and services to the right by lowering the cost of supply per unit. For the individual firm, lowering investment costs through tax, credit, and fiscal incentives does this directly, as would any offsets to regulatory costs. Indirectly, greater investment stimulates productivity increases and R & D, which further lower costs. Lower costs lead to more competitive prices, improved market share, more investment, etc. This is the same beneficial cycle seen in Japan. Japan now has pollution and safety standards at least as stringent as those of the United States, but they are offset by low cost loans from the Japan Development Bank, by rapid depreciation, and even by expensing of such investments. Thus the anti-competitive effect to the individual firm is minimized. The correlation of this offset-payments structure with Japan's continued international competitiveness, price stability, and low user cost of capital is not accidental.

An appropriate list of policies for the United States to help break into this virtuous cycle would include the following: incentives for modernization; more, and more rapid depreciation allowances; expensing of safety and environmental and other mandated investments; elimination of double taxation on dividends from common stock; deductibility of interest on preferred stock to strengthen balance sheets; continuation of Domestic International Sales Corporations; and tax relief for U.S. citizens working overseas. A reduction in corporate taxes or an increase in the investment tax credit would not be as beneficial since this would favor mostly those high technology or service industries which have already been most successful in competing, due to their low capital requirements, their ability to expense R & D investments, and their dependence on deductible labor inputs. The United States must allow basic industry to recapture some of the capital taxed away under the current tax/inflation structure. This recapture could and probably should be tied to increased investment and price stability. The cost to the economy even in the short run would be small as greater competitiveness, increased employment, greater business confidence, and, therefore, greater investment raise the level of economic activity and government revenues, and hence offset any initial revenue reduction. But longer-term positive results of greater price stability, higher growth, greater competitiveness, a stronger dollar, and a reduced budget deficit would be enormous. Like Japan, the United States must begin to think of the economy in dynamic and evolutionary terms.

There are other areas where some restructuring would help the U.S. balance of payments. Anti-trust policy is in need of both clarification and rationalization. Currently, U.S. firms are uncertain of how government will react to rationalizations or overseas cooperation. Often cases brought by the government seem more anti-business than anti-trust and focus on business success rather than on collusion, e.g., IBM or Kodak. This is not true in Japan. Anti-trust policy has in many ways denied economies of scale to U.S. firms and has harmed international competitiveness. In addition, labor should be given some incentives to contain wage demands, e.g., automatic dismissal of dumping suits in industries where wage hikes have chronically exceeded productivity gains. And finally, the United States must develop and implement a comprehensive, cohesive, and expanded energy policy, including a larger R & D effort which will make use of our indigenous energy resources.

The real contribution of the United States toward adjustment of the world balance-of-payments system will come only through changes in these areas. The necessary policies are basically domestic in nature and are closely interrelated as lower costs and increased, investment and productivity can result in lower prices, more moderate wage demands, greater competitiveness, and a better ability to pay for and conserve energy through modernization. It is ironic that they should have to be advocated as part of an intelligent balance-of-payments policy. But in fact the U.S. balance of payments will largely take care of itself once rational microeconomic policies are adopted at home. Indeed, what Japanese want most from the United States is not a verbal commitment to free trade but an improvement in the underlying efficiency of the U.S. economy so that foreign competition is no longer a threat, but merely a challenge.

SUMMARY AND CONCLUSIONS

Japan's growth strategy for the 1949-71 period, concentration in basic industries, was a great success. The major problems of the 1950s—capital scarcity, low income, and the balance-of-payments constraint—were solved, as the industrial structure was transformed by strong private investment and consumption demand, combined with progressive government policies. It was an appropriate strategy for an expanding world economy. Plant and equipment investment was strong throughout the period, even during "recessions" when growth fell as "low" as 6%. Export growth and competitiveness were also major factors; export markets provided justification for additional plant and equipment investment once domestic demand was basically satisfied. Concomitantly, fiscal policy was conservative. By 1971, though, major economic imbalances had surfaced; poor social security and welfare systems, pollution, lack of social overhead capital, raw material shortages, and increasing trade surpluses were exacerbated by widening bilateral imbalances and maturing domestic and international demand across a broad range of basic industries. Just as the economy was coming to grips with these problems, several shocks accentuated the change in Japan's economic situation—currency fluctuations, raw materials and food shortages, the oil crisis, and recession. Though to some degree these events directed attention away from the fundamental evolution, on the whole they prodded rethinking and reformulation of national goals. The government and business community are still struggling to work out a consensus and implement it.

Japan's policy formulation and implementation problems in the 1979-85 period will be complex. Economic fundamentals have changed; unlimited exports of certain products cannot continue; anticipatory plant and equipment investment has been curtailed; and fiscal conservatism is increasingly costly in terms of unused capacity. But on top of these problems, the political structure that allowed high growth is changing. Agriculture's political strength is harming other sectors, and, as the agricultural labor force is rapidly aging, the basic coalition of agriculture and business underlying LDP rule is under strain. Moreover, international cooperation is becoming more difficult, as transnational interest groups are at times in conflict with national policies, and as more government agencies are involved in economic planning and policy. This will increase adjustment difficulties and the need for multiple solutions. Yet, Mr. Ohira is known as a consensus-builder, which would indicate that the basic economic fundamentals will play a large role in determining policy, and hence that achieving a consensus will be difficult. Recent events have not changed the problems of inadequate private investment demand, lack of real export growth, and needed structural readjustments. All will continue to put policy pressures on the new cabinet.

Nevertheless, certain economic and political continuities will help Japan. Capital costs remain low and industrial productivity extremely high relative to competitors, so that the differential with other major producers in basic industries will continue for some time. In fact, as many foreign producers fail to invest and their equipment becomes increasingly antique, the relative gap may grow. This will contribute to continued domestic and export price stability in Japan. Nor have the basic drives for corporate survival and improvement abated; while many massive new plants in basic industries are unlikely, existing facilities will be upgraded through introduction of labor-saving machinery, robots, and new designs, while new facilities will be built abroad. Labor market conditions and the permanent employment system should continue, keeping workers receptive to various improvements. All this, of course, assumes a stable world geopolitical situation, especially in East Asia, facilitating a strong, prosperous, but non-military Japan. Further, society's basic cohesiveness will not change, and political continuity is likely eventually to achieve consensus on the economic scenarios outlined above.

However, the changes are important. Japan is now an economic superpower with major multinational corporations and responsibilities to promote world equilibrium and development without unnecessary tensions. The world is less open to Japanese growth based on exports while more eager for Japanese investment and development aid. At the same time that capital flows out, Japan's capital-output ratio will rise as technology is developed and as more investments are nonproductive. This process will lower growth. New mechanisms will have to be developed for economic planning and guidance, and a major change is needed in government attitudes toward spending for structural change, demand management, and import stimulation.

Japan was astute between 1949 and 1971, but still lucky. Diligence, effort, and wisdom were important, but a stable world environment was certainly a major factor supporting the various forces that dovetailed so systematically. And there were also special boosts from the Korean and Vietnam wars. The mutually self-supporting system developed during the period sustained Japan through the oil crisis and subsequent recession, so that the nation at present stands in a relatively strong economic position. But Japan's high productivity cushion grows less comfortable as others drift toward protectionism and as domestic demand deteriorates. Continued economic and political stability are still essential to further development. A concerted effort by all, including an effort by the United States to rationalize its economy, will be needed for Japan to maintain appropriate growth, both for its own sake and for that of a more harmonious, efficient, and prosperous world.

NOTES

1. Conversions are made at ¥190/US$. Most data used in this article are from the following four sources: Bank of Japan Statistics Department, *Economic Statistics Monthly,* various issues; hereafter cited as BOJ Monthly. Bank of Japan Statistics Department, *Economic Statistics Annual,* 1976 and other years; hereafter cited as BOJ Annual. Bank of Japan Statistics Department, *Hundred Year Statistics of the Japanese Economy,* 1966; hereafter cited as BOJ

Hundred Year Statistics. Bureau of Statistics, Office of the Prime Minister, *Japan Statistical Yearbook,* 1973-74 and other years; hereafter cited as PMO.

2. Most comprehensive is Hugh Patrick and Henry Rosovsky, eds., *Asia's New Giant: How the Japanese Economy Works* (Washington: Brookings Institution, 1976). A shorter account is Andrea Boltho's *Japan, An Economic Survey 1953-73* (London: Oxford University Press, 1975). A general overview of article length is Hugh Patrick's "The Phoenix Risen from the Ashes: Postwar Japan," in James Crowley, ed., *Modern East Asia: Essays in Interpretation* (Harcourt, Brace, and World, 1970) pp. 298-336.

3. BOJ Annual.

4. Hans Mueller and Kiyoshi Kawahito, *Steel Industry Economics,* International Public Relations Co., Ltd. (Japan Steel Information Center, January, 1978), p. 7.

5. BOJ Annual.

6. BOJ Monthly.

7. Tsuneo Iida, et al., *Gendai Nihon Keizai Shi: Sengo Sanjūnen no Ayumi* (An Economic History of Modern Japan: The Course of 30 Postwar Years) (Tokyo: Chikuma Shobō, 1976), p. 136.

8. PMO.

9. BOJ Annual.

10. *Ibid.*

11. *Ibid.*

12. *Ibid.*

[151]

13. *Ibid.*

14. PMO.

15. BOJ Annual.

16. Calculated from BOJ Annual.

17. BOJ Annual.

18. Iida, et al., *op. cit.,* p. 312.

19. BOJ Annual.

20. President Directory.

21. BOJ Annual.

22. Patrick and Rosovsky, eds., *Asia's New Giant;* data on parks and roads are from Patrick and Rosovsky, "Japan's Economic Performance: An Overview," p. 36; datum on flush toilets is from Edwin S. Mills and Katsutoshi Ohta, "Urbanization and Urban Problems," calculated from data on pp. 707-708.

23. PMO.

24. BOJ Annual.

25. Gary Saxonhouse, "Employment, Imports, the Yen, and the Dollar," in Henry Rosovsky, ed., *Discord in the Pacific: Challenges to the Japanese-American Alliance* (Washington: Columbia Books, 1972), pp. 84, 88.

26. BOJ Annual.

27. International Monetary Fund, *International Financial Statistics,* various issues; hereafter cited as IFS.

28. Bank of Japan Statistics Department, *Balance of Payments Monthly*, various issues.

29. Council on Wage and Price Stability, *Prices and Costs in the United States Steel Industry* (U.S. Government Printing Office, October, 1977), p. 37.

30. IFS.

31. IFS.

32. BOJ Monthly.

33. BOJ Annual.

34. President Directory.

35. BOJ Annual.

36. In the early 1970s Dow applied to MITI for a large investment (about 25% of contemporary Japanese capacity) in the caustic soda business, a fully liberalized industry. Dow's membrane process was both more efficient and more sound environmentally than the Japanese industry's mercury process. Due to Japan's increasingly stringent pollution controls, the caustic soda industry was under some pressure to change and modernize, but Dow refused to license its technology for sound competitive reasons. As a result, the industry became concerned about potential real competitive difficulties and put pressure on MITI and local governments to resist Dow's entry. After several years of protracted negotiations, Dow's application was approved. But given the adjustments U.S. industries have had to make to Japanese competition, the Dow case left U.S. businessmen and policy-makers justifiably irritated.

37. See Industrial Structural Council (advisory body to MITI), "International Trade and Industrial Policy for the 1970s," May,

1971, and "Japan's Industrial Structure: A Long Range Vision," June, 1975.

38. See Keidanren (Federation of Economic Organizations), "Confused World Trade and Industrial Structure," Tokyo, 1975.

39. BOJ Annual and newspaper releases.

40. James Abegglen, "Why Many Fail in Japan," *Far Eastern Economic Review,* November 11, 1977, discusses the difficulties foreigners have selling in Japan, and emphasizes the need for more effort by foreign firms.

41. Council on Environmental Quality, *1977 Annual Report,* Washington, 1978.

[FOUR]

Trends in Japan's Foreign and Defense Policies

Martin E. Weinstein *

Japan's alliance policy, its strategy and its relative military capabilities are little different at the end of the 1970s from what they were at the beginning of the decade or, for that matter, in the 1950s. Bipolarity may have given way to triangular or quadrilateral political arrangements in Northeast Asia, the confrontations of the Cold War may have been replaced with détente and the Shanghai Communiqué, but the Mutual Security Treaty remains the proverbial cornerstone of Japan's foreign policy, and Japan continues to depend for its military defense not so much on its own Self Defense Force, as on the U.S. Seventh Fleet and the Fifth Air Force.

Although the Sino-Soviet dispute has become a major factor

* Proffessor Weinstein served as Special Assistant to the United States Ambassador to Japan from August 1975 to August 1977. This chapter reflects his observations and experiences during that service.

in Japan's security environment and changes in American policy toward the Soviet Union and China have given Japan more room for maneuver, the government of Japan has shown little inclination to take major initiatives or departures toward the Asian Communist giants. Significant developments occur from time to time, such as the 1978 Treaty of Peace and Friendship with Peking, which followed the Petroleum and Trade Agreement with China reached in early 1978, or Japan's periodic negotiations with Moscow over trade or political issues. Yet the impact of actions such as these on the organization of Japan's economy and the direction of its foreign policy are limited. Close, cooperative ties with Washington still take clear precedence over relations with Peking and Moscow; and the widening of Japan's relations with the Russians and the Chinese is constrained by uncertainty about how far and how fast the Americans are moving.

When one compares them, it becomes apparent that Japan's foreign and defense policies have changed less during the past decade than have those of the United States. In part, the reason is that the Japanese had less to change. Their relations with Peking were never as economically restrictive or as bitter as ours, nor did they have powerful military forces deployed in East Asia, which they could withdraw. Nevertheless, the pendulum of American policy swings on a wider arc than does that of Japan, and the swing from Cold War toward détente and rapprochement has gone further in Washington than in Tokyo. In a policy planning conference of American and Japanese officials in early 1976 one Japanese, after discussing the limitations of our openings to Moscow and Peking, asked what the U.S. government planned to do after détente, particularly if it were unsuccessful. The American officials were put off by the question. The senior American present patiently explained that détente would continue indefinitely, because there was no acceptable alternative. The Japanese nodded politely but skeptically. In their minds the question remains unanswered.

In the 1950s and 1960s, there were pro-American, politically conservative Japanese, staunch defenders of the Security Treaty, who were concerned that American military predominance in the Western Pacific, combined with our anti-Communist fervor and Yankee toughness, could lead to an unnecessary war with the Soviets and Chinese—an unnecessary war into which Japan would have been unavoidably drawn. The thrust of Japanese policy then was to keep the shield of the Security Treaty raised while seeing to it that the American sword stayed safely and unprovocatively in its sheath. This was the purpose of the Prior Consultation Notes appended to the 1960 Security Treaty by the Kishi Cabinet. In the Prior Consultation Notes, the U.S. government agreed to consult with the government of Japan and to gain its approval prior to making any major changes in the force structure or weaponry of the U.S. forces stationed in Japan, or prior to deploying these forces to a combat area outside Japan.[1]

In 1978 the questions in the minds of Japan's ruling conservatives are of an entirely different order. These men are still pro-American, and they still support the Security Treaty, but they wonder whether the treaty and the American forces which stand behind it are adequate for Japan's defense. Given the changes that occurred as a result of Vietnam and Watergate in America's world outlook, in congressional and bureaucratic attitudes toward overseas military interventions, and, perhaps most importantly, the shrinking of American military strength in the Western Pacific, Japanese now wonder what the Mutual Security Treaty means to the United States, and what it will mean in the 1980s. Does it represent an unequivocal commitment to fight in Japan's defense, or does it mean something less? If so, how much less? Are the Seventh Fleet and the Fifth Air Force an effective deterrent against the Soviet Pacific Fleet and air forces? If deterrence fails, will American naval and air forces be able to keep open the lines of communication to Japan and the Western Pacific? What can Japan do?

The most significant change that has occurred in Japanese foreign and defense policy is that moderate, cautious Japanese conservatives are now asking themselves these questions, not in a panicky or even an urgent way, but deliberately and seriously.[2] Ten or twenty years ago they did not. Then, they took American military predominance, nuclear and conventional, in the air and on the seas, as an unshakeable premise upon which Japanese policy could be built. Now, they do not. No one in Japan has yet proposed clear, convincing answers to the above questions. And in view of the demonstrated success and enormous inertia of existing policies, dramatic departures in Japanese foreign and defense policy do not appear imminent. Nevertheless, we should realize that fundamental changes have occurred in Japanese *perceptions,* and that these perceptual changes are opening the possibility of substantial alterations in Japanese policy in the 1980s.

It should be noted that during the past few years, a number of respected writers have argued that the Japanese government has already made basic changes in its foreign and defense policy, or is in the process of doing so. These arguments are built on interpretations of the economic quarrels that have beset the United States and Japan, on the issues that have continued to divide Japan and the Soviet Union, on improvements in Sino-Japanese relations, and on evidence of growing Japanese involvement in Southeast Asia. While government spokesmen in Tokyo and Washington insist that their two countries have never been closer, some scholars and journalists tend to argue that Japan has adopted or is adopting new, basic policies of greater economic and political independence from the United States, that Japan is assuming a leadership role in Southeast Asia, and that Japan is moving toward cooperative economic and possibly even security ties with China.[3]

This essay, in contrast, was written in the belief that while fundamental changes in Japan's foreign and defense policies are likely, they have not yet taken place, nor have they been decided upon by the Japanese government. On the contrary, the senior Liberal Democratic Party (LDP) politicians who rule Japan are struggling to preserve as much as they can of the domestic and international positions Japan gained in the 1950s and the 1960s. Moreover, as Gerald Curtis makes clear in Chapter 2, there are no substantial domestic pressures which are likely to cause a major shift in foreign policy. Fundamental policy changes are not likely to take place gradually or incrementally; they are more likely to occur suddenly, should the reversal of the U.S.-Soviet military balance in Northeast Asia and the Western Pacific be unmistakably brought home to the Japanese, perhaps by an American failure to honor a security commitment in that region. That is why this chapter focuses on the changing Japanese perceptions of the U.S.-Soviet military balance, and on the military contingencies in the 1980s that could shock Japan into making basic changes in its foreign and defense policies.

Differing Perceptions of the Security Environment and the 1976 Defense White Paper

In June 1976, the Japan Defense Agency issued its second White Paper.[4] In the first, which had appeared in 1971,[5] Mr.

Yasuhiro Nakasone, who was then Director General, had called for expanded Japanese forces to fill the gaps being left by the reversion of Okinawa and by the reduction and consolidation of American forces in the Far East. His White Paper had also made a strong plea for a heightened defense consciousness among the Japanese people. Mr. Nakasone had a reputation as a hawk and as an aspiring Prime Minister, and many Japanese viewed his White Paper as an effort at self-promotion. In any case, it became clear in the ensuing defense budgets that Prime Minister Sato's Cabinet was *not* going to act on Mr. Nakasone's proposals. In contrast to its 1971 ancestor, the 1976 White Paper was a model of bureaucratic caution and blandness. It received less media attention, and one is tempted to pass it over as having little significance for Japanese foreign and defense policy.

There are, however, two aspects of the 1976 White Paper that deserve attention. First, the preparation of the White Paper led to a revealing disagreement between the Foreign Ministry and the Defense Agency on the future strategic environment in the region. Second, the 1976 White Paper had an unprecedented and unusual set of statistical tables and charts appended to it.

When the paper was drafted in the Defense Bureau of the Defense Agency in late 1975, it had a clear, consistent purpose and argument. Defense Agency Director General Michio Sakata wanted to gain public approval and greater legitimacy for the Self Defense Forces.[6] The budget outlook was unpromising, and the price of weapons was rising rapidly. Moreover, between 1972 and 1976, personnel costs in the Defense Agency had risen from 47 to 56 percent of the defense budget, while procurement outlays had dropped from 25 to 16 percent. In these circumstances, Mr. Sakata saw no likelihood of substantially improving the Defense Force's weapons and equipment, or even of reaching the procurement goals of the modest Fourth Defense Plan (1972-76). Consequently, instead of clamoring for budget increases that were certain to be refused, he set out to gain greater public acceptance and legitimacy for the Defense Agency and the Self Defense Forces. Minister Sakata directed the Defense Bureau to prepare a White Paper that would reassure the Opposition and the doves—a White Paper free of the hawkish arguments that characterized previous Defense Agency publications.[7]

The early drafts of the White Paper took the line that Japan could look forward to ten years of peace and security in an era of détente. There was no mention of "gaps" and no discussion of U.S. force reductions. The United States was expected to continue to improve its relations with both the Soviet Union and China. Japan would follow suit. With the major powers behaving peacefully, war was improbable in Korea, and the level of tension there would drop. Given the stable, secure international environment predicted in the draft, there would be no need for expensive improvements or expansion of the Self Defense Forces. Instead, the draft White Paper proposed a modest cut in SDF personnel during the coming decade, and the application of the funds freed by these cuts to a moderate upgrading of weapons and equipment. The new, undemanding Defense Force, in the new, safe, secure world of détente, was to be known as the "basic standing force."

The thrust of Mr. Sakata's approach to the Liberal Democratic Party (LDP) doves and to the Opposition was that since he was not pushing for more powerful, expensive Defense Forces, it was only appropriate for them to respond by giving the Defense Agency a more respectable place in Japanese political life. His suggested quid pro quo was the establishment of a Diet Committee on Defense, which was still under consideration by the government in late 1978.

Since the draft White Paper's analysis of the international

[161]

Defense Spending Trends

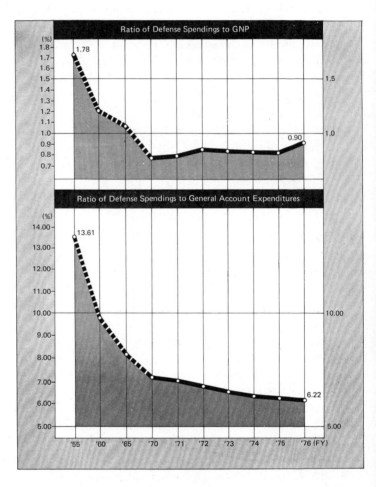

Source: *Defense of Japan, 1976,* Defense Agency, Tokyo, p. 129.

Changes of Composition of Defense Budget Under The Fourth Five-Year Defense Plan

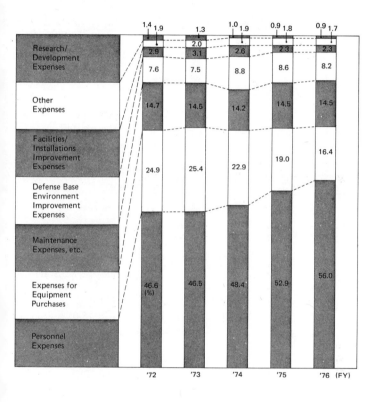

(Note) 1. Procurement includes Weapons and Vehicles, Aircraft and Ships.
       2. Operation and Maintenance includes Living cost, Clothing, Fuel,
      Maintenance and Repair.

Source: Ibid., p. 132.

[163]

Trend of Forces Around Japan (Approx.)

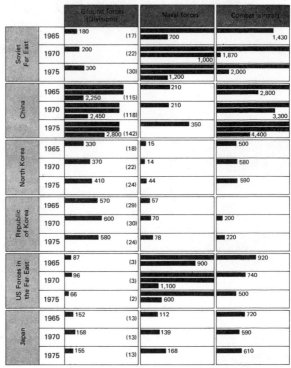

		Ground forces (Divisions)		Naval forces	Combat aircraft
Soviet Far East	1965	180	(17)	700	1,430
	1970	200	(22)	1,000	1,870
	1975	300	(30)	1,200	2,000
China	1965	2,250	(115)	210	2,800
	1970	2,450	(118)	210	3,300
	1975	2,800	(142)	350	4,400
North Korea	1965	330	(18)	15	500
	1970	370	(22)	14	580
	1975	410	(24)	44	590
Republic of Korea	1965	570	(29)	57	
	1970	600	(30)	70	200
	1975	580	(24)	78	220
US Forces in the Far East	1965	87	(3)	900	920
	1970	96	(3)	1,100	740
	1975	66	(2)	600	500
Japan	1965	152	(13)	112	720
	1970	158	(13)	139	590
	1975	155	(13)	168	610

(Note) 1. The figures for Ground forces (10 thousands persons) and Air forces (Combat aircraft) are quoted mainly from the Military Balance published in the corresponding year.

2. The figures for Naval Forces (10 thousands tons) are quoted mainly from the Jane's Fighting Ships published in the corresponding year.

3. The figures for Chinese divisions do not include Artillery, and railway construction engineer divisions.

4. Naval Force of the U.S. Forces in the Far East is the 7th Fleet. Air forces include carrier borne elements of the 7th Fleet.

5. U.S. Forces in the Far East are in Japan, the Republic of Korea, Taiwan and Philippines.

6. The figures for Japan indicate actual strength.

Source: Ibid., p. 15.

Deployment and Basing Around Japan

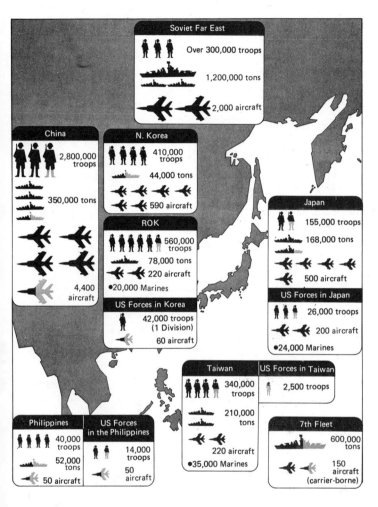

(Note) 1. Aircraft is "combat aircraft" from Military Balance, it comprises bomber, fighter-bomber, strike, intercepter, reconnaissance, etc.; it does not include helicopters.

Source: Ibid., p. 14.

political trends and of Japan's strategic environment dealt with broad foreign policy questions, copies of the draft were sent to the Foreign Ministry. There, it landed in the Security Treaty Division of the North American Affairs Bureau, and in the Research and Analysis Bureau. In both offices the draft White Paper was sharply criticized for being unrealistic and excessively optimistic. The Security Treaty Division people argued that the international political and strategic analysis was so completely at odds with the actual situation that it was beyond salvage and repair. They urged that it be completely rewritten to take into account what they saw as the deterioration in U.S.-Soviet relations, the uncertainties of Chinese domestic politics and foreign policy, and the continuing tension and instability on the Korean Peninsula. The Defense Agency's prediction of a ten-year period of peace and security came under especially harsh criticism. It was quickly scrapped.

The Research and Analysis Bureau agreed with these criticisms but felt that the Defense Agency's draft could be salvaged if it were revised. The analysts proposed a number of substantial revisions which were intended to balance and hedge the Defense Agency's assessments, most of which were incorporated into the final version of the White Paper. As a result, the Defense Agency was left with its "basic standing force" concept, but without most of the analysis and predictions that made it a logical response to Japan's international environment.

Oddly enough the inter-agency hedging and balancing process did not extend to the tables and charts appended to the White Paper. Among these were a table of the "Trend of Forces Around Japan" and a chart on "Deployment and Basing Around Japan." The deployment and basing chart showed the Soviets holding an approximate 2:1 advantage in naval combat vessels and combat aircraft in the Western

Pacific. The table on Force Trends showed that while the tonnage and numbers of Soviet naval and air forces in the Far East had grown by approximately 80 percent between 1965 and 1975, those of the United States had declined by about 70 percent.[8] In brief, the figures showed a reversal of the U.S.-Soviet military balance around Japan, and Soviet naval and air predominance.

There was nothing classified or secret about these figures. Most of the data in the charts and tables were taken from *The Military Balance* published by the Institute for Strategic Studies in London, and from *Jane's Fighting Ships*. The data were consistent with statements, published in October 1975, by the Chief of Naval Operations, in which Admiral James Holloway declared that the Sea of Japan had become a Soviet lake, and that it was uncertain whether U.S. naval and air forces could keep open the lines of communication in the Pacific west of Hawaii should the Soviets attempt to interdict them.[9] The Defense Agency had begun to feed this information to the Japanese press in the autumn of 1975, together with reports of Soviet naval operations in the waters close to Japan.

In the course of the Foreign Ministry-Defense Agency discussions on the draft White Paper, the diplomats pointed out that these data on the balance of military forces around Japan seemed inconsistent with the Agency's rosy analyses and predictions about Japan's future security. The Defense Agency agreed: they did seem inconsistent. The diplomats asked whether the reversal in the U.S.-Soviet balance might not have serious strategic implications for Japan. The Defense Agency replied that based on their talks with U.S. defense officials, they did not believe that the actual shift was as dramatic as the statistics suggested, and moreover, that the Soviets did not intend to take any military actions in Asia and the Pacific against Japan and the United States. They believed,

[167]

therefore, that the main significance of the changed balance of forces around Japan was, as they put it, more political and diplomatic than military. They suggested that the Foreign Ministry ought to address itself to these changes. The buck had been passed, but the Foreign Ministry let it drop.

The Defense Agency's draft analyses and predictions were based on President Nixon's 1972 and 1973 Foreign Policy Reports, and on discussions held in 1973-75 with Defense Department and State Department officials. As the Japanese diplomats pointed out, however, by late 1975 and early 1976, when the White Paper was being revised, Secretary Kissinger's statements on U.S.-Soviet relations had become decidedly less optimistic. The debacle in Saigon had contributed to this change. So had the Soviet-Cuban intervention in Angola. SALT had bogged down, and so had U.S. relations with Peking. And President Ford was preparing to present Congress with the first real defense budget increases since 1969.

The table on the "Trend of Forces Around Japan" and the chart on "Deployment and Basing Around Japan" were published, without alteration or comment, with the White Paper. In a conversation with a Foreign Ministry official who participated in its preparation, I asked whether he and his colleagues had thought of explaining and accounting for the alarming statistical data in the analysis section of the White Paper. The official smiled and said, "Certainly not. You know what is in those tables. What could we have said? We could have quibbled with some of the numbers, or gotten into a discussion of Soviet intentions, but that only would have made it worse. We would end up looking ridiculous if we tried to make that data harmless."

Perceptions and Trends since 1976

Since the publication of the Defense White Paper in June 1976, events and trends in the world and in the Asian-Pacific region have done little to reassure the Japanese foreign and security policy community about the balance of forces around Japan or about American resolve and reliability. American Asian-Pacific military deployments have continued to shrink. Although Soviet naval and air forces have increased only slightly in numbers, their range and sophistication have improved.[10] The 1978 White Paper on Defense, while taking the same general position on Japanese defense as the 1976 White Paper, placed more emphasis on the Soviet military buildup and its implications.[11]

Moreover, the Soviet Union has taken an increasingly tough line toward Japan in recent years. Prime Minister Miki's government (December 1974 - December 1976) was surprised at the virulence of Soviet opposition to a Sino-Japanese Peace and Friendship Treaty, at the adamant Soviet refusal to negotiate the Northern Islands issue, and at the vehemence of the Soviet reaction to Lt. Victor Belenko's defection to Japan, with a MiG-25, in September 1976. Soon after taking office, Prime Minister Fukuda found himself in an unprecedentedly harsh negotiation with the Soviets on the application of the Soviet Union's 200-mile fishery zone.[12] In the spring of 1977, the Soviets forbade Japanese boats to fish in the Soviet zone until the Japanese government had agreed to a highly restrictive fishery agreement. During March 1977, while the negotiations were deadlocked, more than 1,500 Japanese fishing craft remained idle at the docks, while Soviet fishing boats operated *within* Japan's three-mile territorial sea. A

[169]

Japanese official who participated in these negotiations, and who had years of experience dealing with the Soviets, told me that the Russian negotiators were unusually high-handed and aggressive. As he put it, "They seemed to want to make it clear to us that the Soviet Union is now the predominant super-power, and that Japan is a small, weak, defenseless country."

Following President Carter's inauguration in January 1977, the Japanese government made several attempts to discuss Soviet military strength and Soviet fishery policy with the incoming Carter Administration. They were turned politely away, on the grounds that the U.S. government had not yet concluded its own assessment of Soviet capabilities, and because it would not be useful to treat fishery questions as a political issue. More importantly, however, in the spring of 1977, the Carter Administration wanted to keep itself clearly and firmly focused on the global issues to which the President would address himself at the May 1977 Summit Meeting in London. These global issues, as defined in Washington, were economic recovery and nonproliferation. As I. M. Destler points out in Chapter 5, these issues were to generate friction and strain between Washington and Tokyo. They have been dealt with by interim, inconclusive compromises that leave both the trade imbalance and the future of nuclear energy unresolved.

In brief, while the Soviets have been getting stronger and tougher, the military foundation of the U.S.-Japanese alliance has eroded, and the alliance has been beset by quarrels. In these circumstances, the Fukuda Cabinet has leaned as far as it can to work toward a cooperative relationship with Peking, to the point of finally concluding the long delayed Peace and Friendship Treaty. However, it would be mistaken to conclude on the basis of the Sino-Japanese Treaty of Peace and

Friendship, signed in August 1978, that Japan's leaders are trying to solve their international economic, political and strategic problems by forming a partnership with China. They want to help alleviate Japan's economic doldrums by increasing exports to China and to use Chinese petroleum, if possible, to help diversify Japan's energy imports. They also want to position Japan to participate in a more active, cooperative U.S.-Chinese relationship if that should materialize. They are aware, as William Barnds points out in Chapter 6, of the limitations as well as the potentials in the area of Sino-Japanese cooperation.

In the field of security, however, the most disturbing development has been President Carter's announced policy of withdrawing American combat ground forces from the Republic of Korea. The first stage of the withdrawal was scheduled for 1978, and the last of these troops are expected to be out by 1981-82. Japanese doubts and reservations over the purposes and wisdom of this withdrawal policy have been publicized in the United States. Just before and after President Carter's election, then Foreign Minister Zentaro Kosaka, and Ambassador to Washington Fumihiko Togo, publicly criticized the proposed American troop withdrawal.[13] Yet it is important to realize that the Korean issue has been intentionally muted by the Japanese government.

By the time of Vice President Walter Mondale's visit to Tokyo at the end of January 1977, the new Prime Minister, Takeo Fukuda, although himself deeply concerned over the announced withdrawal, had put a stop to critical public statements by Japanese officials. Prime Minister Fukuda came to believe that President Carter was personally committed to the troop withdrawal. Since he did not want to initiate his relations with the President by quarreling, either publicly or privately, and since there were several more urgent and

[171]

immediate issues on the diplomatic agenda, such as the operation of the Tokai Mura nuclear reprocessing facility and the curbing of television exports, Prime Minister Fukuda decided not to press on Korea. This downplaying of the issue should not lead us to forget that anxiety and opposition to the troop withdrawal run much more deeply and strongly than the public dialogue would suggest.

Moreover, it became evident upon reflection that Japanese objections to the withdrawal of U.S. ground forces from South Korea would raise disturbing and divisive questions about Japan's basic foreign and defense policies. For if the Japanese government were to oppose, or even sharply question the withdrawal, what would happen? It was almost certain that the Americans would say that if the Japanese government were worried about the security of Korea and East Asia, then it should *do* something about it: increase Japan's defense budget, strengthen the Defense Forces, or take a more active role in the military defense of the Republic of Korea. Since Prime Minister Fukuda was not prepared to take any of these steps, it seemed pointless to make an issue of Korea. Not only would it generate an unseemly quarrel with President Carter, but it could also stir up deep and passionate divisions among Japanese voters, in the Diet, and among Prime Minister Fukuda's own supporters in the fragile Liberal Democratic Party.

Although President Carter and Prime Minister Fukuda discussed the withdrawal at their Washington meeting in March 1977, and Secretary of Defense Harold Brown and General George Brown, Chairman of the Joint Chiefs of Staff traveled to Tokyo in summer 1977, to explain the Administration's Korean policy, Japanese officials and many among the public continue to feel that the United States has made a major change in its Far Eastern policy without consulting Japan. It is widely believed in Japan that Mr. Carter made up his mind to withdraw the Second Division, completely without benefit of Japanese advice or opinion, in the spring of 1976, when he was Candidate Carter; and that in the "consultations" that have taken place since winter 1977, the Americans have simply been notifying the Japanese government of the timing and modalities of the withdrawal. In fact, in an effort to rationalize this unpleasant condition, Prime Minister Fukuda stated in January 1977, that the troop withdrawal is a bilateral issue to be negotiated between the United States and the Republic of Korea. This position releases Japan from formal responsibility for the result of American policy, but does not remove a deep sense of concern over the future of Korea.

Despite all the administration's assurances that the American defense commitment to the Republic of Korea remains unaltered—that it will be supported by American air and sea power, that an additional increment of American F-4s will be dispatched to South Korea, and that the Second Division's tanks and weapons will be transferred to ROK forces-most Japanese, in and out of government, believe that the American commitment to South Korea has been weakened and put in doubt. In March 1977, Japanese reporters acquired a copy of Presidential Review Memorandum (PRM) 13, the National Security Council study of the troop withdrawal. In its analysis of that document, the *Mainichi Shimbun* pointed out that of the memorandum's 80 pages, 20 were devoted to "the human rights problem, the effects of the withdrawal of U.S. forces upon the political oppression of the Park Government, and the likelihood of Congressional support for aid to the Republic of Korea." [14] Since then, the human rights issue has been overshadowed by Koreagate and the wrangling over Park Tong Sun's testimony. From this persistent stream of criticism and investigations, the Japanese have quite naturally concluded that the U.S. government, the Congress and the people must view the Republic of Korea as an oppressive, corrupt Asian dictatorship, not morally worthy of defense. The Japanese ask: Will Americans fight and shed their blood in defense of South Korea? They doubt that we will.

Among Japanese officials and specialists on foreign policy and defense, the Administration's Korean policy has raised other questions and doubts, which are not easily answered. Since 1953, North Korea together with the Soviet Union and China have been demanding the withdrawal of American forces from the Korean Peninsula. Is the U.S. government now going to give them a large part of what they have been clamoring for, without a single reciprocal concession? Or are there negotiations and understandings about which the Japanese government has been kept in ignorance? The implication, of course, is that our government is either softheaded or deceitful.

Finally, Prime Minister Fukuda and many other Japanese officials have not been convinced by the American strategic argument in support of the troop withdrawal. The essence of that argument is that U.S. ground forces are *not* necessary to maintain the military balance between North and South Korea; that with additional American weapons and continued U.S. air and naval support, South Korea and North Korea will remain in a stable military equilibrium. The official American analysis and argument largely discounts Soviet and/or Chinese involvement in another Korean war, and ignores the apparent reversal which has occurred in the U.S.-Soviet military balance around Korea. In 1950, when the Americans went to South Korea's defense, U.S. naval and air forces in the region had unchallengeable superiority on the seas and in the air. Soviet and Chinese help to North Korea was largely confined to support and assistance on the ground. In the early 1950s, American naval and air superiority assured that the lines of communications and logistical support to South Korea were uninterrupted and, indeed, unchallenged. Now, however, as Admiral Holloway has pointed out, the Sea of Japan has become a Soviet lake, and Soviet naval and air forces are a serious threat to American lines of communication west of Hawaii. In these circumstances, Japanese ask, is it realistic for the U.S. government to plan for the security of South Korea as though it were simply a matter of maintaining a balance between Seoul and Pyongyang?

All these questions about Korea and the U.S.-Soviet balance lead back to the question of Japan's future security. For the present, however, the government of Japan holds firmly to the Security Treaty, and encourages Japanese businessmen to keep their position as the biggest source of foreign investment for South Korea, while rescheduling North Korea's Japanese bank loans and keeping open nongovernmental channels to Pyongyang. Japanese officials are concerned that North Korea's economic difficulties, if not alleviated, may lead President Kim Il-Sung to take desperate, reckless military action. Furthermore, being uncertain about the prospects for U.S.-North Korean relations, the Tokyo government wants to keep the door open to Pyongyang in order to avoid the kind of embarrassment that followed the sudden shift in U.S.-China policy in 1971.

Ten years ago one could predict with few qualifications that Japan would hold to the basic lines of its foreign and defense policy through this decade.[15] Despite the Vietnam War, it seemed likely that the Japanese government would want to continue its policy and that the two premises upon which it rested would remain intact. These premises were: (1) American naval and air predominance in the Western Pacific, which was the basis of our security guarantee; and (2) a strong, shared sense of mutual indispensability, closely related to security considerations, which had in the 1960s tempered the economic quarrels that appear to be inevitable between major trading partners. Although the policy prediction appears to have been correct, the premises upon which it was based have been upset by the events of the past decade. The military premise has been knocked down, and the economic premise has been weakened and placed under great strain. In the changed circumstances, what are the prospects in the 1980s for the United States-Japan alliance? Will it continue, and will it be effective in maintaining regional security? Will Japan in the 1980s be more likely to rearm on a large scale—meaning a defense budget in excess of 3 percent of GNP—or to developing nuclear armaments?

Gerald Curtis has persuasively argued that domestic political factors are not likely to push Japan into basic changes in its foreign and defense policy. Consequently, the answers to these questions are going to be shaped by the Japanese perception of and response to their international environment. In their discussion of the 1976 White Paper on Defense, the Foreign Ministry and the Defense Agency put forward two alternative future environments, neither of which required a change in Japan's alliance policy or in its modest, inexpensive defense posture. Let us briefly reconsider those two optimistic futures, as well as two more pessimistic scenarios.

Japanese Options in a Changed Environment

1. *Successful Détente:* The most desirable international environment for Japan in the 1980s would approximate that described in the early Defense Agency draft of the 1976 White Paper. In their prediction of a decade of peace, the Defense Agency writers did not postulate an international

utopia, founded on love and fellowship. They anticipated that the United States, the Soviet Union and China would continue to be competitive, suspicious nuclear powers. They expected, however, that intelligent, skillful diplomacy would succeed in creating such an effective, stable equilibrium among them that the threat of military confrontation and war between the major powers would recede to a remote improbability. Assuming that this stable, relatively relaxed equilibrium would be achieved, they reasoned that North and South Korea would have no choice but to co-exist peacefully. In such an environment, the Soviet advantage in naval and air power would not pose a significant threat to Japan. The Soviets would be inhibited by their need to maintain a global détente with the United States, and by their fear that an aggressive policy in Asia would provoke a Washington-Tokyo-Peking alignment against them. The Defense Agency concluded, therefore, that the U.S.-Japan Security Treaty, backed by reduced American forces and by the existing Self-Defense Forces, would be adequate to maintain regional stability and to protect Japan in the 1980s.

Although the Foreign Ministry convinced the Defense Agency in 1975-76 that this view of the future was excessively optimistic and unrealistic, and although it is not at all clear that the prerequisite stable equilibirum has been achieved, it now appears that U.S. policy in Northeast Asia is following this scenario. The United States is in the process of withdrawing its ground forces from South Korea and is reducing its military presence in Japan, while attempting to court Peking and keep alive its global détente with Moscow.

2. *More of the Same:* The Foreign Ministry's view of the future differed from the Defense Agency's in several important respects. The Foreign Ministry officials believed that the equilibrium in Northeast Asia in the 1980s would not become

more stable or relaxed than it was in 1975, or than it had been before the Vietnam War. They believed that war in Korea, involving the superpowers, would continue to be a real possibility. They hoped, therefore, that the United States would consolidate and gradually strengthen its naval and air forces around Japan in order to counter the Soviet buildup and to support the American commitment on the ground in Korea. This view was consistent with the tenor of President Ford's Pacific Doctrine speech of December 1975, and with the increase in the 1976 U.S. defense budget, including the supplement to the naval appropriation.

In this scenario, the Japanese Defense Forces also go through the 1980s at approximately their present strength. The Security Treaty is supported by a gradual and moderate U.S. naval and air buildup, which demonstrates U.S. intent to restore the U.S.-Soviet military balance. Japan is shielded by American ground troops in South Korea. The United States and Japan continue their efforts to improve their relations with both the Soviet Union and China, but the American military presence in Korea and Japan is not reduced *unless* the Korean issue has first been defused by a negotiated settlement which is accepted in both Seoul and Pyongyang.

Although American policy is currently moving away from this scenario, it is conceivable that increased tensions in Korea, or among the United States, the Soviet Union and China, or pressure exerted by Congress, could reverse the direction of American policy and move it back to this position.

The common characteristic of the "Successful Détente" and "More of the Same" scenarios is an essential, underlying optimism about the prospects for maintaining stability and peace in Northeast Asia in the 1980s, *without re-establishing U.S. (and/or Japanese) dominance in the air and seas around Korea and Japan that existed in the 1950s and '60s.* This optimism was most obvious in the Defense Agency's approach, but it also permeated the more sober thinking of Foreign Ministry officials. The Foreign Ministry officials were caught in a dilemma. On the one hand, they believed that war in Korea, involving the superpowers, will continue to be a real possibility; and that, given the recent trend in the balance of U.S. and Soviet naval and air forces, the United States will not be prepared to wage war successfully in Korea should one break out in the 1980s. On the other hand, these same officials know that the Japanese people and government are not prepared to build up Japan's naval and air forces to compensate for the American decline, nor are they eager to change alliance policy. Consequently, what the thinking of these Foreign Ministry officials boils down to is the *hope* that the continued presence of American ground forces in Korea, combined with modest increases in U.S. naval and air capabilities, will convince the North Koreans and the Soviets that the United States remains able and determined to fight in Korea, and will thus successfully deter another test of strength in the peninsula. The optimism of this approach resides in the fact that these same officials seriously doubt that the consolidation and modest augmentation of American forces which they favor would be adequate to re-establish a safe military balance around Japan, since a safe balance is not a numerical balance between U.S. and Soviet forces, but rather American ability to protect the lines of communication to Japan and Korea. Given the existing balance and trends in American policy, however, they believed that consolidation and modest augmentation were the best they could realisticaly hope for.

Japanese optimism is largely a reflection of the optimism that has dominated U.S. policy assumptions about Northeast Asia since the end of the Vietnam War. American optimism, which expresses itself in the belief that policy statements and diplomatic maneuvers can substitute for military forces, can be understood as overcompensation for the exaggerated "worst case" planning of the 1950s and 1960s. The "worst case" approach to strategic planning and military preparations has been criticized for generating needless tensions, excessive armaments, and in some cases for bringing about the very "worst case" which it was intended to prevent. Let us assume that these criticisms are justified. The worst cases which could befall Northeast Asia and Japan include: (1) global nuclear holocaust; (2) Soviet attacks against Japan; (3) Soviet interference against shipping to Japan; (4) general, nuclear war between China and Russia; (5) a cut-off of Middle East oil; (6) another full-scale Korean war. Let us put these contingencies aside and consider several less catastrophic, but perhaps more plausible possibilities.

If, in the 1980s, the military balance in the Western Pacific and Northeast Asia continues to shift toward the Soviet Union, there is a better than even chance that the stable, secure regional equilibrium postulated in the optimistic scenarios will not materialize, and that the level of tension and military confrontation in and around Korea will be heightened rather than eased.

3. *Moderate Deterioration:* Following the withdrawal of American ground groops from South Korea in the early 1980s, North Korea will want to test the U.S. defense commitment. It might do so on its own, calculating (probably correctly) that Moscow would provide some support. Or it might seek prior Soviet approval and backing. The Soviets, who in the 1970s were opposed to actions that heightened tension in Korea, will be less cautious as a result of their growing military strength. Thus Moscow will acquiesce in North Korea's proposal on the condition that the testing process stops short of another Korean war. In this scenario, North Korea agrees not to

undertake a full-scale invasion or to attempt to take Seoul. It will limit its test to a dramatic reinforcement of its forces along the Demilitarized Zone (DMZ), followed by prolonged skirmishes along the DMZ, probes into South Korean air and sea defense systems, and a major effort at infiltration, sabotage and subversion.

For Pyongyang, the object would be to demoralize Seoul by demonstrating that the United States does not have the will or the military capability to support South Korea effectively. For the Soviets, the objectives would be: (1) to drive a wedge between Washington and Peking, assuming that Peking would have to fall into line and back Pyongyang; and (2) to demonstrate not only to South Korea but more importantly to Japan that the U.S. defense commitment is of doubtful value.

The idea that the Soviet Union would let itself be party to a limited adventure of this nature in Korea is frequently rejected on the grounds that a North Korean probe supported diplomatically and logistically by the Soviet Union would perforce reflect a major Soviet challenge to the United States, a challenge which would either be part of or provoke a global crisis. It should, however, be kept in mind that: (1) a Soviet-North Korean understanding on such a policy would be made and kept in secret; (2) the Soviet Union would probably publicly deplore the increased tension and violence in Korea, would charge South Korea with provocations and aggression, and would call for negotiations and peace, while it was covertly assisting North Korea; and (3) the Soviet Union, in this scenario, would not initiate direct military action against American forces. In brief, the Soviets might well see a test of this kind in Korea in the 1980s as being of relatively low risk, particularly since they could back quietly away from North Korea if they were to decide that the test was becoming too dangerous. There would be no necessity for a U.S.-Soviet

[181]

global crisis over Korea, unless the United States government decided to have one. When one considers the highly critical view of South Korea which has pervaded the Congress and the media for several years, and when one considers the persistent efforts of the U.S. government to avoid confrontations and to cultivate détente despite the Soviet Union's aggressive armaments policies and its interventions in Africa, one wonders whether the U.S. government would automatically treat a series of skirmishes along the 38th parallel as a major Soviet challenge. Let us assume, therefore, that the test begins. The Soviets give diplomatic backing and covert logistical support to Pyongyang. They also call for a negotiated settlement, and at the same time warn the United States of the dangers of intervening directly and escalating the conflict. They demonstrate by the deployment of their Pacific Fleet and air forces that they can interdict the lines of communication to South Korea in the Straits of Tsushima.

In this scenario, the North Korea-Soviet test is only partially successful. The United States disappoints Pyongyang. Washington promptly announces that it will stand firmly behind its defense commitment to South Korea, and makes an energetic effort to stage a logistical buildup in Korea and Japan in preparation for a serious North Korean attack. Due to inadequate naval transport shipping scarce supplies of weapons and material, and poorly maintained depots in Japan, the U.S. effort produces a weak, faltering logistical buildup. Since there is no serious, prolonged fighting in this test, however, South Korea and the United States suffer no humiliating military defeats, and there is no rupture in the Washington-Seoul relationship.

The Soviets find the results more satisfying. China gives reluctant diplomatic support to Pyongyang, and charges South Korea and the United States with aggression. Announcements from Washington about the common strategic interests of the United States and China cease. Sino-American relations become strained and unfriendly. Moreover, although the United States does not suffer a military defeat, Seoul, Tokyo and Washington discover with a shock that they got by this test only because North Korea did not escalate—partly because of Soviet restraint—and because the Soviets refrained from intervening to block the Tsushima Straits.

In this scenario, it becomes clear to the Japanese that their existing defense arrangements are inadequate. The question, then, is how Japan will respond to this moderate deterioration. Will it react within the framework of the Security Treaty, or by moving away from the treaty? Loud voices will be heard in Japan calling for accommodation with the country's Communist neighbors, and foreign and defense policies will become divisive issues once again. Opponents of a military buildup will argue that Japanese democracy will be endangered, and that such a buildup will have an adverse effect on Japan's relations with most Asian countries. (China, which is at present urging Japan to build up its military strength, could be an exception.) Yet if the United States responds by undertaking a deliberate, long-term naval and air buildup and urges Japan to do the same and to cooperate in a strategy that promises to effectively counter the Soviet threat, Japan will probably hold to the alliance. Moreover, as the Japanese realize that even a deliberate, long-term American naval and air buildup is not going to restore assured American control of the sea lanes around Japan, Japan's own defense budget will jump from approximately 1 percent of GNP to 3-5 percent of GNP. Japan's rearmament would be conventional, primarily in naval and air forces intended to cooperate with the United States in gaining control of the Tsushima and La Perouse Straits, and for protecting Japanese coastal shipping in the Sea of Japan as well as along Japan's Pacific coast. The U.S. nuclear umbrella would still suffice. The size of Japan's naval and air contribution to the alliance would necessitate joint military planning and coordinated operations. There would be no more talk of "free rides," but the U.S. government would have to learn to deal with Japan as a military partner, not as a dependent.

One can imagine several other scenarios that could be classified as moderate deteriorations of Japan's international environment. What they have in common is that they shock Japan into a large-scale rearmament, without scrapping the Security Treaty or going nuclear.

4. *Radical Deterioration:* This scenario has the same point of departure as the preceding one. The United States goes into the 1980s with a dwindling military presence in Asia, believing that its commitments to Korea and Japan are protected by a regional equilibrium that holds the Soviets and the North Koreans in check. The equilibrium proves illusory when the North Koreans and Soviets conduct their test of post-withdrawal security arrangements. Moderate deterioration shades off into radical deterioration if the United States either fails to respond to the test, or if after the test it fails to rebuild its military position in the Western Pacific. One can easily envision the latter case. During the testing in Korea, there would be widespread and vocal criticism in this country and in Japan of any American "intervention" in Korea. The Japanese government would quibble and procrastinate over the use of bases in Japan and the provision of logistical support for operations in Korea. In this case, the U.S. government would probably conclude that it could not hope to defend Korea against a full-scale attack because of Japan's unwillingness to cooperate; and in view of Japan's failure to cooperate in the defense of Korea, why should we go to the expense of building up our forces in the Western Pacific to defend Japan? In this

scenario, the Security Treaty is abrogated or becomes a scrap of paper, and Japan is left to defend itself in a hostile, unstable environment.

Although the Japanese government's initial reaction might be a policy of lightly armed neutralism, it is unlikely, given the deep-seated mutual antagonism that has historically characterized Russo-Japanese relations, the growing preponderance of Soviet military power around Japan, and the Soviet predilection for making military threats and probes, that Japan would long remain lightly armed. Unless the Soviet Union were to display unprecedented sensitivity and tact in dealing with Japan, the Japanese perception of massive Soviet military power directed threateningly at a weak, vulnerable Japan—a Japan without a strong, reliable ally—would probably generate a powerful movement toward large-scale rearmament. Moreover, since in this scenario the American nuclear umbrella has lost much of its credibility, and no longer automatically covers Japan, Japan's rearmament program would in time most likely include nuclear weapons despite the Japanese nuclear allergy and the domestic divisiveness such a move would cause.

Large-scale, nuclear rearmament would not preclude diplomatic efforts by Japan to ease its isolation. The Japanese government might well attempt to negotiate a *modus vivendi* with the Soviet Union, or to form a cooperative security relationship with China, and/or to retain even a weak, tenuous security link with the United States. The essence of this scenario is that it leaves the Japanese convinced that the United States is no longer a reliable guarantor of Japan's security, and they must rely primarily on their own efforts and military forces as the basis of their defense policy.

Conclusion

We are probably now moving toward a highly unstable international environment in Northeast Asia in the 1980s. In looking at the regional military balance, it is essential to keep in mind that U.S. and Soviet naval and air forces have distinctly different conventional missions. American forces must be able to protect the lengthy lines of communication from the West Coast to Japan and South Korea. If they cannot accomplish this mission, there is no way the United States can take action in defense of Japan and Korea, short of threatening or fighting a nuclear war. The Soviets, however, have no need to maintain secure lines of communication across the Western Pacific. Their conventional mission is simply to be able to interdict the American lines of communication—which is inherently cheaper and easier than protecting them.

The instability of the regional environment stems from the fact that the equilibrium upon which the United States is depending for the maintenance of regional security while it reduces and withdraws its military forces is ultimately contingent on American ability to project military power and support to Japan and to Korea. And it is becoming increasingly improbable that we will be able to keep open the lines of communication to any of these countries in the 1980s if the Soviets should decide to interfere with these lines. The Soviets would be unlikely to threaten or undertake such action under present circumstances. However, a continuation of the past decade's trend in the Soviet-American military balance, both in the world and in East Asia, could lead to a greater Soviet willingness to take risks in the belief that they should test the new "correlation of forces."

[186]

If we continue with our present policy, we will be gambling that a combination of our reputation as a great naval and air power, and of Soviet caution will save us from having to face this test. If that is the case, our Asian policy is in danger of becoming a bluff.

The Japanese are not looking for an opportunity either to rearm, or to move away from their alliance with the United States. In fact, their reluctance to alter their foreign and defense policy is leading Japan into an increasingly vulnerable position. For if American policy becomes a bluff, so does Japan's. And Japan stands to lose much more heavily than we do if the bluff is called.

NOTES

1. For a detailed account of the negotiation of the Prior Consulation Notes, see Martin E. Weinstein, *Japan's Postwar Defense Policy, 1947-1968* (New York: Columbia University Press, 1971).

2. See Henry Scott-Stokes, "Japan Now Debates Arms Issues that Have Been Taboo Since 1945," *The New York Times,* August 6, 1978; and "A New Sun Rising," *The Economist* (London), July 29, 1978.

3. For examples, see Bernard K. Gordon, "Japan, the United States and Southeast Asia," *Foreign Affairs,* Vol. 56, No. 3 (April 1978), pp. 579-600; Sheldon W. Simon, "Japan's Foreign Policy: Adjustment to a Changing Environment," *Asian Survey,* July 1978, pp. 666-86; and Thomas Pepper, "Japan's Asian Policy," *Pacific Community,* April 1978, pp. 411-23.

4. *Defense of Japan, 1976,* Defense Agency, Tokyo.

5. *Defense of Japan, 1970,* Defense Agency, Tokyo.

6. The Director General of the Defense Agency holds the rank of Cabinet Minister.

7. This account of the evolution of the 1976 White Paper is based upon the author's discussions with Japanese Foreign Ministry and Defense Agency officials.

8. It should be noted that the bulk of U.S. military deployments to Vietnam, including naval and air forces, were made in 1966-67.

9. "Interview with Admiral James L. Holloway III, Chief of Naval Operations," *U.S. News and World Report,* October 20, 1975, pp. 61-64.

10. See *Tokyo Asahi Shimbun,* January 9, 1978, p. 1, on operations east of Japan by Soviet TU-16 Badgers armed with AS-6 or AS-7 air-to-surface missiles. This article, probably based on a Defense Agency release, states that these weapons can be used for nuclear attacks on Japan, or for attacks on Japanese naval forces and commercial shipping.

11. *Defense of Japan: 1978,* Defense Agency, Tokyo.

12. Frank Langdon, "Japan-Soviet 200 Mile Zone Confrontation," *Pacific Community,* October 1977, pp. 46-58.

13. For American criticisms see Donald Zagoria, "Why We Can't Leave Korea," *The New York Times Magazine,* October 2, 1977, pp. 17ff.; and Frank Gibney, "The Ripple Effect in Korea," *Foreign Affairs,* Vol. 56, No. 1 (October 1977), pp. 160-74.

14. *Mainichi Shimbun,* Evening Edition, March 7, 1977.

15. See Martin Weinstein, "Strategic Thought and the U.S.-Japan Alliance," in James W. Morely, ed., *Forecast for Japan: Security in the 1970s* (Princeton, New Jersey, Princeton University Press, 1972).

FIVE

U.S.-Japanese Relations and the American Trade Initiative of 1977: Was This "Trip" Necessary?[1]

I. M. Destler

If viewed in the perspective of previous history, the U.S.-Japanese "special relationship" was one of the postwar period's great surprises. Relations between the two countries had alternated between amity and enmity ever since Commodore Perry's "black ship" entered Tokyo Bay in 1853. But there had certainly been no precedent for the close economic and political alliance of the past thirty years.

This alliance continues today, and the best guess is that it will continue for some time into the future. Yet at some time in the early 1970s it entered a new era. In the 1950s and 1960s its formal bases—the 1951 and 1960 security treaties—were a source of constant contention in Japanese politics, their semi-legitimacy imposing both a limit to the scope of cooperation and a threat to its very existence. Now, security relations fully merit the characterization applied by Henry Kissinger (and Gerald Ford) in 1975—they have "never been better." But the same cannot be said of economic relations; they have tended, on the contrary, to grow more difficult, sometimes even bitter, with Japan's rise as a world economic power. And if economic tensions rise too much, they are likely to spill over to affect overall relations between the two governments, and the attitudes of the two societies toward each other.

This chapter pays particular attention to recent difficulties, and to the U.S. effort to address them in late 1977. But it seeks also to put that experience in context: by considering the nature of the postwar alliance and how it has evolved; by assessing relations on other current. issues; by evaluating the uses and limits of "external pressure," or the "black ship" scenario, in conflict resolution with Japan.

The Alliance Until 1967

When the United States and Japan entered into the security treaty of September 8, 1951, the relationship was one of extreme inequality: militarily, economically, and psychologic-ally. Japan was a defeated and devastated nation only begin-ning to recover; the United States was at the height of its powers. For virtually all Japanese the fundamental lesson of World War II was that their country must renounce military action outside its borders. The great majority felt, in addition, that Japan's defense forces needed to be quite limited, at least in the years immediately ahead. The basic political and intellectual cleavage in Japan was between socialist-oriented "reformists" who believed renunciation of armaments should be accompanied by "neutralism" in international relations, and the conservative political and bureaucratic leadership which was taking a very different course. For these conservatives, a close alignment with the United States appeared as an absolute necessity. Not only had the Americans the power to grant or delay Japan's return to formal sovereignty, and to provide a security shield, but they also had the means to facilitate a viable new world role by supporting and encouraging Japan's postwar economic construction and resurgence.

Americans, by contrast, were fighting in Korea and reaching out militarily to a worldwide network of alliance commitments. For them, the security treaty was not just useful; it was the predominant purpose of the relationship. With the onset of the cold war, Americans saw international politics overwhelmingly through bipolar lenses. Japan's strategic location, large population, and potential economic and political strength made it an important ally, particularly since China was "lost." Moreover, bases in Japan proved indispensable in the Korean War, and U.S. troop deployments on the main islands and in Okinawa were central to the overall American military posture in the Far East. For Japanese, by contrast, the security relationship carried considerable costs in domestic divisiveness. This peaked in 1960, when opposition to its renegotiation and the way Prime Minister Nobusuke Kishi managed the Japanese ratification process forced Kishi's resignation and the cancellation of President Eisenhower's planned Tokyo visit. And the volatility of defense issues—combined with the semi-legitimacy of Japan's own defense forces—made inconceivable any serious operational defense cooperation like that within NATO. The alliance was also troubled by the China issue. For many Japanese believed that America's nonrecognition policy was blocking Tokyo from developing a relationship with Peking that would prove politically, economically, and culturally fruitful.

But notwithstanding these sources of tension, American dominance and Japanese deference on security issues did complement one another. Even more complementary were the economic policy conceptions which predominated in the two capitals. Unlike the Americans, Japanese leaders gave priority to matters economic after the war—first survival, then rapid growth. Only the Americans had the economic strength and the political inclination to support and nurture this resurgence, to accept a growing flow of Japanese exports, to provide a reliable source of advanced technology, and to push for Japan's entry into GATT and later into groupings of advanced industrial countries like the OECD. And because U.S. leaders saw some degree of Japanese economic success as indispensable if Japan's democracy and pro-Western policy orientation were to be maintained, providing such support was consistent with U.S. political purposes. Thus, Americans and Japanese pressed for nondiscriminatory treatment of Japanese *exports,* but Americans as well as Japanese saw justification for restrictions on Japanese *imports.* Similarly, Americans tolerated Japanese restrictions on foreign investment while giving Japan preferential access to U.S. capital markets (through exemption from the interest equalization tax) as late as 1965.

In the United States, general support of free trade did not of course preclude special restrictive arrangements for those product areas where Japanese exports aroused political reactions strong enough to threaten both the larger U.S. free trade policy and amicable U.S.-Japanese relations. Thus John Foster Dulles could, in 1955, oppose legislated quotas on cotton textiles as a threat to the U.S.-Japanese alliance, and at the same time urge the Japanese to make their own accommodation to U.S. industry pressure through "voluntary" export limitations. And the Japanese government and industry acceded. But such specific product concessions did not unduly disrupt the overall economic and political relationship, partly because many other countries were discriminating far more flagrantly against Japanese products. Rather, "voluntary" limitations served to buy protection for the relationship by limiting its threat to vocal U.S. interests.

This asymmetrical dependence relationship was consistent with Americans' idea of their country as leader and example to the world—the United States was seen as the forgiving, postwar benefactor of a Japan democratized through American occupation. And the dependence relationship was consistent also with Japanese *amae* psychology, definable roughly as a feeling that a stronger party in a relationship has a particular obligation to protect the weaker. Thus, the inequality of power justified for Japanese the unequal application of trade rules. Since Japan was the weaker party, it was fair to seek open access to American and other foreign markets on "free trade" grounds, and at the same time to restrict access of others to the Japanese market on "protectionist" grounds. And in fact, Japan was running a substantial deficit in its trade with the United States until 1965, and also in its trade worldwide.

In the 1950s and early 1960s, to sum up, economic relations were basically harmonious. American interest in Japanese recovery fostered overall trade policies favorable to Tokyo; specific product issues were handled by "voluntary" side deals for export restraint. Security relations were more precarious, threatened in Japanese politics by limited acceptance of the security treaty and by the widespread belief that the United States was pursuing an unrealistic China policy and forcing Tokyo to do likewise. The Vietnam war strengthened the view that the alliance was both dangerous and morally objectionable for Japanese. There was also a mounting campaign against continued United States administrative control of Okinawa.

By the early 1970s, however, this pattern was essentially reversed. The old sources of security tensions had been defused, though Japanese conservatives now worried about the reliability of the U.S. security commitment. But the economic relationship had, unexpectedly, generated the most serious sustained bilateral crisis since the occupation.

Post-1967 Relations: The Primacy of Economics

The causes of this shift were long-term: the rapid growth of the Japanese economy; the relaxation of bipolarity in world politics and of the cold war orientation in American policy thinking. But if one searches for transition years, 1967 is one good candidate. It was then that Prime Minister Eisaku Sato won from President Lyndon Johnson formal recognition of the Japanese desire for agreement "within a few years" on return of administrative rights over Okinawa.[2] That same year, presidential aspirant Richard Nixon published an article in *Foreign Affairs* that cautiously espoused a "long-run" policy of "pulling China back into the world community."[3] It was also in 1967 that the Kennedy Round trade talks concluded, bringing about the largest tariff reductions in history but also, by their very conclusion, unleashing pressures for trade restrictions which the talks had held at bay.

In November 1969 President Nixon agreed to reversion of Okinawa.[4] In July 1971 he "shocked" Tokyo with his opening to Peking, but also liberated Japanese to shape their own China course, with the new government of Kakuei Tanaka leaping to negotiate full diplomatic relations with

Peking in September 1972. These steps combined to remove the Okinawa and China issues as burdens on the security relationship, and the opposition parties' challenges to the *desirability* of the relationship became weaker, relatively pro forma. Over the same period, Japanese conservatives began to worry about the *reliability* of the American connection, in the wake of the "Nixon Doctrine" of 1969-70, the ground troop withdrawal from Vietnam in 1973, and the victory by Hanoi in 1975.

In this new political climate, opposition parties felt constrained to modify or de-emphasize their formal anti-treaty positions in order to demonstrate they could be "responsible" repositories of government power, as Gerald Curtis has pointed out in Chapter 2. Experiments in joint defense planning and coordination were also inaugurated in the mid-1970s without generating great controversy in Tokyo. And episodes that might earlier have caused deep bilateral crisis did not have this effect. In September 1974, for example, retired U.S. Admiral Gene LaRocque told a Congressional committee that American ships "do not offload [nuclear weapons] when they go into foreign ports such as Japan," [5] a statement which precipitated a predictable uproar in the Tokyo press in view of Japan's continuing "nuclear allergy" and the government's policy of minimal disclosure on such issues. But despite the fears of some with memories of 1960, the "LaRocque Statement" never seriously threatened President Ford's visit a month later. Nor did the much more important and protracted "Lockheed Incident" do much damage to Japanese-American security cooperation, even though it dramatized links between U.S. aircraft manufacturers and corrupt "money politics" in Tokyo.

On economic issues, however, the road after 1967 grew rockier. President Nixon moved quickly in 1969 to deliver on his promise to the American textile industry to negotiate restraints on the export of Far Eastern wool and man-made fiber products to the United States. Using the leverage of the still unresolved Okinawa issue, he won sweeping secret concessions from Sato—which Sato proved politically unable to implement in a domestic atmosphere of rising economic nationalism and resistance to "unreasonable" American demands. Further U.S. pressure, combined with serious tactical blunders, only stiffened Japanese resistance, and helped generate a protectionist backlash on Capitol Hill. A highly restrictive trade bill passed the House in 1970—and almost passed the Senate. The dispute poisoned bilateral relations on other issues also; it was one important cause, by several reports, of Nixon's callous treatment of Japan, and of Sato, when he announced his plans to visit Peking.[6]

The textile dispute remained unresolved in August 1971 when the President delivered his second "Nixon shock": the 10 percent import surcharge and the floating of the dollar. Tokyo was the major international target of this "new economic policy," and it generated alarm among Japanese political, business and financial leaders. They responded with policy changes and concessions to repair the frayed American connection. A textile settlement was reached in October, on American terms. In December, the multilateral Smithsonian accord was concluded, which contained an upward revaluation of the yen of 17 percent in relation to the dollar.

The Nixon shocks also alarmed many Americans. Such tactics might be effective in winning immediate policy concessions, whether they be important and long-overdue (e.g., yen revaluation, import liberalization) or simply accommodations of unreasonable U.S. demands (e.g., textiles). But more importantly, such tactics threatened the trust and confidence on which the Japanese alliance ultimately depended. So while 1972 and 1973 brought continued tension on economic issues, punctuated by a "record" bilateral trade imbalance in 1972 and the "soybean shock" of 1973, these years also saw conscious efforts initiated on both sides to repair the damage. Henry Kissinger began consulting and cultivating Japanese leaders, even delivering a modest *mea culpa* before the Japan Society in 1975.[7] There were serious differences over energy, dramatized when Kissinger visited Tokyo in the fall of 1973 just as Japan was tilting sharply toward the Arabs to protect its oil supplies. But each government determined to live with and mute this policy tension. And higher oil prices also brought Japan's current account into deficit for a while, making "fragile blossom" seem a more apt metaphor than "emerging superstate."[8] Japan was not perceived as a major current force for global economic disequilibrium. Trade issues were multilateralized and defused, as the Tokyo Round talks opened in 1973. Floating exchange rates appeared to be reducing the trade imbalance. And the U.S. Congress gave the Administration broad, if constrained, bargaining authority in the Trade Act of 1974.

By 1975, the sum total of these events suggested a conclusion that the alliance had survived a shaky transition and was now on firm ground once again. Perhaps, some felt, it has even built a firmer basis for partnership and cooperation: on security issues, in a better accepted if still unequal relationship; on economic issues, stressing reciprocity of rights and obligations in a liberal, multilaterally managed world order.[9] But an underrated contributor to the peace of mid-decade was the relative absence of difficult issues where domestic politics and priorities generated important bilateral tensions. The Fukuda government and the Carter Administration would not be so lucky. Indeed, they had to address three such issues in 1977, their first full year in office. These were Korea, nuclear energy, and the trade imbalance.

The Carter-Fukuda Period

One issue that was not causing them major problems was defense cooperation. The Mutual Security Treaty had virtually vanished as a source of serious political contention in Tokyo. And actual defense cooperation was growing. The purpose of Japan's self-defense forces remained defense of the home islands; the pace of collaboration was limited to what Japanese domestic politics could absorb. Many Americans continued to feel that Japan was getting something of a "free ride" militarily, and ought perhaps to move more rapidly to strengthen its forces and increase its contribution to American base costs. But major controversy was avoided, and while the two nations' defense forces were far from having achieved an operational basis for effective joint action should the need arise, no major threat requiring such action appeared imminent.

Nor did the other serious potential issue of 1950-67, China policy, generate major difficulty for U.S.-Japanese relations. The Carter Administration moved very cautiously in 1977 toward normalizing diplomatic relations with Peking.

The official Japanese preference that year remained the status quo—a continued U.S. liaison relationship with Peking and the security treaty with Taipei. But Tokyo's ability to protest was limited by the fact that it had normalized in 1972. Moreover, as Washington accelerated its normalization efforts in 1978, Tokyo moved also, concluding the Sino-Japanese friendship treaty in August. Finally, Carter's recognition of Peking (effective January 1, 1979) was accompanied by continuing "unofficial" relations with "the people on Taiwan," and a pledge of sales of defensive arms as needed. Thus Japanese concerns about Taiwan's future viability were assuaged.

[199]

Korea was more difficult. It remained, as Gerald Curtis notes in Chapter 2, the one issue where Japanese opposition parties still took strongly ideological stances, and yet also the area whose security, to conservatives, was most vital to the security of Japan. Japan's divided Korean community, and allegations of financial links between South Korea and pro-Seoul elements of the LDP, compounded the difficulty. And while candidate Carter had promised, in May 1976, to consult in advance with Japan on major policy actions affecting Japan, he also reaffirmed between election and inaguration, without such consultation, his campaign promise to withdraw U.S. ground combat forces from Korea. Inevitably, as Ambassador Mike Mansfield recently acknowledged, "the *perceived* abruptness of our action for a time undermined Japanese confidence in the constancy of American policy." [10] The Japanese Ambassador to Washington, Fumihiko Togo, was among those expressing strong concern, and some Japanese feared this was one more step in a longer-term American withdrawal from Asia. But the Japanese government was constrained by domestic politics in its response; indeed, there were even risks to that government in serious consultations, because these would give the Japanese government some "responsibility" for eventual U.S. policies, and thus subject it to attack at home.

However, Carter found his decision meeting strong resistance also from the U.S. security community, including officials in the State and Defense Departments. He responded by reiterating very strongly the American commitment to defend Korea from attack, and by agreeing both to postpone the withdrawal and to compensate for its impact. It would be phased over five years, with the "teeth" of the Second Division removed last. The Koreans would be compensated for the equipment and matériel that the withdrawal would remove from the front. Such steps have done much to alleviate

Japanese anxiety, particularly since they were paralleled by extensive informal discussions in Tokyo. However, congressional approval of the proposed arms transfers became intertwined with the "Koreagate" bribery scandal. In response to this delay, President Carter reduced even further the number of troops scheduled for withdrawal in 1978.

Generating much more direct and explicit bilateral difficulty was an issue bridging security and economic concerns—Japan's plans to begin experimental reprocessing of spent nuclear fuel to extract plutonium at Tokai Mura. Japan, with very limited indigenous energy sources, wanted to explore technologies pointing toward a possible future "plutonium economy," where breeder reactors would produce more fuel than they consumed. The attraction was an apparently inexhaustible source of nuclear energy, reducing or eliminating dependence on outside uranium sources. The danger was that plutonium usable for breeders was also usable for weapons, without the delays required to convert the low enriched uranium used in conventional reactors to weapons material. Thus existing international safeguards to assure timely detection of any diversion of nuclear fuel for weapons would be ineffective. And Carter had made nuclear proliferation a top priority issue. So while previous U.S. administrations had encouraged Japanese nuclear development, including reprocessing, the Carter Administration came to office determined to take a tougher, more cautious line.

The Tokai Mura plant was scheduled to open in mid-1977. But the United States, as the provider of Japan's enriched uranium, had the right under the operative bilateral agreement to pass on the uses of spent fuel. Carter Administration policy was now temporary deferral of commercial reprocessing at home. Americans would have preferred, therefore, that Japan defer reprocessing also. Some felt that it was incumbent on the

United States to use all its leverage to prevent or defer development of plutonium technology wherever possible; Tokai Mura provided one such opportunity. Arguing against such a U.S. stance, however, was the importance of energy development to Japan both economically and politically, and the fact that European states—including Germany—were already proceeding with similar reprocessing experiments which the U.S. lacked the power to halt.

Negotiations on the issue were intense and often difficult. During Fukuda's March visit, Carter recommended to him a Ford Foundation study stressing the economic costs as well as the proliferation risks of breeder technology. On April 7, 1977, the President announced a new anti-proliferation policy. Ultimately, however, the United States government moved to a compromise position. A strong assist came from Ambassador Mansfield, who argued that Japan should not have restrictions imposed on its nuclear development which would appear discriminatory vis-à-vis Western Europe. In the agreement signed September 1, 1977, the United States assented to the opening of the Tokai Mura plant for a test period of two years, employing the reprocessing technology planned by Japan but providing for intensive research during these years on safeguards, and on an alternative technology ("co-processing") which does not directly produce weapons-grade material.[11] Only time would tell whether the issue had been resolved or postponed; most experts appeared to feel it was the United States which had yielded the most, and that it would be difficult for the Americans to insist on a shift to an alternative, "safer" technology when the two-year period expired. Among the factors that will affect the outcome are current multilateral consultations (including the new International Fuel Cycle Evaluation Program), and the implementation of the rather restrictive nuclear export legislation passed by Congress in early 1978.

Other issues caused bilateral difficulty during this period, including fisheries and aviation. But the most troublesome problem in 1977 and 1978 was trade. Before 1977 ended, Japan and the United States were deep into their sharpest economic dispute since the "Nixon shock" era. The immediate formal outcome was a January 13, 1978, statement containing a number of general and specific new Japanese policy commitments; it was hailed by the President's Special Representative for Trade Negotiations, Robert Strauss, as "a major move on a new enlightened course" that "redefined" U.S.-Japanese economic relations. But that hyperbole was tempered by caution: if the U.S. didn't press for full implementation, Strauss told the Senate Finance Committee, "we will end up with a few minor trading concessions."[12] In both the substantive and political complexity of the negotiations and the ambiguity of the result, the episode may be typical of the difficulties faced by the contemporary relationship. A more detailed account and assessment therefore is in order.

The Trade Crisis of 1977

The core of the dispute was the trade imbalance. Japan was running a huge worldwide current account surplus, the United States a record trade deficit. Bilaterally, the trade balance had been generally in Japan's favor since 1965, but the "record" gap of $4 billion in 1972 had closed to below $2 billion in succeeding years as American sales to Japan skyrocketed, particularly in farm products, and as currency revaluation had its effects. But Japanese exports rose sharply in 1976 while imports stagnated; the bilateral gap rose to $5.4 billion, a record which lasted only until 1977 brought the figure to $8.1 billion. In the same year, the worldwide United States trade deficit was leaping to $26.7 billion, more than four times the previous record of $6.4 billion set in 1972.[13]

When senior economic officials of the Carter Administration came to office in January 1977, they brought with them worries about the Japanese imbalance. With the OPEC nations running a large surplus, they felt it very important that the stronger among the advanced industrial economies share the burden of the rest of the world's deficit. Moreover, if recovery from world recession were to succeed, they thought it necessary that the three strongest, "locomotive" economies—the United States, Japan, and Germany—stimulate domestic demand so as to draw in imports from elsewhere, thus pulling other, weaker economies to recovery also. The Japanese (and German) trade surplus and slow domestic growth worked against this goal. Vice President Mondale carried this message in his post-inaugural trip, including discussions with Prime Minister Fukuda and with German Chancellor Helmut Schmidt. This theme was pressed also at the London economic summit in May.

At London, Fukuda reiterated his government's determination to achieve its goal of 6.7 percent growth in the 1977 fiscal year. He also responded to American and European concerns about Japan's current account surplus by citing a Japanese projection that it was in the process of disappearing, to be replaced by a $700 million deficit. The growth target was a serious political commitment, important in Japanese politics; the current account projection was not. But when, contrary to that projection, Japan's current account surplus in fact grew larger, frustration grew also in the United States and Europe. Reports circulated that Fukuda was reneging on a promise.[14] More widespread was the belief that the Japanese were not, at minimum, taking their obligations to world economic recovery very seriously. In Tokyo, meanwhile, discontent grew also,

[204]

centering on the cause of the burgeoning surplus—the fact that domestic demand and investment were not picking up sufficiently to maintain the recovery that the export boom had inaugurated.

The need for Japan to act to rectify its global imbalance was stressed by Under Secretary of State Richard Cooper and Assistant Secretary of the Treasury C. Fred Bergsten when they visited Tokyo in September 1977. But concern was also rising in Washington about specific product issues—products being *exported* to the United States in record amounts; products *not* being *imported* very substantially by Japan. Color television was an early case of the former, resolved when Special Trade Representative Robert Strauss negotiated an orderly marketing agreement with Tokyo in April, which reduced sales sharply from their abnormally high 1976 levels. And when the U.S. trade imbalance continued to worsen, increased attention was paid to Japan's barriers against imports—particularly by officials in the Department of Commerce. Secretary Juanita Kreps also visited Tokyo in September and labelled the trade deficit "simply unacceptable"; her preferred remedy was increased Japanese imports. One promising result was establishment of a binational Trade Facilitation Committee to investigate complaints of specific impediments encountered by firms seeking to export to Japan. But the overall Japanese response to these U.S. initiatives was limited. Once again, the view that Japan saw trade too much as a one-way street, pushing exports while impeding imports, became widely popular in Washington. And its adherents included officials essentially sympathetic to Japan and specializing in dealings with that country. Many of them felt that the Tokyo government was simply not dealing seriously and sincerely with the international economic problems to which it was contributing.

[205]

In this generally discouraging context, an interdepartmental group of U.S. officials began to meet informally around September to address U.S.-Japanese trade relations.[15] The initiative apparently came from the State Department; the level of the gatherings was the deputy assistant secretary and country director; the premise was that the United States lacked a clear, concrete sense of what it wanted economically from Japan, and that the Japanese government would not respond to general admonitions like those Cooper and Bergsten had conveyed. So the officials began an effort to set forth the types of actions they felt were desirable, beginning with a "laundry list," then refining and focusing their priorities. As work proceeded, the interagency structure became somewhat more formal—there was an assistant-secretary level group chaired by Deputy Special Trade Representative Alan Wolff, supported by a group chaired by Deputy Assistant Secretary Erland Heginbotham of State's Bureau of East Asian Affairs.

Around the same time Henry Owen, White House coordinator of international economic policy, was among those American officials worrying about what they saw as a deteriorating political climate toward Japan in the United States: in the country, in the Congress, and within the executive branch. Quietly settling issues one by one might not suffice to arrest this deterioration; what was needed instead was a broad, visible agreement on a range of economic issues. This idea was broached in October with a senior Ministry of Foreign Affairs *(Gaimusho)* official.

While all this was happening in Washington, the rise of the yen—encouraged by American policy—was having its effects in Tokyo. Because it weakened export price competitiveness of certain important products, it ended any glimmering hope that the 6.7 percent growth target for FY 1977 (April 1977-March

1978) would be even approximately achieved. It therefore increased the interest of the business community, and Ministry of International Trade and Industry (MITI) officials, in economic and trade policy steps that might arrest further upward revaluation and stimulate growth. So United States officials got what they read as signals, from the *Gaimusho* and especially from MITI, that prospects for Japanese policy change had increased and that stronger American pressure might be helpful in facilitating it. And they were also getting signals in Washington that pressures for trade restrictions were rising. There was what one official involved characterizes as the steel "firestorm" of October; plant closings, which manufacturers blamed on imports, spurred intensified industry and congressional efforts to limit such imports. There was also a continuation of industry petitions for relief on a range of other products, while the Multilateral Trade Negotiations (MTN) at Geneva, intended to provide a political counter-weight to such pressures, were only beginning to awaken after years of earnest slumber. The job of balancing all of these pressures belonged to Special Trade Representative (STR) Robert Strauss, who was also becoming the Administration's most powerful international economic official.

To this point, Strauss had been only intermittently involved in Japanese trade issues. But he had a once-postponed trip to Japan pending, and the Japanese—appreciating his strong Washington position—saw him as the logical person with whom to deal. So they suggested he come to Tokyo to conclude an agreement. But Americans saw this as premature until they had gotten more on specifics. So when the Administration's Cabinet-level Economic Policy Group (EPG) met on November 9 under Treasury Secretary Michael Blumenthal's chairmanship to review Japanese trade issues, it heard a proposal that a mission headed by Deputy

STR Wolff go to Tokyo to present a strong series of suggestions, akin to demands, about what steps the Japanese government should undertake. At least two EPG members protested that this would be too high-level, too formal, too visible. So it was decided to send the next-ranking STR official, General Counsel Richard Rivers, whose lesser status and low-key personal style would reduce the chances of a sharp Japanese reaction.

Rivers arrived in Tokyo the following week, accompanied by Heginbotham and Japan Country Director Nicholas Platt of State. The policy message they carried was strong—almost certainly stronger than those Japanese who were signalling for such pressure must have expected. The Japanese government should set a growth target of 8 percent for the coming fiscal year; it should make a specific commitment to move toward ending Japan's worldwide trade surplus, tied to an explicit timetable; it should liberalize remaining import quotas, most of which were on agricultural products; it should take a range of steps to facilitate imports of manufactured products; it should commit itself to advance tariff reduction on a broad list of items, and play an active, forceful role for trade liberalization in the MTN talks. Contrary to several press reports, U.S. officials insist that Japanese export restraint was not on their list, though they did give strong play to the fact that other Americans were advocating just such a solution. But the tacit political message conveyed by the substance of the "suggestions," however diplomatically they might be delivered, was that U.S.-Japanese trade relations were under very severe strain. A Japanese failure to take strong action would place the economic relationship in serious jeopardy, with likely spillover to relations on other issues.

U.S. officials were thus trying to turn the unfavorable trends of American trade politics to their advantage. The "protectionist threat" would provide leverage with the Japanese; an agreement won through such pressure would then be turned against the "threat" at home. But they seem to have assumed the message would be delivered quietly; hence they sent Rivers rather than Wolff. But so strong a set of suggestions was almost bound to leak and create sensational headlines in Tokyo, given the range of Japanese officials and ministries involved. Moreover, it is unclear how the pressure would have served U.S. purposes if it had remained quiet. Japanese politicians and bureaucrats could hardly use it as a pretext for painful policy changes unless the fact of U.S. pressure were widely known—a visible, threatening "black ship."[16]

In any case, the mission proved anything but quiet. The substance of the message, cabled ahead so the ministries could prepare an informed response, leaked quickly to the Tokyo dailies. And then, by coincidence, a delegation of *Komeito* Diet members was having meetings in Washington with Strauss, Vice President Mondale, and Defense Secretary Harold Brown. After each meeting, the Japanese delegation head called a press conference to convey what Americans insist were exaggerated, inaccurate accounts of what was said: Strauss was reported as declaring U.S.-Japanese economic relations at the "bursting point," Mondale as accusing Fukuda of welching on a promise made at London to eliminate the trade deficit, and Brown as saying America intended to withdraw troops not just from Korea but from East Asia generally. These stories broke in Tokyo just as Rivers was beginning his rounds, and his mission became, contrary to intentions, a sensational media event. When he met Fukuda, the Prime Minister dubbed him "the most famous person in Japan." His behavior at particular meetings was portrayed in the press as fierce and demanding, and the atmosphere of the meetings as one of confrontation, though American officials involved insist that Rivers was careful and low-key and the tone of the meetings was constructive. The fact that the growth rate issue was central to the American program made U.S. pressure appear even more outrageous. For even in this age of interdependence, such policies are normally viewed as domestic matters.

Japanese bureaucrats leaked a stream of reports of the meetings in order to influence their internal policy debate. Those in the Ministry of Finance who opposed greater deficit spending portrayed Rivers as absolutely outrageous, hoping perhaps to generate a nationalist backlash. But MITI and *Gaimusho* officials sympathetic to some of the proposals also painted Rivers as a "bad guy": they wanted to intensify the sense of U.S. pressure, and thus its power in generating policy change. And the Japanese dailies, themselves interested in shaking up the government on economic policy, further amplified the reports.

The Japanese coverage generated coverage by the American media, causing serious concern in Washington. U.S. officials, understandably shaken by the press storm, debated whether pressure was backfiring; State Department officials, including Ambassador Mansfield, were interestingly among whose who argued that it was not, that pressure needed to be maintained if results were to be forthcoming.

In Tokyo, meanwhile, there were several sorts of reactions. There was resentment of the arbitrary, demanding behavior of the Rivers mission as reported; there was a belief that Japan was being given discriminatory treatment, as evidenced by the absence of similar U.S. pressure on Germany. Some sophisticated "America watchers" saw the Carter Administration as both weak and unclear as to its priorities. As *Asahi* columnist Yasushi Hara saw things, first Cooper and Bergsten had delivered a strong general message of concern, but foresworn an effort to prescribe on details. Two weeks later, Treasury Secretary Blumenthal began "talking down the dollar," exerting unanticipated pressure on the yen. Now with the Rivers mission, the United States was taking yet a third tack. One possible explanation was Carter's overall political weakness—his Administration, embattled on many policy fronts, was scratching for some sort of economic policy "success" vis-à-vis Japan in order to buttress itself internally.[17]

The first major official Japanese action after the mission returned to Washington was the reorganization of the Fukuda Cabinet. Like most such reshuffles, this one had been long in preparation, and it responded to a range of political and policy concerns in addition to the trade crisis of November. But to American eyes it offered hope. Fukuda gave important positions to persons favoring a more expansionist and liberal course: Kiichi Miyazawa at the Economic Planning Agency; Toshio Komoto at MITI. And he appointed a new Minister for External Economic Affairs, former Ambassador to the United States Nobuhiko Ushiba, who was inevitably labelled a Strauss counterpart. This was true only in form: Ushiba lacked Strauss' domestic political base, and he lacked the established coordinating role and supporting staff that STR had built up over fifteen years. But the new Minister was known and respected by Americans, and he had a mandate to help bring together, for presentation in Washington, a "package" of policy concessions.

The new Cabinet set to work on the content of this package; to some, it was a race to see how many policy changes they could secure before being "captured" by those bureaucrats—particularly in Finance and Agriculture—most resistant to change. For U.S. pressure had quickly precipitated counterpressure from potentially affected groups, above all the heavily protected agricultural community on which the ruling Liberal Democratic party relied disproportionately for support. The new Minister of Agriculture was exposed very quickly to this pressure and it took its toll. On trade, the package proved modest: an "eight point program" whose most concrete steps were unilateral tariff cuts on 124 items and expansion in import quotas for oranges, citrus juice, and beef for hotel consumption. Ushiba himself confessed his disappointment with the package before leaving for Washington, and U.S. officials ran a quick computer analysis of its likely impact on the trade imbalance and found it slight. Strauss called a press conference on December 12, the first day of Ushiba's four-day Washington mission, and "very candidly" labelled the package "insufficient," falling "considerably short of what this country ... feels is necessary."[18] But this problem was in part of Washington's making. Despite the public emphasis given to relaxing Japanese import barriers both visible and invisible, this was not the route to rapid change in the trade balance; such institutional adjustments would take time to be felt. Thus to measure such concessions in terms of short-run trade effects was almost to guarantee that they would prove "insufficient."

Later in the visit, Ushiba unveiled the remainder of his package: an increase of Japan's growth rate target for the fiscal year beginning April 1978 to 7 percent, and a lifting of the previous 30 percent limit on deficit financing in order to attain it. These issues were being decided at Cabinet level in Tokyo even as Ushiba made the rounds in Washington, and MITI officials were pressing American "allies" to stand firm on the growth rate issue, to counter "softer" signals being exploited by the Finance adversaries that the United States might find 6 percent acceptable. Thus had the politics of the two governments become intertwined.

The new Japanese growth policy helped Strauss maneuver

his way out of what threatened to become a serious political bind. The specific concessions on imports had proved modest. And Strauss needed such concrete gains because these were most useful to him politically within the United States. But it was here that Japanese interests were resisting most effectively. A continuation of headline-generating U.S. pressure could strengthen the backlash, not only tying the hands of the rather weak Fukuda government on trade, but threatening to precipitate a broader crisis of confidence in U.S.-Japanese relations. The growth package gave Strauss something that could immediately be dubbed "promising." He wanted and needed to reach some form of agreement in January for his own political purposes: something he could use to demonstrate concrete accomplishment, to hold protectionist pressures at bay. And he was pressed also in this direction by those within the U.S. government who felt enough was enough, that U.S. pressure was rapidly becoming counterproductive in Tokyo as well. So between the conclusion of Ushiba's Washington talks on December 15 and Strauss' Tokyo arrival on January 11, U.S. rhetoric began to shade in a more positive direction. "A closer look at the Japanese proposals," the *Washington Post* reported on December 22, convinced U.S. officials that Japan was "ready to make a greater effort to slash its surplus than they first believed." Aided by modest further Japanese concessions, they began to generate expectations that an interim agreement would be reached, with enough in it beyond the Ushiba "package" to give the agreement credibility, and Strauss credibility in signing it. This effort was successful. The crisis element was relaxed but the pressure was maintained, aided by the not entirely coincidental appearance of no less than four U.S. Senators in Tokyo in early January to press strongly and publicly for opening up Japanese markets. After two days of tough personal bargaining in Tokyo,

[213]

including suggestions to Ushiba that it might be better not to issue a communiqué at all, Strauss won enough in addition to give some substance to the claim he had raised the outcome from the "C-plus or B-minus effort" he had expected to "an A result, a major move on a new enlightened course."[19] The 7 percent growth target was included in the January 13 Joint Statement, and Japan "stated its intention to take all reasonable and appropriate measures" to achieve it. The relatively modest tariff reductions on 124 items were apparently identical to those in Ushiba's December package, covering $2.6 billion in 1976 Japanese imports. But further specific concessions were gained on import quotas; the most measurable was a 10,000-ton increase in hotel beef imports, compared to the 2,000 tons Ushiba had offered in December. And by pressing very hard, Strauss won both a recognition that, "in the present international economic situation, the accumulation of a large current account surplus was not appropriate," and a commitment to steps aimed at "marked diminution" immediately, and further reduction "aiming at equilibrium" in FY 1979 and beyond.

There was also a joint commitment, considered very important by U.S. trade officials, "to achieve basic equity in their trading relations by affording to major trading countries substantially equivalent competitive opportunities on a reciprocal basis." And there were other specific provisions: Japanese reiteration of plans to double foreign aid and to increase imports of manufactures; a "sweeping review" of Japan's foreign exchange control system; "expansion of credit for imports into Japan"; dispatch of Japanese missions to the United States to explore such things as increases in purchases of lumber and electric power plant machinery. Concessions from the U.S. side were limited, but there were general commitments to pursue "non-inflationary economic growth" and to "improve its balance of payments." And the Japanese

[214]

managed to extract from Strauss a declaration of his "confidence that in the next 90 days an effective energy program would be enacted by the Congress."[20]

With this package under his belt, Strauss adroitly defended the agreement before the Senate Finance Committee, countering its members' evident skepticism over the depth and breadth of his accomplishments by: (1) stressing the enormous "potential" of this "entire change in [Japan's trade] philosophy," and (2) exhorting committee members to keep up the pressure to help assure that the potential would be realized.[21]

The Trade Initiative in Retrospect: Was This "Trip" Necessary?

Thus U.S. trade diplomacy in the October 1977–January 1978 period was a conscious and calculated, if not always coordinated, effort to seize the initiative in both the bilateral and domestic political arenas. Externally, there was stepped-up pressure in pursuit of goals U.S. officials had been pushing all year, reflecting a widely shared belief that Japanese trade and economic policies constituted an inadequate response to severe and growing international problems. Internally, there was an effort to package the Japanese negotiations and their outcome in a way that would brake pressures for trade restrictions at home. As international diplomacy, the effort was conducted with considerable care—certainly more than a reading of news accounts would suggest. Mistakes were made, but on the whole U.S. officials were sensitive not just to the uses of pressure but to its limits. They knew when to ease off. As domestic politics, the initiative was a rather unusual effort to anticipate and contain what was seen as an emerging crisis. It was nurtured particularly by middle-level professionals, and the State Department was centrally involved: alert to domestic political concerns, arguing not against pressuring its foreign "clients," but rather advising on the form and quantity of pressure that would prove most effective. They saw their role, quite properly, as *mediation:* between the needs of the relationship and other urgent priorities in both countries.

But even if the tactics were adequate and the goals both good and sophisticated, the question remains: Was this "trip" necessary? Was it useful?

Granted that any U.S. administration would have sought Japanese action to reduce the trade surplus, was this particular campaign a useful means to this end? Did it improve prospects for managing trade relations in the future, or might it make a difficult set of problems even more intractable? More generally, how much should Americans and Japanese employ the high-pressure "black ship" scenario to resolve difficult political issues? How effective was the campaign in (1) dealing with the *short-run* political and policy situation, and (2) facilitating the *longer-range* management of issues, and of U.S.-Japanese relations more generally?

In Tokyo, the campaign was certainly effective in bringing some immediate policy concessions, more than would have taken place without it. It also appears to have strengthened the hand of those Japanese favoring a more aggressive growth strategy, not just in December but in the months thereafter. There was justifiable concern, expressed well by Gary Saxonhouse, that U.S. pressure might backfire by compounding "the malaise and uncertainty in which the Japanese private sector is mired" because it shook confidence in the American connection: "As much or more aggregate demand might be lost this way as can be gained from whatever Tokyo is forced to do."[22] But in the early months of 1978, the Japanese economy did appear to be improving its growth performance, and the 7 percent target for fiscal 1978 seemed at least within the realm of possibility. On specific product issues, however, no such overall shift in political power or policy seems to have resulted: Liberalization steps were taken, but U.S. pressure generated counterpressure—particularly by farmers—which confirmed the strength of Japanese protectionists as well. This strength continued into mid-1978, limiting Japanese concessions on import barriers as the Tokyo Round approached its climax. But on balance, Washington pressure did have useful, if modest, positive short-run results in Tokyo.

In United States politics, the immediate utility of the "trip" is harder to discern. There was undeniably a "protectionist threat"; though the phrase is often loosely employed, it is convenient shorthand for a considerable number of pressures, in the United States and other countries, to relieve particular economic problems by erecting new trade barriers, at cost to overall global (and usually overall national) economic welfare. Such pressures have been fueled since 1974, as is well known, by the prolonged recession and slow recovery. But the Japan initiative does not seem to have been particularly relevant to either the *form*, the *scope*, or the *timing* of this "threat" as it manifested itself in the United States.

American negotiators portrayed Congress as the potential villain in the piece; the picture painted at least implicitly was of a strong legislative movement for trade restrictions, very likely to act decisively in the months ahead if the Japanese did not come across with concessions. If not, why push in the fall of 1977, and why treat the January reopening of Congress as a deadline date? But 1977's upsurge in industry efforts to win relief from foreign competition was primarily in the *form* of *quasi-judicial efforts:* escape clause appeals, anti-dumping and countervailing duty petitions, lawsuits. The arenas were the International Trade Commission, the Treasury Department, and the Customs Court. Congress in some cases had the right

[217]

to override their decisions, and Presidential decisions, with respect to these petitions. And there were of course individual industry efforts to win legislative action, sometimes following failures to win the desired results elsewhere. But such efforts were generally unsuccessful. Legislatively, Congress was just not very active on trade policy in 1977.

The one important exception was the upsurge of concern about steel, which included a substantial and effective industry campaign for legislative backing. The symbol was the Congressional steel caucus, and a disturbing harbinger perhaps was Jacob Javits' decision to join it. But there was no comparable legislative effort underway on other products, and the steel issue was not being handled through U.S.-Japanese negotiations, despite Japan's willingness to enforce export restraints. Rather, it was being countered by unilateral U.S. action: development of a reference price system for steel imports. And if the *scope* of the legislative threat in the fall of 1977 was thus quite limited, this suggested that the *timing* of the real danger was more likely in 1979 or 1980: after specific product groups organize further and begin perhaps to build inter-industry alliances; after the results of the MTN begin to come to Congress for approval. Thus, while a "protectionist threat" undeniably exists, and may well grow stronger, more than a little skepticism seems justified about the particular "threat" and its timetable which American officials apparently conveyed to Japanese.

All of this leads to the second, longer-term question: the effects of the "trip" over time on the two governments' capacity to address the problems substantively and manage them politically in a mutually responsive way.

Even granted the lack of any immediate, overriding protectionist threat in Washington, the trade initiative might still have longer-term political usefulness if (1) it headed off pressures that would otherwise have grown stronger; or even if (2) if could not head off such pressures but nonetheless put the Administration in a better position to cope with them. But it might also, conversely, strengthen U.S. forces for trade restrictions rather than contain them

U.S. officials complained with some justice that they were sometimes condemned, like the ancient messenger, for causing the bad tidings they merely conveyed. And they certainly did not create the underlying economic and political problems. But their political orchestration inevitably focused much greater public attention on the issues within the United States, affecting the perceptions of Americans (including politicians) who do not normally pay close daily heed either to trade problems, or to problems with Japan. Taking care that senators and congressmen conveyed a sufficiently tough message to Minister Ushiba may well also have affected these legislators' perceptions, or at least the priority they gave the trade issue.

What were the net effects? On the positive side, the initiative generated action enabling the administration to assert it was addressing trade problems with Japan and making some progress on them; Strauss was fighting for American interests, with Congressional backing, and would continue to do so. Thus he could argue against legislative pre-emption of particular issues while negotiations continued.

In other respects, however, the publicity generated by the Japan enterprise strengthened U.S. protectionist forces. It dramatized U.S. problems with the Japanese and the flaws in Japanese trading practices, tending to give legitimacy to other voices seeking far more drastic solutions. It was in January, not October, for example, that columnists Jack Anderson and William Safire wrote misleading and (in the Safire case) inflammatory columns on Japanese trade practices.[23] More

[219]

generally, the fact that the Administration evidently took the "protectionist threat" so seriously could only send signals to legislators that they should raise their own estimates of its importance, and of how much they should yield to it on particular trade issues.

Finally, there is the question of whether the agreement itself may not prove counterproductive in American politics, raising expectations which it cannot satisfy. The key target of American negotiators was the trade imbalance. But the impact of all the specific trade concessions was likely to total only a fraction of a billion dollars in increased Japanese imports in 1978, set against the 1977 bilateral trade imbalance of $8.1 billion, and the much larger worldwide current accout surplus.[24] Yen revaluation and domestic stimulus were relied on to reduce the surplus much more markedly, but the magnitude and timing of their impact would be neither foreseen nor controlled. In rightly giving priority to the aggregate trade figures, yet also perpetrating the "myth," in Tad Szulc's words "that the remedial measures" agreed to "during January can change the [overall] situation very much in the near future," [25] the two governments risked very serious future trouble. Strauss obviously recognized the danger. He sought to hedge against it, telling senators that "I am skeptical" about Japanese estimates of a "five to six billion reduction in a year," even suggesting that it was an eight-year problem. But these were the same senators whom Strauss had encouraged to tell Ambassador Ushiba in December that time was running out.

In fact, there was no significant "diminution" in Japan's worldwide current account surplus for fiscal year 1978; instead, it remained roughly the same. And the bilateral trade deficit for *calendar* year 1978, by far the most important single statistic to congressional eyes, rose to $11.6 billion from $8.1 billion in 1977.[26] The final months of 1978 brought, at long

[220]

last, some favorable movement in the monthly data; the imbalance was no longer growing. But it promised to remain very high by pre-1977 standards, even though the rise of the yen to the unheard-of level of around 200 to the dollar had already affected the *volume* of trade substantially: the quantity of Japanese goods moving to the United States was stagnating, and the quantity of American exports to Japan was up sharply.

As 1979 began, the Japanese government of the new Prime Minister, Masayoshi Ohira, had abandond the 7 percent growth target as no longer practical, and was feeling new heat from the Carter Administration. On Capitol Hill, legislators and their staffs were preparing to review the multilateral trade agreement and related issues, amid growing impatience with the Japanese imbalance and amid proposals for drastic action to deal with it.[27] With an Ohira visit to Washington scheduled for spring and a multilateral economic summit in Tokyo for the summer, the best hope for officials on both sides of the Pacific was not that they would resolve the trade issue, but that they could continue to manage it politically through what looked like a particularly threatening year.

The persistence of the trade imbalance offers a final basis for placing the "trip" of late 1977 in broader perspective. As already noted in this chapter, the imbalance is the sort of economic/interdependence issue that has been the prime source of Japanese-American tension since around 1967. Tokai Mura was another. The nuclear reprocessing and trade disputes of 1977 may therefore be harbingers of what lies ahead. This does not mean, of course, that every year will feature such difficult bilateral negotiations. But many will. We had best get used to it.

By definition, such issues involve strong "domestic" policy concerns: e.g., Japan's energy needs; American industrial in-terests and pressures; both countries' overall economic growth and evolution. They also can involve competing foreign policy concerns: e.g., non-proliferation of nuclear weapons. Set against these concerns, the needs of U.S.-Japanese relations risk neglect. Officials responsible for these relations, and for assessing the impact of one country's actions on the other, will not automatically be major players on these issues unless they assert themselves—as they did within the U.S. government in 1977, but did not in such earlier episodes as the "new economic policy" of 1971 and the "soybean shock" of 1973.

Such issues also have major multilateral as well as bilateral dimensions. In some cases, like Tokai Mura, the bilateral conflict will become sharper because one country is concerned with worldwide effects and precedents. In others, like trade issues between 1974 and 1976, bilateral concerns' will be subsumed or incorporated into the agenda of multilateral forums. This can reduce their immediate volatility, but it may also lead to immobility—pressure is defused, but for that very reason results are harder to attain. And this in turn brings a renewal of efforts through bilateral channels, as the recent trade negotiations demonstrate.[28]

Finally, such issues tend to resist definitive resolution. Unlike the reversion of Okinawa or the Panama Canal, decisive settlements are the exception. Interdependence issues involve competing policy values; politically they usually require not the final triumph of certain values over others but the capacity to strike workable balances, tolerable trade-offs which will need further adjustment when they cease to be tolerable.

In coping with such issues, the Japanese and American governments may well suffer from opposite vices. Well-known is the Japanese tendency to adapt to the world rather than try to shape it, to see foreign policy as reluctant but necessary accommodation to the world environment rather than seize the initiative to affect that environment. Well-known also is the American tendency toward activism, toward exaggeration of our capacity to manage and manipulate events. Thus American officials, and their countrymen who watch them, are attracted by action programs which seem to provide handles on the evolution of the world, and intellectual constructions which provide a framework within which such action programs can fit. In the 1960s it was Atlantic partnership and a declaration of interdependence; in the 1970s we have the three "locomotive" economies leading the world to the promised land of recovery. The point is not that such conceptions are necessarily wrong or unuseful; it is that Americans tend to assume their rightness and press them on others who see the world through different lenses.

Those opposing "vices," if such they can be fairly labeled, color bilateral dealings in many negotiations. Americans press their views and initiatives and seek to universalize them; Japanese do not respond in kind, but instead measure the seriousness of each new American thrust and how much Japan should or must adjust to it. And both Americans and Japanese, for complementary reasons, are attracted to the high-pressure, "black ship" scenario played out most recently from November 1977 to January 1978. It is not so much that they explicitly decide to employ it; there was no such conscious decision, in fact, in 1977. But they are pulled toward taking steps which bring about its enactment.

Americans slide into the scenario for obvious reasons. It is a way for them to be active and to get results. And any discomfort or guilt from making Japan a particular target is assuaged by evidence that Japanese both need and want such pressure, however it may be portrayed in headlines.

For Tokyo politicians, external pressure offers to an

exceptional degree the refuge it offers politicians everywhere—they can shift blame to others for particular policy changes and the pain imposed, even if such politicians favor these changes themselves. And to a lesser degree it offers the same attraction to Japanese bureaucrats, who also become expert in orchestrating the impact of American pressures because this is a way to move their ministers.

The problem is that the scenario may easily become too attractive. It may come to be used far more than it should. Japanese who speak to Americans will continue to explain apologetically that their government does not change policy easily, without strong impetus—as if any other government does. Americans might tend toward the belief that Japan will not move unless leaned upon, but will concede almost anything if sufficient pressure is brought to bear. Ignored would be the fact that such pressure only seems to work under a fairly limited set of political conditions. Ignored also would be the danger that its repeated application could have very bad cumulative results.

The preconditions for the scenario seem at least two: (1) the existence of strong Tokyo allies with their own reasons for doing what the Americans want; (2) the credibility of the threat, of the costs to Japanese interests in not yielding. The first precondition offers one insight into why continued American pressure was largely counterproductive in the textile confrontation of 1969-71. No important Japanese political figure saw his personal or policy interests served by concessions.[29] In 1977-78, by contrast, Americans exerting pressure did have strong Japanese allies. This was due importantly to the greater strength of their substantive case and its greater compatibility with important Japanese domestic interests.

The second, more troubling precondition is a credible

threat. The up-front threat in 1977-78 was a protectionist surge in Congress, and executive branch officials made reasonable efforts to ensure that senators and representatives did their part in getting Minister Ushiba, among others, to take this seriously. But the more serious, tacit threat is that the viability of the American connection is to some degree at issue. U.S. officials do not express it this way or even intend to send this message, but that is the way the message tends to be publicly perceived in Tokyo. This is why it generates such headlines. Its likely effect in the short run is concessions—by January 1978, the Fukuda government was at the point where it would have been very badly damaged had it failed to reach an accord. But over the long run, the combination of both humiliation and threat cannot but expand the political market in Tokyo for alternative, less pro-American policies and stances. This is particularly true because it casts the United States in the role of ogre in Japanese political drama, and because it shakes faith in the durability of the American connection. Exacerbating matters is the fact that it not only risks, but may well require, a major public outcry for its effectiveness.

This suggests that the "black ship" scenario should be reserved for exceptional situations in which a Japanese policy shift is at once: (1) *important;* (2) *attainable;* (3) *decisive,* either in putting an issue to rest politically or in changing its substantive shape in a very substantial, even irreversible, way. It should not be employed for ephemeral or symbolic results, because when the problems re-emerge or worsen it cannot be so easily employed again.

Yet the interdependence issues which complicate Japanese-American relations will only rarely offer opportunities meeting all three of these criteria. The trade issue of 1977 clearly did not. However one regards the substance of the Strauss-

[225]

Ushiba accord, it was certainly not decisive in addressing this enormous, intractable problem. Was this "trip" then necessary and useful? The answer here, on balance, is "No."

Escalating the issue to the level of political crisis certainly got Japanese attention, gained some modest policy concessions, and perhaps bought time. But it is not at all clear why political time needed to be bought in October 1977 rather than later. And using the scenario then essentially precluded its use later, for another dramatic Straussian effort to "redefine" U.S.-Japanese relations would almost certainly strain Administration credibility in Washington and generate a serious backlash in Tokyo. Furthermore, for reasons already stated, it is not at all clear that the January agreement, together with the political spin-off from the diplomatic campaign, puts advocates of liberal trade and intelligent Japanese-American relations in a stronger position to face the continuing substantive problems than they would have held had the trip never been taken.

What then was, and is, the alternative? There is, of course, no easy one—that is the problem. For Americans, the need domestically is to take stronger policy steps in those areas where we contribute to the trade deficit—inflation, high oil imports, slow growth in industrial productivity, inadequate export marketing. Internationally, the need is to exert continuing pressure in a wide range of forums, to emphasize Japan's co-responsibility for helping maintain an open international economy, to insist that Japanese action go beyond attractive rhetoric or reassuring projections. But at the same time, we must avoid the belief that any quick fix is possible. And we must resist the temptation to treat Japan as singularly guilty on trade matters; there is more than enough guilt, and responsibility, to go around.

Notes

1. This essay draws on discussions with a number of American and Japanese officials involved in current bilateral relations. It also draws, in its general introductory analysis, on *The Textile Wrangle: Conflict in Japanese-American Relations 1969-1971* (Ithaca: Cornell University Press, 1979), which the writer co-authored with Haruhiro Fukui and Hideo Sato.

2. Communiqué of November 15, 1967, reprinted in *Department of State Bulletin,* December 4, 1967, pp. 744-47.

3. Richard M. Nixon, "Asia After Viet Nam," *Foreign Affairs,* October 1967, p. 123.

4. Communiqué of November 21, 1969, reprinted in *Department of State Bulletin,* December 15, 1969, pp. 555-58.

5. U.S. Congress, Joint Atomic Energy Committee, "Proliferation of Nuclear Weapons," Hearing, September 10, 1974; T.J. Pempel, "Japan's Nuclear Allergy," *Current History,* April 1975, pp. 169-73ff.

6. These events are treated at length in Destler, et al., *The Textile Wrangle.*

7. Kissinger's address is reprinted in *Department of State Bulletin,* July 7, 1975, pp. 1-2.

8. These phrases are from the titles of books on Japan published early in this decade by Zbigniew Brzezinski and Herman Kahn. The Japanese editions of both were bestsellers.

[227]

9. See, for example, Philip H. Trezise, "The Second Phase in U.S.-Japanese Relations," *Pacific Community,* April 1975, pp. 340-51.

10. Address to the Japan Society, New York, February 2, 1978 (emphasis in original).

11. Ambassador Mansfield cited the Tokai Mura talks as "a model of successful negotiations between equal partners." Address to the America-Japan Society Welcoming Luncheon, Hilton Hotel, October 14, 1977.

12. *New York Times,* January 14, 1978; U.S. Senate Committee on Finance, "United States/Japanese Trade Relations and the Status of the Multilateral Trade Negotiations," Hearing, February 1, 1978, p. 12.

13. Statistics provided by U.S. Census Bureau, Department of Commerce, f.a.s. value basis.

14. See, for example, James Reston, "Did Japan Mislead Carter?" *New York Times,* December 14, 1977.

15. The discussion which follows draws substantially on discussions with several U.S. officials involved.

16. The metaphor recalls Commodore Perry's steaming into Tokyo Bay in 1853. His "black ship" has become a symbol of the role of the ostensibly unwanted but irresistible external pressure in producing Japanese policy change.

17. Yasushi Hara, "Japan-U.S. Trade," *Asahi Evening News,* December 2, 1977.

18. *Washington Post,* December 13, 1977.

19. *New York Times,* January 14, 1978. According to *Washington Post* economic correspondent Hobart Rowen, Strauss described it to the President differently, as "a C-minus agreement that he'd present as a B-plus" to the public. *Washington Post,* February 5, 1978.

20. For the text of the Joint Statement, see *New York Times* January 14, 1978, and Senate Finance Committee, "United States/Japanese Trade Relations," pp. 45-47.

21. Senate Finance Committee, "United States/Japanese Trade Relations."

22. *New York Times,* January 11, 1978.

23. *Washington Post,* January 15, 1978; *New York Times* January 19, 1978.

24. For example, the U.S. Department of Agriculture estimated that the "five specific measures in the agreement relating to agricultural trade . . . along with Japan's announced intentions to . . . make additional purchases of grain, could together stimulate as much as $100 million in additional agricultural imports to Japan, with the United States possibly taking as much as 60 percent of the total increase." *(Foreign Agricultural Trade of the United States,* April 1978, p. 18.)

25. "The Strauss Round," *The New Republic,* February 11, 1978, p. 9.

26. Commerce Department figures, f.a.s. value basis. Bank of Japan statistics put Japan's global current account surplus for *calendar* year 1978 at $16.6 billion, up from $10.9 billion in calendar 1977. Because of a drop-off in early 1979, the *fiscal* 1978 figure seems likely (as this is written) to be roughly equal to the $14 billion of fiscal 1977.

27. Senator Lloyd Bensten, generally a moderate on trade questions, argued in January 1979 for consideration of a "surcharge or other barriers" directed specifically toward Japan. The most comprehensive recent congressional treatment of U.S.-Japanese trade issues is the January 1979 report of the House Ways and Means Committee's Task Force on United States-Japan Trade, a group chaired by Representative James R. Jones (D-Okla.)

28. For further development of this theme, see my "United States Trade Policymaking During the 'Tokyo Round,'" in Michael Blaker, ed., *The Politics of Trade: U.S. and Japanese Policymaking for the GATT Negotiations,* East Asian Institute, Columbia University, 1978.

29. The situation changed in July 1971 when Kakuei Tanaka became MITI Minister and saw bearing the brunt of the issue as a way to strengthen his candidacy for Prime Minister. Partly for this reason, an agreement was reached three months later. (See *The Textile Wrangle,* Chapter 12.)

[SIX]

The United States
and Japan in Asian Affairs

William J. Barnds

The strength and durability of the U.S.-Japanese relationship has been one of the central elements behind the prosperity and stability that East Asia (excluding the former French Indochinese states) has known since the end of the Korean War. In view of the great differences in culture, history, and geography between these two countries—combined with the legacy of World War II—it is remarkable how seldom there have been major problems in postwar Japanese-American relations

Even when serious problems have developed, they have been transitory. The dramatic Tokyo riots over the security treaty in 1960, which forced the cancellation of President Eisenhower's planned visit to Japan, had little lasting impact. The Nixon "shocks" in the early 1970s had a greater impact, if only because there were several of them—the opening to Peking, U.S. restrictions on Japanese textile shipments, the conflict over yen revaluation, and the U.S. soybean embargo.

For a time many Japanese feared that the Nixon Administration was making a fundamental shift in its Asian policy by making better relations with China the cornerstone of America's East Asian policy. Yet it soon became clear that no such dramatic change was intended. Within a few years Foreign Minister Ohira and Secretary of State Kissinger claimed that the difficulties had been overcome, that both countries had learned valuable lessons, and that relations had never been better.[1]

There was considerable truth in these optimistic assertions, but they largely overlooked two important points. *First,* The United States and Japan were becoming so deeply involved with each other, especially in the economic sphere, that frictions and strains were periodically inevitable. The real issue was not whether such strains could be avoided, but whether they could be managed so as not to undermine the basic relationship. The magnitude of this problem was masked in the years 1974-76 when Japan was struggling to adjust to the oil price increases, and the upsurge in demand for U.S. products—especially foodstuffs—temporarily strengthened the U.S. balance of trade. Japan's $17-billion trade surplus in 1977 (of which over half was with the United States) was an important element in the dramatic increase in the U.S. trade deficit that year, and the magnitude of the problem increased in 1978.

Second, the relative power and self-confidence of the two nations was changing. This would require readjustment in their respective roles, but given the elusiveness of such concepts as power and self-confidence, the appropriate changes would be hard to define and to agree upon. The change was obviously greatest in the economic sphere and least in the military arena. The economic change involves more than Japan's trade surplus with the United States, for

Japan's economic role in Asia has increased more rapidly than has that of the United States. Between 1965 and 1975 U.S. trade with the countries of East and Southeast Asia (excluding Japan) increased from $4.2 billion to $22.7 billion, while Japan's trade increased from $4.3 billion to $31.7 billion.[2] Yet even in the economic sphere the Japanese basically see themselves as weak and dependent upon an uncertain world economic environment, while they view the United States as strong and more in control of its own destiny. American perceptions have moved in the opposite direction. Moreover, the Japanese still view international as well as interpersonal relations in hierachical terms, and a relationship of equality is difficult for Japanese. The United States, because of its domestic troubles and uncertainty about its role in the world, is no longer regarded as a model or a "big brother" by the Japanese. Yet it certainly is not a "little brother." What is it? Finally, the field in which the United States has changed course most dramatically is its attitude toward its military role in Asia, and this is the area in which it is most difficult for the Japanese to see how they could successfully take over any substantial part of the U.S. role.

These changing circumstances and perceptions have already affected many aspects of Japanese-American relations to some extent, and their future impact may be even more substantial. If we analyze the relationship we find that it consists of three separate but interrelated aspects: (1) the bilateral relationship; (2) the relationship of the two countries in world affairs generally, which is chiefly concerned with global economic issues, but which at times involves policies toward such regional matters as the Arab-Israeli dispute; and (3) the respective roles of Japan and the United States in Asian affairs. One need not be a proponent of a linkage *strategy* in foreign policy to recognize that major achievements or strains in one

[233]

aspect of the relationship can have significant impact on other aspects. Thus, with differences between the two countries over their respective responsibilities toward the world economy (the "locomotive" strategy and the fall in the value of the dollar), and with their bilateral economic relations likely to remain troubled, it is particularly important that U.S. and Japanese policies on the key issues in Asian affairs be dealt with carefully and skillfully.

This third aspect of the relationship is sometimes downplayed or neglected because of the great importance of the other two and because of Japan's low-profile foreign policy. Yet Japan is not simply an advanced industrial nation, and thus part of the trilateral world of North America, Western Europe, and Japan. Nor is it merely part of the North when North-South issues and a "new international economic order" are being discussed. Its geography, history and culture make it an integral part of Asia, although a part that is unique in many ways. There are differences within Japan over how *active* a political role the country should play in Asian affairs; but as Japan assumes a more significant political role in the world, its primary focus will be on Asia.

Thus the overall Japanese-American relationship will be significantly affected by the extent to which there is a basic harmony between the policies of the two countries on key Asian issues. This does not mean that they must—or even should try to—follow identical policies. Each country has interests beyond maintaining harmony with its ally. In fact, there probably would be a danger in attempting to achieve an identity because of their differing interests and the different domestic pressures and constraints weighing upon the two governments on some issues. It is important, however, that the two countries do not actively pursue sharply conflicting policies on key political issues, which will be difficult since their economic competition is becoming sharper throughout Asia.

What are the key issues confronting the United States and Japan in Asian affairs? What are the respective interests, roles and policies of the two countries? What opportunities and problems lie ahead? There appear to be *six* key issues, which are: (1) policies toward conflicting jurisdictional claims of Asian states in the seas; (2) policy toward Vietnam and its Communist neighbors; (3) relations with the Association of Southeast Asian Nations (ASEAN); (4) the Taiwan issue and normalization of relations with the P.R.C.; (5) Japanese and American policies toward the Soviet Union and the People's Republic of China—a balanced approach or a tilt; and (6) the Korean peninsula and its role in East Asian affairs.

U.S.policy on these issues cannot—or at least should not—be made simply on a case-by-case basis, but should be a function of a larger conception of the appropriate American role in East Asia. It is obviously beyond the scope of this essay to attempt to set forth the concepts, priorities, and guidelines that would enable the United States to carry out a successful policy toward East Asia. Yet unless the basic considerations underlying U.S. policy are touched upon, any judgments on the key issues listed above would exist in a vacuum.

Overall U.S. policy will of necessity be more complex than it was at the height of the Cold War when particular policies and activities could be assessed according to whether or not they contributed to the strategy of containment. Now the United States needs to pursue a more subtle and complicated balance-of-power policy as well as a broader "world order" policy. As to the former, the United States wants China to be strong enough to serve as a check on Soviet power, but we should avoid supporting China so extensively as to undermine any chances for less antagonistic relations with the Soviet

Union. We also want to continue to maintain close ties with our Asian allies and friends (especially Japan) so as to prevent any single nation—including China—from becoming dominant in Asia. While cooperation between the United States, Japan and China may gradually increase, differing perspectives and interests make it unlikely (and undesirable) that any de facto alliance will result—so long as there is no substantial increase in Soviet strength and assertiveness. Thus, such matters as the appropriate nature of U.S. relations with Peking, and particularly the feasibility of Western moves to enhance Chinese military capability, will be difficult to determine because of their differing impacts on different countries.

As regards "world order" politics, the top priority should continue to be given to fostering economic integration and political cooperation between ourselves and the non-Communist Asian states, which has made possible the stability and prosperity of the area. It is now also desirable to move beyond this by trying to draw China gradually into constructive efforts to deal with problems of regional and global concern. Yet Chinese and American perceptions and outlooks differ greatly, and U.S. ability to influence Chinese views on such matters will remain very limited. The ambiguities that will exist in giving due weight in policy formulation to the diverse considerations involved will not be easy for the United States to resolve, in view of its history, diversity, and structure of government. Yet any attempt to escape from these dilemmas by adopting neat formulas or a single overarching principle—such as giving top priority in all situations to maintaining the alliance with Japan, or doing whatever is necessary to strengthen China vis-à-vis the Soviet Union—is bound to lose touch with reality and lead to failure.

One final point should be kept in mind. U.S.- Japanese relations will be affected in subtle but important ways by the evolution of America's position in the world. Japan has been attempting to reduce gradually its heavy dependence on the United States. Tokyo would like to carry this process somewhat further, in a way that does not undermine the prospect for continued cooperation with the United States. At the same time, Japan's policies over the long term will be conditioned by its view of American determination and ability to maintain a strong position in the world.

Disputes in the East Asian Seas

The subject of conflicting claims in East Asian seas and to the resources of the seabeds is a complex set of issues that requires considerable analysis to be dealt with comprehensively. However, a few key points soon become apparent. The nature of the American and Japanese interests is quite different. Some of the disputes involve Japan directly, especially the overlapping claims of Japan and of both the People's Republic of China (P.R.C.) and the Republic of China (R.O.C.) in the East China Sea. The United States, on the other hand, is involved in two less direct ways. The first concerns the policy to adopt toward possible exploration by U.S. oil companies in disputed areas. The second and related issue involves whose claims—or what principles—to support in disputes between various nations, some of whom are allies while others are adversaries with whom we want to improve relations. There is obviously a potential for U.S.-Japanese friction here, although it has not yet become a serious problem.

Basically, the policy of the U.S. government has been to discourage American companies from undertaking exploration or drilling activities in those disputed areas regarded as most sensitive to Peking.[3] This policy has had to be applied chiefly

[237]

in regard to areas involving disputes between the P.R.C. on the one side and Taiwan or the Republic of Korea on the other, for the latter two countries have tried to involve U.S. firms for both political and economic reasons. At the same time, exploration in the Taiwanese Straits or the Yellow Sea has not been discouraged by the U.S. government in areas beyond what could be termed the maximum Chinese claim on the median-line principle.

Japan has proceeded more cautiously than has South Korea or Taiwan for two reasons. First, it would like to reduce its heavy dependence upon the major international oil firms by encouraging Japanese firms to develop the competence to undertake offshore exploration and production on their own where possible, and in partnership with Western firms where the latter's knowledge and experience are necessary. Second, Tokyo has been uncertain whether it should give top priority to seeking large-scale oil imports from the P.R.C. as part of a general policy of expanding its economic and political relations with Peking, or should place primary emphasis on developing offshore production in the areas it claims.

Peking, while never stating its claims in the East China Sea with precision, has argued that "the continental shelf is the natural extension of the continental territory" and therefore that the P.R.C. "has inviolable sovereignty over the East China Sea continental shelf...."[4] The continental shelf extends well beyond the median line, which Tokyo asserts should be the determining factor in the location of the boundary. Moreover, in the draft Law of the Sea treaty the rights of the coastal state may be extended beyond the continental shelf itself. Thus the potential for a major dispute clearly exists.

In addition, the P.R.C. and Japan claim the Senkaku Islands (Tiao-yu T'ai), located some 200 miles southwest of Okinawa, which have been controlled by Japan. Ownership of these islands by one party or the other would have an important bearing upon their rights in the East China Sea. Until 1978 the two governments had set aside the dispute over the Senkakus. Both Tokyo and Peking had basically played a waiting game regarding the East China Sea while they explored the possibilities of expanding trade further and while each country developed its capacity for more advanced offshore oil operations. However, in April 1978 armed Chinese fishing vessels carrying signs asserting Chinese claims anchored in waters around the Senkakus despite orders from Japanese patrol boats to leave.[5] The motivations behind the Chinese action are uncertain. The move could have been a Chinese reaction to efforts early in 1978 by pro-Taiwanese forces within the Liberal Democratic party to push the Japanese government toward closer relations with Taipei; it could have been pressure on Japan to accept Peking's terms in the long drawout negotiations for a peace treaty; or it could have been a Chinese move to assert its territorial claims more forcefully whatever the consequences to Sino-Japanese relations. Whatever the cause, the Chinese move highlighted the importance of the conflicting claims of Tokyo and Peking to the Senkakus.

The decisions facing the United States are complicated for several reasons. Various corporations have different interests and press the United States to take stands or to adopt principles that favor their particular interests. For example, the main interest of the major international oil companies lies in continuing to supply petroleum to the large Japanese market, although their interest in developing Chinese offshore oil fields has increased as the P.R.C. has turned to foreign sources to spur its development effort.

Other companies are primarily interested in exploration and/or production in areas claimed by Japan, China, Taiwan

[239]

or South Korea. Most American oil companies want the United States to retain full authority over as large an area off the U.S. coasts as possible so as to limit the role of any international seabed authority. At the same time, those granted concessions from Japan in the East China Sea find that acceptance of the median line principle by Peking would be to their advantage.

What should be the U.S. stance on the two general policy questions: the disputes between the countries in the area and the activities of U.S. companies in disputed areas? As to the jurisdictional claims, four broad choices are possible. The first would be to side with the P.R.C., chiefly as a means of strengthening Sino-American relations in order to counter the U.S.S.R., but also because of a U.S. desire to strengthen the rights of coastal states to extend their jurisdiction seaward. The second would be to support Japanese claims so as to strengthen the U.S.-Japanese alliance. The third would be to adopt a hands-off posture, allowing the matter to be settled—de facto or de jure—by negotiations and/or a test of strength between Tokyo and Peking. Finally the United States could attempt to serve as a mediator or intermediary in an effort to help the parties reach agreement.

The arguments for and against each of these stances are too complex to discuss in detail here. (Moreover, any position adopted should be weighed by considering its impact on the claims and positions of Taiwan and South Korea and on America's overall East Asian policy.) Briefly, however, the gains accruing to the United States from siding with either China or Japan would be more than offset by the damage to our relations with the other. Only if Peking makes a sustained effort to enforce its most ambitious claims would it be appropriate for the United States to tilt in favor of Japan, for such a stance on Peking's part probably would develop in the context of a general hardening of Chinese foreign policy. It would be beneficial to the United States, as well as to China and Japan, if the two parties were to arrange a compromise settlement. If such a settlement occurs, however, it is likely to result more from a complicated series of trade-offs that reflect the basic nature of Sino-Japanese relations than from adherence to any particular Law of the Sea principle. In such circumstances a detached (rather than an involved) U.S. position would be more appropriate, except in the unlikely event that *both* parties want the United States to play a role.

As regards the activities of U.S. firms, there would appear to be little reason for any basic change in policy—at least as far as exploration in Japanese-claimed areas is concerned. Exploration closer to the P.R.C. would be provocative to Peking and thus unduly costly, relative to the potential gains. Continuation of the present policy may involve some friction with the P.R.C.; but unless the United States is to make the avoidance of any disputes with Peking its top priority, we shall have to accept such an outcome on occasion.

Policy Toward Vietnam

Japanese and American long-term interests in Vietnam—as well as in Laos and Cambodia—are essentially similar. Both Japan and the United States want to see those countries pursue a policy of accommodation rather than confrontation with the ASEAN nations. More immediately, both want to see Vietnamese troops withdrawn from Cambodia and an end to the Sino-Vietnamese military conflict. Their reasons for this are not only the danger that such a military conflict may spread, but also that it is undesirable for Hanoi to feel compelled to line up completely with Moscow—particularly to the extent

[241]

that it permits the U.S.S.R. to establish a naval base in Vietnam. Hanoi avoided complete reliance on any single power until 1978, but conflict between Vietnam and China over Vietnamese-Cambodian disputes and over Hanoi's treatment of ethnic Chinese will make it difficult for Vietnam to reduce its heavy reliance on the Soviet Union. The provisions for military cooperation in the 25-year Soviet-Vietnamese Treaty of Friendship and Cooperation signed in Moscow on November 3, 1978, may limit the scope of a Sino-Vietnamese war, but the treaty probably convinced Hanoi that it could invade Cambodia without undue risk.[6]

Vietnam's troubles with China in 1978 increased Hanoi's desire to improve relations with the ASEAN nations. But Vietnam's growing links with Moscow create fears among ASEAN leaders that the U.S.S.R. will assume too large a role in Southeast Asia. The best way to contribute, however modestly, toward furthering U.S. and Japanese interests would be for both countries to have normal relations with Hanoi so as to increase the latter's stake in a peaceful Asia and provide it with some diplomatic maneuverability vis-à-vis Moscow and Peking. Japan, which has diplomatic relations with Vietnam (and has extended it some small loans) is obviously ahead of the United States on this issue.

The establishment of normal diplomatic and trade relations with Vietnam would also be helpful as a symbol that the United States has moved beyond its preoccupation with the old issues and animosities that led to and grew out of the Vietnam war. Nonetheless, establishing relations with Vietnam stands far down in the hierarchy of American interests in Asia. There has been no bloodbath in Vietnam—in contrast to Cambodia—but conditions have been bad enough to prompt a substantial flow of refugees. The enactment of laws by Congress forbidding U.S. aid to Vietnam probably is an accurate reflection of the attitude of the American people. Establishing diplomatic relations should not be regarded as a "reward" to another nation for good behavior, but such a move coming on the heels of Vietnam's invasion of Cambodia would be widely misinterpreted and would serve no constructive purpose.

In the circumstances obtaining in early 1979 there is little the United States can or should do to move toward normal relations with Hanoi, even if reports that the latter has dropped its demand for aid or reparation as the price of diplomatic relations prove correct. The United States should take China's views into account in formulating American policy toward Vietnam, but should not take China's side in its dispute with Hanoi.

Over the longer term, the United States should periodically probe Vietnam's intentions regarding their bilateral relations and should try to make further progress on the issue of American soldiers missing in action. If Hanoi's occasional hints in 1978 that it would no longer demand economic aid as a precondition to diplomatic links become official Vietnamese policy—and if the Vietnamese-Cambodian conflict subsides—the United States should move to establish diplomatic and trade relations. In the meantime, the United States should accord top priority to efforts to settle the refugees in Asian or European countries where possible and in the United States when necessary.

The United States has little reason to object to Japanese policy—except for its stringent restrictions on the entry of Vietnamese refugees. Tokyo understands the constraints that have affected U.S. policy. While Tokyo probably would like to see the United States be somewhat more flexible in dealing with Hanoi's demands, differences over relations with Vietnam are unlikely to place serious strains on U.S.-Japanese relations in the absence of a major shift in the pattern of

[243]

Hanoi's relations with the other Southeast Asian nations—or a major escalation of the Sino-Vietnamese-Cambodian conflict.

Relations with the Association of Southeast Asian Nations (ASEAN)

American and Japanese interests in Southeast Asia have much in common, and the roles and policies of the two countries are complementary to a striking extent. Both Japan and the United States want to see the ASEAN nations (Indonesia, Thailand, Malaysia, Singapore and the Philippines) continue their rapid economic growth, retain their present orientations in world affairs, and develop political institutions that provide stability and greater popular participation. They also want to see ASEAN succeed as an institution in view of the contribution it can make to regional stability and progress.

Yet there are also differences in roles and interests that should not be overlooked. The area is more important economically to Japan than it is to the United States. A much larger proportion of Japanese than of American foreign investments are located in the ASEAN states. Southeast Asia accounts for 12 percent of Japan's total trade, but only 4 percent of America's. Nearly all of Japan's oil comes from or passes through the area, while only a small part of U.S. oil imports originates in or is shipped through the area. At the same time, the United States continues to have a significant, if reduced, military presence in the area by virtue of its military bases in the Philippines—backed up by U.S. military links with Australia. Moreover, the area's importance to Japan increases its importance to the United States, something that is often overlooked by those who argue that in the post-Vietnam era American interests in Southeast Asia are insignificant.

Nevertheless, it is difficult if not impossible to assign any precise weight to the importance of Southeast Asia to the United States. About all one can say of the area as a whole is that it is of modest or moderate importance to the United States, fully recognizing that such words convey more of a flavor than a guide for policy. Clearly, U.S. (and Japanese) interests are much greater in insular than in mainland Southeast Asia, and the disparity becomes even more marked if one includes the Malay peninsula with the offshore nations. Trade is much greater with the insular countries, where U.S. investments are also concentrated, and, together with the Malay peninsula, they have important natural resources in large amounts. They also sit astride the lines of communication into and through Southeast Asia, which gives them considerable strategic importance. Yet Thailand's location makes it too important to ignore or neglect.

At present, Japan's more active economic role and its closer links to ASEAN as an organization are somewhat "balanced" by the U.S. military presence. An important issue, however, is whether this is an appropriate or durable division of labor. While U.S. trade with Southeast Asia increased more than five-fold between 1965 and 1975 (a sizable growth even allowing for inflation), Japan's trade increased over seven times in the same period and is now nearly twice the amount of U.S. trade with the region. (Southeast Asia has a modest trade surplus with both the United States and Japan.) Does such a situation leave Japan too exposed politically for its good, and for the good of the area? Is, as one long-time observer has argued, the U.S. position too heavily concentrated in the military sphere relative to other American activities there? Bernard Gordon has commented that:

. . . in Southeast Asia American policies may have become so heavily involved with security that they threaten to lose sight of the interests that defense policies are intended to protect.

For an American foreign policy, dependent ultimately on public acceptance and support. this raises questions of balance. Until recently, the U.S. presence in the Pacific has been evident across a wide spectrum: in assistance, in trade and investment, in education and cultural effort, *and* in defense. Now there has been a decline in most of those roles, with only defense remaining a high-priority official concern. The result, accelerated and reinforced by Tokyo's own initiatives, is that Japan increasingly is the dominant presence in economic as well as other activities, while present trends will leave the United States with its military role in Southeast Asia the foremost aspect of the American presence.

If that develops, it has to be questioned whether Americans, in the absence of other functions, will accept the role of principal buttressing power in the Pacific—particularly since within the United States the constituencies that might argue for a broad-gauged American role are themselves in decline.[7]

Even if one thinks that this appraisal exaggerates the dangers of the present situation (since U.S. trade with Southeast Asia increased some five-fold between 1965 and 1975), problems could arise out of too neat a division of labor. Yet it is easier to say what should not be done than what should, and can, be done. No country would be a net beneficiary if Japan were to cut back its economic activities in the area, despite the psychological and political strains that such heavy dependence on Japan creates. The outlook for Tokyo's relations with the area will, of course, depend upon Japan's willingness to conduct its economic activities in a manner that promotes broad-based development as well as short-term profits for Japanese firms and their local partners.

Nor is it feasible for Japan to assume any direct security role in the area despite the gradually diminishing suspicions about Japan's intentions. If Japan does build up its military forces, this will be to enable it to defend its own territory and nearby sea lanes. Thus if a change is to occur in the present structure of relationships, it probably will involve a shift in U.S. activities. Is this necessary and possible? The United States could reduce its military presence further, but in view of the withdrawal from Vietnam and Thailand and the fighting between Vietnam and Cambodia and China, further reductions in the next few years probably would be destabilizing. The current U.S. military presence in the area—chiefly the Philippine bases—is not so expensive that the American people are unwilling to support it, although there are obviously limits to what Congress will or should provide in the way of aid in order to retain these bases. It would be useful if the United States could play a more active role in the economic development of the area, especially since the ASEAN countries have been among the moderate southern forces in the North-South negotiations. Yet it would be unrealistic to think that major American efforts are likely in view of the many problems with higher priority that any U.S. administration will face.

But if no major expansion of U.S. activities is likely, some modest increases probably are possible. If this occurs, should the United States focus these activities in such a way as to give direct support to ASEAN *as an institution* along the lines Japan is doing with its $1 billion credit under the "Fukuda Doctrine"? A move in this direction is underway, but we should let the ASEAN countries take the initiative in the matter. This is not to downgrade ASEAN's importance or the possibility that it may become stronger. Rather it rests upon the conviction that ASEAN is more likely to endure and progress if it does so on the basis of its member states' own efforts than if it becomes—or even appears to become—heavily dependent upon U.S. support and is viewed as a tool of U.S. policy. Moreover, if Japan and the United States act as one in the area, this could alarm the Southeast Asian countries without yielding offsetting benefits.

There are a few potential sources of difficulty that could create problems for Japanese-American relations. Failure of the U.S.-Philippine base negotiations and relinquishment of Clark Field and Subic Bay would have increased the apprehension in Japan that the United States was withdrawing from Asia rather than simply being more selective in its commitments, but the new base agreement should put such fears to rest. Trouble would also arise if the United States were to assign such a high priority to human rights issues as to undermine its generally good relations with the ASEAN states. The Carter Administration's growing awareness of the complexities of the human rights issue combined with the fact that the faults and failures of the ASEAN states are not as dramatic as in many other countries suggest that the Administration is unlikely to initiate moves that would seriously damage U.S. relations with the ASEAN states. However, this issue—as well as the implementation of the new U.S.-Philippines bases agreement—involves Congress as well as the Administration, and Congress has been pushing for a tight linkage between U.S. support for a country and the local human rights situation. Finally, economic or political deterioration within the individual ASEAN states could in time lead either to revolutionary upheavals or to much harsher repression by beleaguered governments. Such developments—or a conflict between Vietnam and Thailand or spread of the Sino-Vietnam-Cambodian conflict—could obviously upset the relatively relaxed attitude that Japan and the United States were able to adopt in dealing with the area from the time of the Communist victory in Vietnam until the outbreak of large-scale military conflicts between the Asian Communist states late, in 1978.

The Taiwan Issue and Normalization of Relations with the P.R.C.

The fact that it took nearly seven years after the signing of the Shanghai Communiqué in February 1972 to "normalize" relations with the P.R.C. indicates the inherent complexity of the issue as well as the degree to which decisions were dependent upon the congruence of favorable domestic political environments in both the United States and China. Watergate and the resignation of President Nixon in 1974, the Communist victory in Vietnam in 1975, constraints during the presidential election year of 1976, and President Carter's preoccupation with other issues and his uncertain standing with Congress and the public during 1977 and most of 1978 made it politically impossible for the United States to move until December 1978. Similarly, the death of Chou En-Lai in January 1976, followed by the political uncertainty connected with the death of Mao Tse-tung in September 1976 and the turmoil surrounding the rise and fall of the "Gang of Four," prevented the P.R.C. from dealing with the Taiwan issue until Teng Hsiao-ping established a power base and Peking made a basic decision to seek closer relations with the major non-communist nations to enable it to carry out its modernization program and to face the U.S.S.R. from a stronger position.

The normalization agreement was a major achievement, but it would be a mistake to think that the Taiwan issue has been permanently settled in a way that is satisfactory to both the United States and China. (Indeed, the use of the term "normalization" can be misleading if it leads people to believe

[249]

that all will be well between the two countries once the process is completed.) A brief examination of the complexities and arguments involved, Japanese and American interests and attitudes, and the explicit and implicit terms of the normalization agreement will illuminate the issues and conditions that still require attention.

The Taiwan problem was complex and difficult because there never was—nor is there today—a completely satisfactory or risk-free solution, for too many clashing interests and principles were involved. The principle of self-determination for Taiwan conflicted with the traditional American position of support for China's national unity and territorial integrity, and espousing the former would have been a direct challenge to the powerful force of Chinese nationalism. Yet the United States had pledged itself by treaty with the R.O.C. to protect Taiwan's security, which was only endangered by the P.R.C. Because of the many complexities in this intractable issue, the best we could hope to do was to deal with the matter in such a way as to reduce it to manageable proportions. It was clear that American skill in handling this issue would have a profound effect upon the assessment by Asian nations of our political skill and maturity.

Japan was especially concerned about U.S. moves dealing with Taiwan, although this issue was and is of such importance to American foreign policy that the likely Japanese reaction to our moves could not be the determining factor in our policy. Tokyo took advantage of the U.S. opening to China to shift diplomatic recognition from Taipei to Peking in 1972 as part of a major Japanese effort to expand relations with the P.R.C. Yet Japan retains strong and growing economic links to Taiwan. Until 1978 its trade with Taiwan was about as large as its trade with the mainland, although the latter offers a greater potential for growth.[8] However, a separate Taiwan complicates Tokyo's dealings with Peking on such issues as jurisdictional claims in the East China Sea.

Most Japanese, like most Americans, were ambivalent about how the United States should deal with the Taiwan issue. The great majority of people in each country probably preferred that the United States handle the matter in a way that preserved the *de facto* status quo. However, many leftists in Japan desire to see Peking gain control of Taiwan, or are at least indifferent to the matter. No politically significant group of Americans shares these views; but some Americans have been willing to take greater risks with Taiwan's security than have others. The Japanese government occasionally warned against any rapid or substantial shift in U.S. policy, as in July 1976 when Foreign Minister Miyazawa told Senator Mansfield that the United States could lose credibility in Asia and undermine the East Asian balance of power if it normalized relations with the P.R.C. without giving due weight to the issue of Taiwan's security.[9]

Yet as Japan's relations with the P.R.C. expanded, and especially after it signed the Sino-Japanese peace treaty in August 1978, it became increasingly difficult for Tokyo to object to a U.S. move to normalize relations. Nonetheless, Japan would be alarmed if Peking ever attempted to seize Taiwan by force or conducted a blockade of the island, although Tokyo regards such action as unlikely in the foreseeable future. However, Tokyo would do virtually nothing itself in such an event and would be reluctant even to support any U.S. moves that were made to protect Taiwan. In such circumstances, there would be major strains in U.S.-Japanese relations if U.S. policy eventually leads either to a P.R.C. takeover of Taiwan *or* to a return to active Sino-American hostility as a result of U.S. military support for Taiwan in a future crisis.

[251]

During the course of Sino-American negotiations it became clear that Peking was unlikely to alter its position that normalization required the removal of U.S. military forces from Taiwan, the ending of U.S.-R.O.C. diplomatic links, and the termination of the security treaty. Nearly all U.S. forces had been withdrawn from Taiwan by late 1978, and removal of the several hundred men remaining was unlikely to create serious problems. The switching of diplomatic representation from Taipei to Peking was unlikely to create unsurmountable problems, although legislation by Congress to provide Taiwan with continued access to U.S. markets and financial institutions on favorable terms would be necessary.

The key issue involved Taiwan's security, and the 1955 U.S.-R.O.C. Mutual Security Treaty had become for many the symbol of U.S. determination on this matter. Many Americans—and Japanese—argued that the status quo was quite a satisfactory arrangement and should be maintained unless and until Peking promised not to use force in seeking to reunify Taiwan with the mainland. Those stressing Taiwan's importance argued that if Sino-Soviet relations remained hostile, Peking could not afford to alienate the United States. If there were a basic shift in Sino-Soviet relations and the two countries again joined forces against the non-Communist world, the United States would need its present Asian allies to maintain an island-chain defense strategy. Finally, U.S. trade with Taiwan would remain larger than trade with the P.R.C.

Other Americans believed that it was a mistake to think that Taiwan's security rested upon a treaty signed in vastly different circumstances, and that if U.S. forces ever became actively involved in the defense of Taiwan it would be for geopolitical reasons rather than because of formal treaty ties. Taiwan's security, in their view, was based upon its own defensive capabilities, the P.R.C.'s lack of an amphibious force to move against Taiwan, China's preoccupation with the Soviet forces on its northern frontier, and Peking's reluctance to undermine its relations with the United States and Japan by undertaking any military action against Taiwan. The sharp deterioration in China's relations with Vietnam would further constrain Peking. Moreover, such people feared that an indefinite failure to normalize relations with the P.R.C. could result in an increase of Chinese hostility toward the United States or possibly a Sino-Soviet détente, although the latter concern declined as Sino-Soviet antagonism continued unabated after the death of Mao.

There were several reasons behind the U.S. decision to shift diplomatic recognition from Taipei to Peking, quite apart from the fact that the United States had implicitly pledged itself to do so in the Shanghai Communiqué. The first was that it believed that such a move, if properly carried out, could help stabilize the situation in East Asia and thus contribute to U.S. security by reducing potential sources of Sino-American conflicts and diminishing the chances that our Asian allies would be caught up in such disputes. But normalization will prove to be stabilizing only if the United States maintains a strong political, military and economic position in the Western Pacific. If it appears to be part of a continuing U.S. withdrawal from the area, it will be destabilizing. Second, the United States had business to conduct with China, which involved both bilateral and multilateral issues. These could have been dealt with for a time under the previous arrangements, but failure to upgrade the liaison offices highlighted the uncertainties and fragility surrounding the relationship.

A third reason was the possible cost of failing to establish diplomatic relations with Peking. While Peking's view of America's willingness to oppose the Soviet Union was more important to Chinese leaders than winning diplomatic recogni-

[253]

tion from the United States, or even gaining control of Taiwan, a U.S. failure to establish normal diplomatic relations could have led to increased Chinese hostility toward the United States or even over time to a Chinese decision to work for better relations with Moscow.[10] A limited Sino-Soviet détente might ultimately be beneficial to the United States, but *not* if it had come about as an anti-American move before relations with China were normalized.

The fourth reason—and a particularly important one to those most worried by the growing Soviet role in world affairs—was that the leverage U.S. links with China had given Washington in dealing with the Soviet Union probably would increase—it certainly would not decrease—with the establishment of diplomatic ties. Even those officials dubious about the idea of trying to cooperate with China *against* the Soviet Union saw problems for the United States in dealing with the U.S.S.R. if Sino-American relations deteriorated, and hence wanted to place them on a firmer foundation.

The attempt to reach an agreement with Peking received renewed emphasis after Zbigniew Brzezinski, President Carter's National Security Adviser, visited the P.R.C. in May 1978. Peking held to its basic conditions for normalization, but began to treat the Taiwan issue differently in its public statements. Teng Hsiao-ping spoke about the P.R.C.'s desire for unification with—rather than liberation of—Taiwan, and stressed that Taiwan could retain its present economic and social systems and its higher standard of living. In 1978 the P.R.C. for the first time was willing to attend a few international conferences at which R.O.C. representatives were present, and launched new appeals for direct negotiations between Peking and Taipei. All of these shifts could quickly be reversed—a point stressed by Taipei—but they probably were designed both to signal Washington that Peking wanted to reach an agreement on normalization and to make it easier for the United States to move in this direction. These specific Chinese moves probably were less influential in convincing the U.S. government that the time had come for a decisive move than was the general course of Chinese affairs and policy. Dramatic changes were occurring in China, such as Peking's reversal of many of Mao's policies, the rise of the "moderate" Teng Hsiao-ping, China's support of NATO and its search for arms in Western Europe, the P.R.C.'s decision to accord top priority to economic modernization, and Peking's major effort to involve Japan and the West in a long-term program to develop China on terms far more flexible than ever before. The U.S. government apparently concluded that a China embarked on such a course—and lacking the military capability to overcome Taiwan—would pose no threat to the island for the foreseeable future.

Nonetheless, the U.S. government was concerned that a normalization agreement which resulted in a complete and abrupt withdrawal of all U.S. support could create such a domestic political uproar in the United States as to force it to become more, rather than less, deeply involved with Taiwan. It could also so shake Taiwan's confidence in its future as to lead it to take such precipitous actions as producing nuclear weapons, declaring its independence from the mainland, or even attempting to develop political or security ties with the U.S.S.R.[11] Similar Chinese and American interests in preventing such drastic moves offered reasonable hope for dealing with the issue without letting it destabilize the area.

Thus the United States agreed to meet the P.R.C.'s three basic conditions for normalization without any statement from Peking that it would limit itself to peaceful means to acquire control of Taiwan. (Even if Peking had been willing to give such an assurance, it would have carried little weight with

R.O.C. leaders or the Americans most suspicious of the P.R.C., for their belief in Peking's good faith is nil.) The United States agreed to recognize the P.R.C. as the sole legal government of China as of January 1, 1979, to withdraw the few hundred remaining U.S. troops from Taiwan early in 1979, and to terminate the U.S.-R.O.C. security treaty at the end of 1979. The phase-out of the treaty rather than its immediate termination was one step designed to reassure the R.O.C. and America's Asian allies that the United States was not "abandoning" Taiwan, although both the R.O.C. and American critics of the normalization agreement charged that President Carter was in fact doing just that. Similarly, the President's December 15 statement that the U.S. retained an "interest in the peaceful resolution of the Taiwan issue" was designed to indicate that the United States was not adopting a hands-off position in the area.

More important than what the United States says will be what it does to assure those on Taiwan an important role in determining the island's ultimate destiny. The United States must make the changes in U.S. laws that are necessary to enable Taiwanese-American economic relations to continue largely as before. China has spoken favorably of the United States following the "Japanese formula" and continuing its economic activities on Taiwan, so these changes should create few problems with Peking. A more difficult issue concerns U.S. moves affecting Taiwan's military security. The United States should continue to sell defensive arms to Taiwan, and appears determined to do so. Such moves should be played in a low key, but since legislation to permit arms sales to a government we do not recognize will be necessary—and since U.S. officials will have to set forth this policy to congressional committees from time to time—it can hardly be kept secret. Peking has already indicated that it objects to such sales, but not so strongly as to refuse to establish diplomatic relations with the United States under these circumstances. Indeed, it may have agreed to mute its objections in order to secure U.S. agreement to terminate the R.O.C.'s last link with a major power.

The Administration's failure to consult Congress before making this move, while understandable in terms of diplomatic practice, may generate considerable political opposition and even a court case challenging the Executive's right to abrogate a treaty without the consent of the Senate. The Administration probably will prevail in such a conflict, particularly since it seems unlikely that Taiwan will suffer in any tangible way in the next few years. Yet it is well to remember that Peking and Washington are to some extent betting on different ultimate outcomes. Peking probably believes that it will gradually be able to draw Taiwan within its orbit, while Washington probably believes that this will be possible only if China's social and economic systems evolve in a manner that makes Taiwan less fearful of being linked with the mainland. Such a happy development may occur, but unless and until it does Taiwan will remain an issue capable of causing periodic strains in Sino-American relations.

Relations with the Soviet Union and the P.R.C.

The speed with which Japan moved in the early 1970s to normalize its relations with the P.R.C. and to expand its economic links with both China and the Soviet Union, coming in the wake of the Nixon shocks, raised several questions in the minds of many Americans about the basic direction of Japanese foreign policy. Was Japan moving away from the United States and toward much closer relations with its large mainland neighbors? If so, would Japan try—and succeed in—balancing its relations with Moscow and Peking, or would geographic, historical and cultural factors lead Japan to move much closer to Peking than to Moscow? If so, how would the latter react?

No conclusive answer can be given to these questions, for the pattern of East Asian relationships is still evolving. Moreover, Japan is by no means the prime mover in the changes that occur. Tokyo's actions and policies are often less the result of Japanese initiatives than they are reactions to the moves of Peking and Moscow. Both Peking and Moscow have mixed periodic resort to pressure tactics with efforts to seek areas of cooperation with Tokyo, although the Soviet mix has involved a heavier reliance on pressure than has the Chinese strategy. But if no definitive answers to the above questions are possible at this time some interim judgments are feasible.

Japan's relations with both China and Russia have expanded significantly during the 1970s. Trade with each country was just over $800 million in 1970, and together the two accounted for less than 5 percent of Japan's total trade. In 1977, trade with China was $3.5 billion and trade with the U.S.S.R. was $3.4 billion. About half of this four-fold expansion reflects the results of inflation, however, and in 1977 each country accounted for about 2.5 percent of Japan's total trade—approximately what it was in 1970. Sino-Japanese trade rose sharply in 1978, and reached $3.4 billion during the first nine months of the year, while Soviet-Japanese trade rose more slowly to $2.9 billion.[12]

In February 1978 a $20 billion eight-year Sino-Japanese trade agreement—under which Japanese manufactured goods and industrial plants are to be exchanged for Chinese oil and raw materials—was signed. In September 1978 the scope of the agreement was enlarged to provide for $80-100 billion in trade over thirteen years—about $7 billion annually. These agreements probably assure the continued growth of Sino-Japanese trade, particularly if Peking becomes more flexible about accepting the credits it will need to help pay for imports from Japan. China is thus likely to become the more important Communist trading partner of Japan, but it will still account for only a small share of Japanese foreign trade.

Japan has invested in several development projects in Siberia, but Soviet attempts to drive very hard bargains and Japanese wariness of undue dependence on the U.S.S.R. have prevented the two parties from concluding such major agreements as that involving the Tyumen oil project. Yet Japan will continue to work for more trade with the Soviet Union not only for the economic benefits involved but in order to keep its relations with Moscow and Peking as balanced as possible.

The 1972 joint communiqué signed when Japan and the P.R.C. established diplomatic relations specified that the two parties would conclude agreements on trade, navigation, aviation, fishing, and a treaty of peace and friendship. The first four were concluded by 1976, though the fishing agreement placed restraints on Japanese activities. The peace and friendship treaty was stalled for several years because of Japan's reluctance to agree to China's insistence that the treaty contain a clause opposing the efforts of any power to establish "hegemony" in Asia—a clause clearly aimed at Moscow.

The peace treaty was finally concluded in August 1978.[13] Tokyo agreed to the anti-hegemony clause, but tried to placate Moscow and maintain its own freedom of maneuver by insisting on the inclusion of a clause specifying that the "treaty shall not affect the position of either contracting party regarding its relations with third countries." [14] The Soviet Union took little comfort from such a clause, however, and attacked Japan harshly, since Tokyo's acceptance of the anti-hegemony clause represented a major defeat for Soviet diplomacy.[15] Moscow's anger was heightened by Peking's portrayal of the treaty as a key step in forging a close, cooperative Sino-Japanese relationship, a theme stressed by Chinese Deputy Prime Minister Teng Hsiao-ping during his successful visit to Japan for the ratification ceremony in October 1978.

Any attempt to evaluate the trend in Japan's relations with China and the Soviet Union solely in terms of trade, credits, or specific agreements risks overlooking the different atmosphere surrounding Japanese relations with each neighbor. To generalize, Sino-Japanese relations have been *relatively* smooth in recent years, with the desire for cooperation on the part of both outweighing specific disputes and problems. On the other hand, conflict has been more noticeable than cooperation in Soviet-Japanese relations. The contrasting atmosphere is partly due to Moscow's greater rigidity and heavier use of pressure tactics compared to Peking's greater flexibility and its efforts to emphasize areas of accommodation. The Soviets are worried by U.S.-Japanese defense cooperation, while the Chinese favor it.[16] Yet even if the Soviets were to deal with Japan in a more subtle and flexible manner, they would still be handicapped by the legacy of military conflict between the two countries, dispute over the northern territories, and the widespread Japanese mistrust and hostility toward the U.S.S.R. that grows out of many decades of antagonism and conflict. Nor do the Soviets see what benefits a more flexible policy on, say, the northern territories would bring them. Soviet leaders see past conflicts between the two nations quite differently than do the Japanese. Japanese see a persistent Soviet pattern of bullying, as in the 1977 restrictions on Japanese fishing activities. Russians see a Japanese record of aggressiveness in the past and an unwillingness to treat the

Soviet Union as a great power today. The Soviets appear to feel that the "real" Japan—a militaristic nation—is lurking below the surface and will one day burst forth—perhaps even aligned with a militant China against the U.S.S.R.[17] Visits to China by Japanese military officials and, in September 1978, the visit to Japan of the Deputy Chief of the General Staff of the People's Liberation Army only heighten Soviet fears that Sino-Japanese military cooperation—perhaps backed by the United States—is developing.[18] Statements by Japanese Foreign Minister Sonoda just before Teng's visit that Japan understands China's desire to modernize its armed forces drew a sharp Soviet rejoinder.[19]

Nor are these considerations the whole of the story, for two other factors must not be overlooked. The first is that despite Japan's respect for China's traditional culture few Japanese believe they have much to learn from China today. Indeed, many Japanese feel superior and even somewhat disdainful of a people who have had as difficult a time as the Chinese adjusting to the impact of the West and the demands for modernity. China is not a threat, and certainly no model, and many Japanese are concerned that China's current "pragmatic" course will in time give way to more radical policies and another period of instability. The second point is that Japanese do fear the Soviet Union and want to avoid offending it whenever possible. Few Japanese fear a direct Soviet attack or assign top priority to placating Moscow, but the growing weight of the Soviet military presence in Northeast Asia is of serious concern to Japan.

In these circumstances, Tokyo will strive over the long term to maintain some balance in its policies toward China and the Soviet Union, for most Japanese believe their country would gain little and could lose much by lining up completely with either. (Indeed, lining up with one party would reduce its leverage in dealing with that country at the same time that it alienated the other.) This does not mean that Japan will seek a position of equidistance between the two, for such a concept is too rigid and mechanistic to be a useful guide to policy. Japan's relations with China are likely to be closer and more extensive than with the Soviet Union because of lingering Sino-Japanese cultural affinities and Japanese fear of the U.S.S.R., but Tokyo will take care that it is not used by Peking as a club to beat Moscow. Beyond this, Tokyo will lean first in one direction and then in another, trying to use whatever links it develops with Peking as leverage on Moscow—and vice versa—but without any illusions that its influence will be great on either of its large neighbors.

The great difficulty Japan will face in implementing this strategy is that both Moscow and Peking will be intensely suspicious of any Japanese cooperation with the other, and each will attempt to use its own links with Japan against the other. It has been relatively easy for Tokyo to refuse Moscow's effort to set aside the dispute over the northern territories by calling for Tokyo to sign a friendship and cooperation treaty in place of a peace treaty. It proved impossible to refuse Peking's demand that a clause opposing the efforts of any country to establish hegemony in Asia be included in the Sino-Japanese peace treaty despite vigorous Soviet countermeasures.[20] Eventually the national prestige of all three countries became deeply involved. Having yielded to Peking, Tokyo will try to convince Moscow that Japan does not intend to cooperate with China *against* the Soviet Union. The Soviets are unlikely to accept such assurances, and a rise in Soviet-Japanese tensions probably will occur. Yet Soviet reluctance to drive Japan even closer to China probably will limit the duration of such a deterioration in relations. This pattern of a significant but temporary rise in Soviet-Japanese tensions occurred, it should be noted, in 1972 when Japan formalized and expanded its relations with the P.R.C. despite Moscow's warnings that this would seriously damage relations between Japan and the Soviet Union.

One other factor will also influence Japanese policy toward China and the Soviet Union substantially, and that is America's relations with the two Communist giants. At present there is considerable harmony between Japanese and American policies toward the Soviet Union and China even though the U.S. and Japanese roles differ in nature. Japan's relationships are essentially economic, although some of its economic activities have significant political implications. Japan's economic links are also more substantial than those of the United States. Japanese trade with China in 1976 was nearly ten times U.S. trade with the P.R.C. Japanese trade with the U.S.S.R. in 1976 was about 40 percent more than U.S. trade with the Soviet Union. No reliable figures are available, but Japan's trade with Soviet Asia probably was larger than U.S. trade with that region by an even greater margin, since most of America's trade probably is with the European part of the U.S.S.R. In the military arena the U.S. role is obviously greater despite Japan's more direct exposure to Soviet and Chinese military power. Few Japanese see China as a significant threat, but a growing number are becoming concerned about the rise of Soviet military power in Asia and the Pacific.

Japan's ability to expand its relations with the Soviet Union and China simultaneously is based (1) on a continuation of the Sino-Soviet dispute, (2) on an American military presence in the area (and a U.S. nuclear deterrent in reserve) that roughly balances Soviet military power, and (3) on no *basic* conflicts between U.S. and Japanese policies toward Moscow and Peking. There is little reason to expect any substantial shift in

[263]

the nature of Sino-Soviet relations in the next few years, although over a longer period a less hostile relationship could evolve. The growth of Soviet naval and air power combined with declining American military strength in the Western Pacific have eroded the former dominant position of the United States in the area. However, given Moscow's quarrel with Peking and the need for many of its forces in Asia to face China, the balance probably has not yet shifted dangerously in favor of the U.S.S.R. Nonetheless, a continuation of recent trends for a few more years could undermine the balance. In this situation the United States should indicate its willingness gradually to build up its forces in the Western Pacific at the same time that Japan improves its capabilities. This would not require dramatic increases in the forces of either country, but would call for those qualitative and quantative improvements necessary to maintain control of the access routes to and through the Western Pacific. An expansion of Japan's defensive naval and air power would not, it should be noted, alarm other Asian countries the way the development of a long-range offensive military capability would.

A basic conflict in Japanese and American policies would occur if the two countries were to tilt sharply in different directions in dealing with China and the Soviet Union. An evenhanded policy by one party and a moderate tilt by the other probably would not cause major problems in Japanese-American relations. Japan is unlikely to tilt toward the Soviet Union (unless it clearly becomes the dominant power in East Asia, leaving Tokyo little choice), and there is no reason for the United States to favor its major competitor in world affairs by tilting toward the U.S.S.R.

To the extent that a tilt occurs in U.S. policy, it is likely to be toward Peking. A case can be made for such a course since rising Soviet power is—at least under present conditions—

America's major concern. However, there are several arguments against any major U.S. efforts to support China *against* the Soviet Union. The U.S.S.R. is already in a weak political position in most of Asia.[21] Virtually its only source of strength in Northeast Asia is its own military power, which can only be used at heavy cost. A pronounced U.S. tilt toward China could increase Soviet assertiveness throughout the world rather than cause Moscow to react by becoming more accommodating in order to induce the United States to back away from Peking. Finally, such a policy—especially if it involved providing substantial arms or military-related technology to China—could damage our relations with Japan and our other Asian allies. In these circumstances a basic but flexible evenhanded policy is the most appropriate course to follow.

Implementing such a policy will pose many difficult choices. Soviet-American relations have a strategic dimension not present in Sino-American relations, and the U.S.S.R. is a world power whereas China remains essentially a regional power. Questions of economic development are more significant in Sino-American relations than in Soviet-American relations. Yet, despite these and other differences, which make any simple attempt to balance our relations with the U.S.S.R. and the P.R.C. unfeasible, the United States should refrain from trying to use one against the other and should seek areas of mutually beneficial cooperation with both powers. Evenhandedness in this sense, rather than an artificial balance, should be the guide to American policy.

The Korean Peninsula

Japanese and American interests are closely connected on many issues in world affairs today, but in few cases are the inherent complexities as striking as they are with respect to the

[265]

Korean peninsula. Until the Carter Administration announced its plan to withdraw U.S. ground combat forces from Korea, Tokyo and Washington saw their countries' interests as broadly similar and their politics as complementary. Since 1977 strong differences have developed between the views of the two governments in addition to the existing sharp divisions within each country over the appropriate policies to be followed.

One point of agreement among all segments of Japanese and American opinion is the importance of maintaining peace on the Korean peninsula. The presence of U.S. troops in South Korea, the existence of the U.S.-Republic of Korea (R.O.K.) mutual security treaty, the presence of U.S. military bases in Japan, and North Korea's security treaties with China and the Soviet Union make it clear to everyone that a war in Korea could draw in the major powers and endanger the peace in East Asia or even the world at large.

The importance of peace and the deep-seated hostility between the two Koreas have led the Japanese and American governments to conclude that a divided peninsula is inevitable under presently foreseeable circumstances. Unification, which would create a nation of over 50,000,000 energetic and talented people, could hardly come about peacefully in the near future. Nor is it likely that a unified Korea could be a non-Communist (even if neutral) nation on the Austrian pattern. The Soviet Union and China would be unwilling to accept the demise of a Communist state, especially one located on their borders. Japan and the United States would like to see the two Koreas move toward a two-Germanies-type situation rather than remain locked in their present hostility. There are also indications that at least some elements in the Soviet Union would prefer to see events evolve in such a manner. But North Korea remains adamantly opposed, as has China, although

[266]

Teng Hsiao-ping's October 1978 statement to Japanese officials that a dialogue between the two Koreas should be encouraged suggests that there is some flexibility in Peking's stance. Nonetheless, Moscow is unwilling to take actions which risk pushing Pyongyang substantially closer to Peking. Thus all three Communist states have turned down offers by the United States and Japan to recognize North Korea if China and the Soviet Union would reciprocate by recognizing the R.O.K.[22] (Korea is one of the few issues on which Japanese and Soviet policies have been closer than Japanese and Chinese policies.)

If the strategic significance of South Korea (and of the Korean peninsula) is under reassessment, the geographic facts of life make the area of greater importance to Japan than to the United States. Nevertheless, the legacy of Japanese colonialism in Korea, the American role in East Asia in the Cold War years, and Japan's determination not to undertake military commitments outside its own territory resulted in the United States assuming responsibility for South Korea's security. While Japan has gradually taken over part of America's earlier economic role, neither the Japanese nor the Koreans would be willing to see Japan play a direct military role in the foreseeable future. But if Japan is determined to avoid direct military involvement, the presence of U.S. bases in Japan, which would be necessary to the United States in the event of a new Korean war, indicates that Japan could not avoid *indirect* involvement without risking a rupture in its relations with America.[23]

Although the United States is more closely involved with Korean security matters—both deterring North Korea and reassuring South Korea—Japanese involvement with most other aspects of Korean affairs surpasses that of the United States. Geographic proximity presents issues concerning fishing rights, division of the continental shelf and the exploitation of its resources, and many other matters which create possibilities of friction as well as cooperation. Only recently have Koreans begun to emigrate in significant numbers to America, but several hundred thousand Koreans live in Japan, and many are organized and actively support Pyongyang, or, in smaller numbers, Seoul. As B.C. Koh has pointed out:

> The presence of some 600,000 Koreans in Japan with divided loyalties and the anomalous fact that Japan is more accessible to the two Koreas than they are to each other have helped to turn Japan into a base of subversive operations as well as an arena of psychological warfare between Seoul and Pyongyang. And this situation is likely to continue as long as Korea remains divided and Japan keeps its doors open to both Seoul and Pyongyang.[24]

Indeed, the large number of Korean refugees that might try to reach Japan in the event of a new Korean war is a major reason the Japanese are so concerned about peace on the peninsula.

Japan has in recent years moved away from dealing only with South Korea. Japanese trade with North Korea grew rapidly in the 1970s until Pyongyang's inability to pay the large foreign debts it had incurred to finance the trade dampened Japanese enthusiasm. Japanese politicians of various parties, including the Liberal Democratic Party, periodically visit Pyongyang, although Tokyo has refused to extend diplomatic recognition to North Korea. The United States, on the other hand, has had no official dealings with North Korea, partly out of deference to Seoul's opposition to such moves.

These different postures toward North Korea arise partly

out of the different nature of Japanese and American roles in Korea. The U.S. government has traditionally placed a high priority on deterring any North Korean military move, especially one caused by a miscalculation of America's response in the event of North Korean attack. However, the nature of the opposition pressures on the Japanese and American governments also has an important influence. There is substantial American opposition to continued U.S. support of President Park's regime, but there is virtually no American sympathy for Kim Il Sung's totalitarian rule in North Korea, and only a few Americans argue for recognition of North Korea. Many Japanese leftists, on the other hand, are strongly critical of Park's conservative economic policies and suppression of his opposition, while they admire Kim Il Sung's socialism and pay little heed to his failure to permit *any* opposition. This creates a type of pressure on the Japanese government that does not exist in the United States. Many Japanese—conservatives and leftists alike—want Japan and the United States somehow to combine diplomacy with deterrence in their policies toward North Korea.

Official Japanese and American views diverged during the early months of the Carter Administration when the United States announced that it would pull its ground combat forces out of South Korea within four or five years. Tokyo was upset that it was informed rather than consulted, and worried that the U.S. move would end the peace and stability that had characterized the Korean peninsula since 1953. Japanese fears were reduced but not eliminated when the United States announced later in 1977 that its air power in Korea would be increased, that only one of the three brigades of the Second Division to be removed would be withdrawn in 1978 and the other two brigades would remain until 1982, and that South Korea would be provided with enough arms to enable it to deter or defeat any North Korean attack.

Some Americans favored troop withdrawal simply as punishment for South Korean bribery in the United States, or because of President Park's authoritarianism, or because of a "no more Asian wars" attitude. There were more serious arguments in favor of the Administration's policy, although they were not often articulated effectively.[25] South Korea, the proponents of the withdrawal argued, had twice the population of the North and a more rapidly growing economy, and so should be able to provide for its own defense as long as it received adequate U.S. arms. The United States would have greater military flexibility in the event of a war, and American power would be more appropriately used as a strategic counter to Soviet and Chinese power. South Korea would appear less like a client state of the United States, an appearance which had weakened its status in the Third World. Finally, a withdrawal would demonstrate to North Korea that South Korea could stand on its own feet, which might lead Pyongyang to conclude that direct dealings with Seoul were its only hope of influencing the South or moving toward unification.

Yet even many of the proponents of a withdrawal of the Second Division admitted that risks were involved. It weakened the deterrent effect of the U.S. commitment, since American involvement in the event of war would no longer be virtually automatic. Indeed, an American president would find it difficult to send ground troops back into Korea once they had been removed. One need not regard Kim Il Sung simply as a reckless adventurer to be concerned that he might resort to force as a means of realizing his goal of unification if he thought the American response would be half-hearted. Moreover, the talk of American withdrawal in recent years was one factor behind the new arms race on the already heavily armed Korean peninsula. An actual withdrawal probably would further this unhappy development.

However, during late 1977 and early 1978, the Administration's plan became increasingly uncertain as those Congressmen angry about Korean attempts to bribe some of its members combined with those opposed to the troop-withdrawal to delay transfer of important items of military equipment to Seoul. Faced with this situation, the Administration announced in April 1978 that it would withdraw only one-third of the brigade it planned to pull out in that year, although it insisted that the shift involved only the timing of the withdrawal and not the basic decision itself. The Administration was encouraged when Congress agreed in late 1978 to the transfer of the Second Division's equipment to Seoul as the troops were withdrawn. Yet it probably recognizes that unless it can secure continued congressional cooperation over the next several years, its plans will have to be modified again. A particularly dangerous period could arise in the early 1980s when North Korea might conclude that any military move had to be made before South Korea's rapid economic growth and its military buildup made an attack too risky. In such circumstances the United States should be prepared to extend the deadline for the troop-withdrawal for a few years beyond 1982.

Is there any way out of this dilemma which preserves the security and stability of the Korean peninsula and the surrounding areas? No one can be certain, given the deep hostility between the two Koreas, the past inflexibility of the Soviet Union and China, and the divisions within Japan and the United States on how to proceed. Many proposals to reduce tensions have been advanced over the years—cross-recognition, a four-power guarantee to the two Korean states, and several others. Less attention has been devoted to using the possibility of conditioning U.S. troop withdrawal on a limitation on (and in time a gradual reduction of) military forces and arms in both Koreas. The limitation should be negotiated by the two Koreas as well as by the United States and other concerned countries that desire to take part. Such a policy would offer something to virtually everyone. Pyongyang would succeed in establishing diplomatic contact with the United States and could look forward to seeing the arms reduction proposals it has made taken seriously; Seoul would no longer be regarded as an illegitimate state by Pyongyang, and would not need to continue its expensive military buildup; the arms race in the peninsula would be curtailed and possibly reversed; the United States would be able to withdraw its troops (and eventually its air force) without risking the security and stability of the area; Japan would welcome the prospect of a more peaceful and less heavily armed peninsula; and Moscow would see the area moving toward a German-type situation. China probably would not openly endorse what would appear to be a two-Koreas approach as long as the Taiwan issue remained contentious, but it might act with enough restraint to make progress possible.

No one aware of the great difficulties involved in arms control—much less, arms reduction—negotiations would pretend that the chances of succeeding in such a venture were high, or could even be predicted with any confidence. The level of suspicion and uncertainty among those involved in Korean affairs is such that each party would move warily and cautiously at best. The military establishments in both Koreas would inevitably have reservations about proposals that reduce their power, although the shortage of trained manpower in both countries suggests that the favorable employment opportunities for demobilized officers and troops might limit their opposition. Despite these obstacles, such an approach warrants serious consideration. Nothing would be lost by testing it, and it could lead to the gradual transformation of one of the most tense and heavily armed areas of the world. Since the normalization of Sino-American relations, the two Koreas have moved toward a renewal of their 1972-73 dialogue; and if the North-South talks continue, the prospect for progress on arms control measures might improve.

In Conclusion

The strains that will beset U.S.-Japanese relations in the coming years will be particularly serious because they will arise not from one but from several basic and possibly enduring issues. These strains could, if not handled well, erode and eventually undermine what has been an almost uniquely successful relationship. Despite the experience of overcoming past difficulties and the awareness of key groups in each country of the importance of close relations, future problems are likely to be centered on issues particularly difficult for each country to handle. Moreover, resentment and anger are growing in each country over the actions, or in some cases the inaction, of the other. Many Japanese believe the United States is pressuring their country in a manner it would never use when dealing with its European allies. Many Americans, noting that Japan's trade surplus with the United States keeps growing despite repeated Japanese predictions that it will decline, suspect that Japan has no intention of reducing the gap.

Japan's rapidly rising productivity not only curtails U.S. sales to third countries, but its exports to the United States threaten the jobs of American workers and, in some cases, the financial well-being of American firms. The rapid rise in the value of the yen harms Japan's weak industries but does little damage to most of its strong industries. Thus the latter's sales abroad become steadily more important to a nation having to import most of its raw materials and to restructure its economy. Under these circumstances American workers and firms will be able to compete in an open U.S. market only if U.S. productivity rises more rapidly than in the past, a formidable task that will require new attitudes, habits, and government policies. Occasional American resorts to protectionism will not be adequate to deal with the problem, and a basic shift to protectionism would create a crisis between the two countries more serious than any experienced in three decades.

Similarly, a continued weakening of America's military position in the Western Pacific area could undermine Japan's national security and force it to grapple with what would be, under adverse circumstances, the most divisive issue in Japanese public life. Japan can gradually assume a greater responsibility for its own defense. But if such a process is not to damage the alliance badly, it should grow out of a mutually agreed upon redefinition of the respective roles of the two countries rather than represent a frantic response to traumatic events that lead to a drastic decline in Japanese confidence in American strength and resolve. And even if Japan does develop more adequate armed forces, a regional military role would not be acceptable to other Asian nations. Thus the United States will have to continue to play the key security role in the Western Pacific—particularly in ensuring the peace and stability in Korea—even if Japan does undertake an expanded military role.

There are many Americans who believe that the United States can afford to deal rather cavalierly with Japan because of the latter's heavy dependence on the United States for markets and security leaves it no place to go. Such complacency is dangerous. It not only assumes that Japan has no choice but to accept virtually any treatment that the United States hands out, but also that Japan's choices will ultimately be governed by reason rather than resentment or anger. Japan is clearly determined to go to great lengths to maintain its close relationship with the United States, for the alternatives are unattractive. United States pressures will on occasion be necessary, but not if continually carried out publicly without an awareness as to which issues are susceptible to such tactics. Japanese policy has been as rational as that of any nation, but it is dangerous to assume that any large and proud nation can be treated disdainfully without adverse consequences. The erosion of U.S.-Japanese relations would hurt Japan badly, but it would also undermine the American position in Asia.

The dangers in the years ahead will not lie only, or perhaps even primarily, in action taken peremptorily by the United States or irrationally by Japan. Both governments will have to make decisions and take actions that will entail domestic political costs—at least in the short term. The United States will have to maintain its basically liberal trade policy despite the costs this will at times impose on some sectors of the populace, and Americans will have to forego the temptations to blame their economic difficulties with Japan primarily on unfair trading practices rather than on Japanese efficiency. The United States will also have to maintain adequate military forces in the Western Pacific area to convince Japan (and other Asian nations) that it has the strength and determination to carry out the responsibilities it has assumed. Japan will have to accept the fact that its economic strength requires it to abolish the subtle but important restrictive practices that limit its imports of industrial goods, and that it needs to assume a leading role in international economic deliberations and decision making. Finally, Japan needs gradually to assume not only a larger political role in Asia but also greater responsibility for its own defense. Japanese can stress the domestic political constraints involved in military matters; but if they continue to do so, they are in a weak position to complain when Americans let their reluctance to continue to bear heavy military burdens in Asia govern U.S. policy.

The United States and Japan would be overlooking a prime opportunity, however, if they viewed these difficult issues only in the context of keeping the relationship from eroding, for an opportunity exists to put it on a new and more rewarding basis. Indeed, it may well be that the best way to preserve and extend the relationship is to redefine the respective roles of the two countries in the direction of greater equality. Such a shift probably is seen as desirable in principle by many Americans, although if it occurs they will hardly be pleased with all of its specific manifestations. Domestic pressures in Japan, as well as the country's tradition of adjusting to events rather than taking a lead in trying to shape them, will make any substantial changes in Japan's role and policies difficult. Yet Japan may be approaching the time when the task of its leaders is to shape a new consensus in a constructive manner rather than to wait until external shocks force major changes under adverse conditions. Constructive moves would provide Japan with the increased international stature and role that some of its citizens believe desirable and others regard as inevitable.

The United States would also benefit if one of its Asian allies assumed more of the responsibilities of a major power, and that could only be done by Japan. Throughout the postwar period the United States has been handicapped in Asia (in contrast to Europe) because it has lacked the benefits derived from working out its policies in true consultation with a nation that was friendly but strong enough so that its views had to be weighed carefully. Lack of such a partner made it easier for the United States to act as it saw fit in Asia, but deprived it of the insights and constraints that a major Asian ally could have provided. No nation enjoys such constraints, but none is wise enough to do without them.

NOTES

1. Ohira's speech was published in *Japan Report*, Vol. XX, No. 12 (June 16, 1974), pp. 2-4. For Kissingers's speech, see *The Department of State Bulletin*, Vol. LXXIII, No. 1880 (July 7, 1975), p. 3. For a similar opinion by a knowledgable private citizen, see Philip H. Trezise, "The Second Phase in U.S.-Japan Relations," *Pacific Community*, Vol. 6, No. 3 (April 1975), pp. 340-51.

2. IMF, *Directions of Trade*, Annual 1967-68, and *ibid.*, 1969-75.

3. The evolution of this policy and the issues involved are described in detail in Selig S. Harrison, *China, Oil, and Asia: Conflict Ahead?* (New York: Columbia University Press, 1977).

4. Cited in Harrison, *ibid.*, p. 142.

5. *The New York Times*, April 15, 1978; *Far Eastern Economic Review*, April 28, 1978.

6. The text of the treaty is in *The Current Digest of the Soviet Press*, Vol. XXX, No. 44, November 29, 1978, p. 11.

7. Bernard K. Gordon, "Japan, the United States, and Southeast Asia," *Foreign Affairs*, Vol. 56, No. 3 (April 1978), p. 587.

8. Japanese trade with the P.R.C. was slightly larger than its trade with Taiwan in 1974 and 1975, but the situation was reversed in 1976 and 1977 because of internal dislocations in China and Peking's efforts to cut its trade deficit with Japan.

9. *The Japan Times Weekly,* July 31, 1976.

10. For a thoughtful statement on these points, see Richard H. Solomon, "Thinking Through the China Problem," *Foreign Affairs,* Vol. 56, No. 2 (January 1978), pp. 324-56.

11. So far, neither Taiwan nor the Soviet Union appears to have done much more than take a few cautious steps of a largely symbolic nature designed to create concern in Peking and Washington that more significant links might develop if China and the United States forged close ties. For an analysis of the incentives and constraints affecting Taipei and Moscow, see John W. Garver. "Taiwan's Russian Option: Image and Reality," *Asian Survey,* July 1978, pp. 751-66.

12. *The Japan Times Weekly,* November 11, 1978.

13. *The Japan Times Weekly,* August 19, 1978.

14. *Ibid.*

15. *Pravda,* August 13, 1978, in *The Current Digest of the Soviet Press,* Vol. XXX, No. 32 (September 6, 1978).

16. For a Soviet view of Japanese-American relations, see D. Petrov, "The U.S.-Japanese Alliance and the New Situation in Asia," *Far Eastern Affairs,* Nos. 4, 1976 – 1, 1977, pp. 57-71.

17. Soviet concern over Japan's modest modernization program is a frequent theme in Soviet pronouncements. See *The Current Digest of the Soviet Press,* Vol. XXX, No. 3 (February 15, 1978), p. 19, and No. 5 (March 1, 1978), p. 7.

18. Tokyo Kyodo, March 27, 1978, in *Foreign Broadcast Information Service* (People's Republic of China), March 28, 1978; *The Japan Times Weekly,* September 16, 1978.

19. *Pravda,* October 15, 1978, in *The Current Digest of the Soviet Press,* Vol. XXX, No. 4l, November 8, 1978, pp. 1-2.

20. See *The Far Eastern Economic Review,* April 14, 1978, for an example of Soviet tactics which helped delay but did not prevent the signing of the treaty.

21. See Donald S. Zagoria, "The Soviet Quandary in Asia," *Foreign Affairs,* Vol. 56, No. 2 (January 1978), pp. 306-23.

22. Pyongyang's concern over this proposal is analyzed in FBIS *Trends in Communist Propaganda,* January 15, 1975; April 13, 1977; and August 3, 1977.

23. Japanese spokesmen have frequently shifted ground on whether or not the United States would be allowed to operate from Japanese bases in the event of war on the Korean peninsula.

24. B. C. Koh, "South Korea, North Korea, and Japan," *Pacific Community,* Vol. 6, No. 4 (July 1975), p. 218.

25. For a strong statement in favor of the withdrawal, see Franklin B. Weinstein, "The United States, Japan and the Security of Korea," *International Security,* Fall 1977, pp. 68-89. For an opposing viewpoint, see Donald Zagoria, "Why We Can't Leave Korea," *The New York Times Magazine,* October 2, 1977, pp. 17 ff.

Index

110, 126, 198, 232;
exploration and claims in East
Asian seas, 237-41
Okinawa, 11, 67, 160, 195, 197, 222
OPEC, 14, 114, 204
Opposition parties, Japan's, 28-29,
30-43, 161; and foreign policy,
50-52; and Korea, 67-69, 200;
"progressive parties," 31;
prospects, 43, 45-49; and U.S.-
Japan security treaty, 51, 63-
67, 196; and Taiwan, 251
Orderly marketing agreements, 91-
92, 107, 109, 119, 139, 205
Owen, Henry, 206

Park Chung-Hee, 68, 269, 270
Peace Treaty, U.S.-Japan (1951), 9
Petroleum and Trade Agreement,
P.R.C. and Japan (1978), 156,
258-59
Philippines, 244; U.S. bases, 244,
247, 248
Platt, Nicholas, 208
Policy process and Japanese
political trends, 49-52, 77;
bureaucratic in-fighting, 50,
130; interest groups, 51
Protectionism, U.S., 217-18, 219-
20, 225
Public opinion, Japanese, 60-61,
69-77, 81, 83, 84; consensus
by default, 69-72

Reischauer, Edwin O., 9
Rivers, Richard, 208-11

Safire, William, 219
Sakata, Gen. Michio, 160-61

Sasaki, Kozo, 33
Sasaki, Ryosaku, 47, 66, 82
Sato, Eisaku, 160, 195
Saxonhouse, Gary, 216
Schmidt, Helmut, 204
Security environment, Japanese
perceptions of, 158, 159-68;
after 1976, 169-76;
deployment and basing
(chart), 165, 166-67, 168;
force trends (chart), 164, 167,
168; scenarios for Japanese
options in 1980s: moderate
deterioration, 180-84; more of
the same or continued, 177-80;
radical deterioration, 184-85;
successful détente, 176-77;
"worst case," 180
Self Defense Forces, 60, 62, 155,
160-61, 166, 177, 183, 264
Senkaku islands, 59, 238-39
Shanghai Communiqué, 249, 253
Siberia, Japanese investments in,
259
Singapore, 244
Sino-Japanese relations, 156, 159,
178, 192-93, 195-96, 257-58,
260-62
Sino-Japanese Treaty of Peace and
Friendship (1978), 14, 58-59,
156, 169, 170-71, 199, 251,
259-60; "anti-hegemony"
clause, 59, 259-60, 262
Sino-Soviet dispute, 17, 124, 155-
56, 252, 253, 263, 264
Smithsonian agreement, 111, 197
Social change, 7-8, 25-26, 85
Social Democratic League, 33, 46

DATE DUE

DEC 9 '86			
GAYLORD			PRINTED IN U.S.A.